AIR BATTLE FOR DUNKIRK

NORMAN FRANKS

AIR BATTLE FOR
DUNKIRK

26 MAY – 3 JUNE 1940

GRUB STREET • LONDON

Published by
Grub Street
4 Rainham Close
London
SW11 6SS

First published in hardback 1983 under the title *Air Battle of Dunkirk*
This edition first published in paperback in 2000

Copyright © Grub Street 2017
Text copyright © Norman Franks 2017

A CIP record for this title is available from the British Library

ISBN-13: 9-781-910690-47-5

Cover design by Daniele Roa

Printed and bound by Finidr, Czech Republic

Contents

Acknowledgements

As with my previous books I was privileged to meet or to correspond with a number of men who flew with the Royal Air Force. In this case, these men listed below all saw action over France and/or over Dunkirk in May and June 1940. They have given generous help and I wish to record my sincere thanks to them all. Sadly, since the original edition of this book, many of them have flown "for the last time".

Air Vice-Marshal H.A.C. Bird-Wilson, CBE, DSO, DFC*, AFC*, 17 Squadron
Wing Commander G.C. Unwin, DSO, DFM, 19 Squadron
Air Vice-Marshal J. Worrall, CB, DFC, 32 Squadron
Squadron Leader J.N. MacKenzie, DFC, 41 Squadron
Wing Commander E.A. Shipman, AFC, 41 Squadron
Air Vice-Marshal C.G. Lott, CB, CBE, DSO, DFC, 43 Squadron
Air Commodore A.C. Deere, DSO, OBE, DFC*, 54 Squadron
Air Commodore J.A. Leathart, CB, DSO, 54 Squadron
Air Vice-Marshal S.B. Grant, CB, DFC*, 65 Squadron
Wing Commander H.M. Stephen, DSO, DFC*, 74 Squadron
Group Captain A.R. Wright, DFC*, AFC, 92 Squadron
Wing Commander A.C. Bartley, DFC*, 92 Squadron
Air Commodore J.M. Thompson, CBE, DSO, DFC*, AFC, 111 Squadron
Wing Commander J.E. Storrar, DFC*, AFC, AE, BSC, MRCVS, 145 Squadron
Wing Commander P.L. Parrott, DFC*, AFC, 145 Squadron
Group Captain R.N.H. Courtney, CBE, DFC*, AFC, 151 Squadron
Air Marshal Sir Humphrey Edwardes Jones, KCB, CBE, DFC, AFC, 213 Squadron
Squadron Leader H.A. Haarhoff, DFC, 220 Squadron
Group Captain R.A.L. Morant, OBE, 222 Squadron
Squadron Leader G.G.A. Davies, DFC, 222 Squadron
Air Marshal Sir Harold Maguire, KCB, DSO, OBE, 229 Squadron
Group Captain Sir Archibald Hope, OBE, DFC, 601 Squadron
Group Captain J. Ellis, CBE, DFC*, 610 Squadron
J. E. McComb, CBE, DFC, DL, 611 Squadron

Wing Commander Sir Barrie Heath, Kt, DFC, 611 Squadron
Wing Commander K.M. Stoddart, AE, 611 Squadron
Group Captain D.E. Gillam, DSO**, DFC*, AFC, 616 Squadron
Air Chief Marshal Sir Harry Broadhurst, GCB, KBE, DSO, DFC** AFC,
    Station Commander, Wittering.

I also thank the late Air Commodore A.E. Clouston, CB, DSO, DFC, AFC*, Mrs Sonia McComb, Ministry of Defence and the staff of the Public Records Office. My good friends Chaz Bowyer and Martyn Ford-Jones, and of course to Amy Myers and everyone at Wm Kimber & Co, who originally published this book, and now to John Davies and staff of Grub Street Publishers. Also to Graham Day of the Air Historical Branch, MoD, and my friend and fellow author John Foreman.

CHAPTER ONE

Blitzkrieg

Britain and her Empire had been at war for 220 days when Germany finally ended the period known as the 'Phoney War' on 10th May 1940. At dawn on that Friday, German troops suddenly opened their offensive along the Western Front. Across the German frontier came 135 German divisions, streaming into Luxembourg and Belgium while paratroops and gliders descended on objectives in Belgium and Holland. Also in the air came the so far victorious Luftwaffe, attacking Dutch, Belgian and French airfields, and also airfields in France from which British RAF squadrons operated.

Although the advance was not totally unexpected, the attack when it came took the Allied forces by surprise and such opposition that they could muster was soon overwhelmed. In Holland the Dutch Air Force was virtually destroyed by 13th May; Rotterdam was bombed the next day and by the 15th the Dutch Army, though still intact, surrendered.

By this lightning push through Belgium and Holland, the Germans circumvented the famed Maginot Line which separated France from Germany, making this costly defence system impotent.

The British and French had expected an attack to come further to the north and in consequence focussed their attention there. When, therefore, German Panzers pushed through the forested Ardennes region around Sedan, they encountered little opposition. The German spearhead crossed the River Meuse on the night of 11th-12th May, its tanks following. The French troops that were rushed to stem this advance were mostly of low quality and poorly equipped. When scores of Luftwaffe Stuka dive-bombers hit them the way was again open and the split in the Allied forces complete. The Germans made straight for the Channel coast spearheading towards Boulogne and Calais.

Despite spirited fighting in the north, the British and French soldiers were soon pushed back towards Brussels. In the air too the French Air Force and British squadrons of the Advanced Air Striking Force and Air Component were quickly overwhelmed. Although they fought heroically they could not hope to stop the might of the Luftwaffe. The men of the RAF in particular fought themselves to a standstill. Those bombers, Fairey Battles or Bristol Blenheims, not shot down on desperate raids on advancing German columns or bridges, were destroyed on the ground between missions. The Hurricane fighter pilots were quite often totally outnumbered and those who survived moved with the remnants of their squadrons from airfield to airfield as the armies on the ground retreated through the corridor leading to the Channel coast.

These fighter units were re-inforced by other Hurricane and Gladiator squadrons or by flights from British-based squadrons operating in France for short periods or even on a daily basis in France, but against the might of the Luftwaffe whose strength in May 1940 was around 3,500 front line aircraft, including 800 of the latest Messerschmitt 109E single-engined fighters, the odds were just too great.

When the offensive opened the AASF had 135 bombers on strength. Two days later it was down to just over seventy, most of which needed service or repair. Then on 14th May the total remaining bomber force was sent to attack German troops in the Sedan bridgehead. The Messerschmitts and flak were ready for them and forty Battles and Blenheims were shot down.

As the Hurricane squadrons hurled themselves almost hourly against German bombers, dive-bombers and fighters, reinforcements which in number were equivalent to a further twelve full squadrons, also dashed themselves to pieces. They inflicted heavy casualties but sustained severe losses too. By the end of the 15th, the RAF had lost nearly 250 aircraft either destroyed or damaged beyond immediate repair. It could not go on. At home, the Commander-in-Chief of Fighter Command, Air Chief Marshal Sir Hugh Dowding, his establishment in fighter squadrons, fighter aeroplanes and fighter pilots already dangerously below the number set by Air Ministry and the Government, could daily see his fighter force being whittled away with little real effect. To retain a sufficient force to defend the whole of Britain he had to make a stand and deny his fighters being sent to a battle that appeared already lost.

Dowding's course of action was initially accepted. In a letter to his 11 Group Commander, Air Vice-Marshal Keith Park, dated 15th May, Dowding added the comment:

> We had a notable victory on the 'home front' this morning. Any orders to send more Hurricanes were cancelled. Appeals for help will doubtless be renewed, however, with increasing insistence. I do not know how this morning's work will stand the test of time: but I will never relax my efforts to prevent the dissipation of the Home Front fighter forces.

On 16th May, just six days after the German attack began, he wrote to the Secretary of State for Air, a letter which undoubtedly changed the course of the war. However nicely he put it, the message he sent was clear. No more fighters for France!

*

The British Expeditionary Force continued its retreat to the coast. By the 17th the German Panzers were across the River Oise and on their way to St Quentin and the Canal du Nord; the next day came fresh moves by the Allied forces – a staged withdrawal to the River Senne. They would continue retreating; firstly to the River Dendre, west of Brussels, then back to the Scheldt. By the 21st the Panzers, with the Aisne and the Somme rivers to their left flank, reached Abbeville where they turned north along the coast threatening the retreating Allies from the rear.

Amiens had fallen on the 20th and to the north were around a million French, Belgian and British soldiers, now cut off from the main French armies in the south. Despite occasional spirited counter-attacks or valiant holding actions nothing was able to stop the German advance for very long. Boulogne fell. Calais was under attack. The retreating Allies were being squeezed towards Dunkirk and Gravelines on the coast. By the evening of 24th May German Panzer units were just fifteen miles from Dunkirk which would have fallen to the Germans the next day, but luckily for the Allied armies the Panzers were halted and ordered to stand fast. There have been many reasons given for this order which as events proved saved the greater part of the BEF. Terrain unsuitable for tanks, the need to conserve the tanks for the battle against the French in the south, lack of supplies and a need for servicing, shortage of food and ammunition; whatever the real reasons, they are now unimportant. They were halted and the task of finishing off the BEF and the French troops now in the area of Dunkirk was given to the Luftwaffe on the request of its commander, Hermann Göring.

Hitler had been undecided on what to do and when Göring suggested that his Luftwaffe could finish the job, Hitler was delighted to have a solution handed to him. He would be able to conserve his precious tanks, and troop casualties would be kept down as his Air Force could undoubtedly bomb the Allies into submission and surrender.

The boastful, bombastic, sycophantic Hermann Göring, eager to please his Führer, ignored or chose to ignore that his Luftwaffe was in no real shape to take on the task of bombing the BEF into submission. Like the RAF in France, the Luftwaffe had been heavily engaged since 10th May. It had been designed to support the Army in Blitzkrieg tactics – Dunkirk was a different tactic. Field Marshal Albert Kesselring, commander of Air Fleet 2, was totally surprised at the order when it was received. He felt the task impossible. Although the Germans could not know it, the Dunkirk docks and loading facilities had already been knocked out prior to the beginning of the evacuation.

In England the situation was far from clear but it seemed certain now that a decision must be made if the bulk of the BEF was to have any chance of survival. The only course was to mount a rescue operation from the sea. It would be up to the Royal Navy to provide the means. To the general public it was still thought that the BEF were in not too bad a state and that the planned withdrawal was still working out as expected. The men of the RAF who would soon be called upon to cover the eventual evacuation knew only as much as they were able to read in the daily newspapers. The scale of the problem was daunting.

*

Although Hugh Dowding's refusal to send any more fighter aeroplanes to France was initially accepted by Prime Minister Winston Churchill, the pressure of the situation forced Churchill to over-rule the Commander-in-Chief Fighter Command. Approval was given to send four more fighter squadrons to France. The order for this was sent to Air Ministry, where the Deputy Chief of the Air Staff, Air Marshal Sholto Douglas, 'interpreted' this to mean not four squadrons but eight flights. By halving eight squadrons, he felt Dowding could rebuild the units. Certainly this was not clear thinking and it was very much against the wishes of Dowding. He had little time and neither the men nor equipment to rebuild these units. Meanwhile the RAF went through a period of operating 'composite' squadrons, for instance, two flights from different squadrons operating as one unit. The logic behind this is obscure for not only did the two units not know each other, they could hardly operate as a whole unit when they had trained in undoubtedly different ways.

As Dowding himself later wrote:

> This was done under the impression that the loss of eight half squadrons would affect me less than that of four entire squadrons, because it was supposed that I should be able to rebuild on the nuclei left behind. But this assumption was incorrect because I had neither the time nor the personnel available for purposes of reconstruction.[1]

---

[1] 'The Battle of Britain', Air Chief Marshal Dowding's despatch, dated 20th August 1941, to the Secretary of State for Air.

Keith Park too was at a loss to comprehend the sense of this action and wrote to Headquarters Fighter Command on 17th May:

> For future temporary requests for reinforcements for BAFF, may whole squadrons be dispatched to avoid the present situation whereby 14 flights of different squadrons are operating as composite squadrons overseas and at home, under squadron leaders who know only half the pilots in their formations and half the others under their immediate command, and are separated from their Headquarters flights. For example, 111 Squadron has one flight in France, another flight at Kenley and the Head-quarters flight at Northolt with consequent dislocation of maintenance and administration.

No sooner had these half squadrons been instigated than an order came from Churchill, now in Paris meeting the French, for yet more squadrons to go to France. This was totally unacceptable even if there were bases in France from where they could operate. Fortunately, the Chief of Air Staff, Cyril Newall, who had not backed Dowding earlier, now took a stand to stop Fighter Command being thrown totally away. Instead of sending six more squadrons to France he ordered six units to be flown to forward airfields around the southern coast of England, from where they could operate over France and return to England each evening. Churchill finally agreed totally to support Dowding on 19th May; no more fighters would go to France whatever the need of their French allies.

*

The first single-seat fighters to operate from England across the Channel, had been Spitfires of 54 Squadron operating from RAF Hornchurch on 16th May. Led by Squadron Leader E.A. Douglas-Jones, the squadron took off at 10.35 and patrolled Ostend for half an hour. That same afternoon the squadron flew escort over two destroyers as they sailed across the Channel. The following morning 65 Squadron's Commanding Officer, Squadron Leader D. Cooke, (flying Spitfire K9907) led his men to Ostend, then up the coast. Shortly before 8 a.m., Flying Officer J.H. Welford (K9915) was ordered to engage a Junkers 88 near Flushing. Despite return fire hitting his wings, Johnnie Welford forced the 88 to crash onto the beach.

'A' Flight of 145 Squadron carried out a patrol over Belgium from Manston on the 18th, engaged twelve Heinkel bombers and shot down seven. One pilot was reported lost; Flying Officer M.A. Newling was seen to go down east of Brussels but under control. Fortunately he baled out and was back two days later.

> Mike Newling had a room in the Mess and when he failed to
> return I went and procured his cap which was in far better
> condition than mine. I was just coming out of his room when he
> came back.
>
> The first time I encountered enemy aircraft was on 22nd May.
> We were on an offensive patrol over Béthune and Arras and ran
> into a bunch of Ju87's escorted by 109's. The squadron went into
> the attack and I was green about the whole business and just flew
> around looking for something literally to appear in front of me so
> I could shoot at it and was gazing awe-struck at what was going
> on around me. Fortunately no more experienced characters came
> up behind me. I saw one or two aircraft hit the deck, two Ju87's
> and one Hurricane spinning down, very conspicuous with its
> black and white underside as it spun towards the ground. Looking
> back I can't help but think how lucky I was to survive those first
> few flights in which I had my baptism of fire.
>
> *Pilot Officer, J.E. Storrar, 145 Squadron*[1]

These patrols and escorts continued over the next few days, RAF fighter
pilots getting used to looking down at French and Belgian coastal towns
and harbours, not knowing that very soon they would be seeing much
more of one particular French sea port – Dunkirk.

> The German Blitzkrieg was moving forward through northern
> France at a terrifying rate. The roads were continuously blocked
> with thousands of refugees fleeing westward ahead of the Huns.
> A really tragic and terrible sight. Things were in a pretty awful
> shambles and general confusion reigned. By the 21st May forces
> had reached Arras-Abbeville-Amiens – No 32 and No 17
> Squadrons joined forces at Hawkinge and went out together on
> patrol in the area and received accurate groundfire from German
> pom-poms and AA guns around Abbeville. A Germany Army Co-
> op Henschel 126 was sighted and although it was flown with
> considerable determination and skill, it did not return from its
> mission. The German Air Force were now employing large
> numbers of aircraft together and, therefore, the AOC No 11
> Group countered likewise. This rather dispels the myth that No
> 12 Group was the first to join squadrons together.

---

[1] All ranks quoted are those held in May 1940.

I was so disorientated after attacking the Hs 126 that I became totally lost. As my fuel was getting low I fortunately sighted an airfield and quickly landed. The shock in finding that the airfield was Le Havre/Octeville and not one in the Pas de Calais was a serious lesson in navigation and emphasised the importance of learning to steer by the position of the sun. We had already heard of two Hurricane pilots who were last seen heading eastward towards German lines, instead of westward. It was thought at the time that their compasses might have been affected.

By the 24th May most of the airfields in north France had been captured by the Germans. The squadron operating from Kenley carried out fighter escort patrols to Blenheim bombers against targets in the Lille-Arras-Calais areas. Although a gaggle of 60+ Ju87's escorted by Me109's were met on 25th May and battle was joined, there were only a few victories claimed.

Pilot Officer H. A. C. Bird-Wilson, 17 Squadron

*

In England, a plan, code-named Operation Dynamo, was put together in the 'possible but unlikely evacuation of a very large force in hazardous circumstances'. Vice-Admiral Sir Bertram Ramsay at Dover would execute such an operation should it become necessary. As May progressed it soon became evident that an evacuation would not only seem possible but highly probable.

*

With Calais about to fall, the BEF now only had the seaport of Dunkirk to fall back on. Fighting by day and retreating during the night hours, the BEF pulled back towards the coast during the night of 26th May. Totally surrounded and with their backs to the sea, they set up and defended a perimeter. It was now apparent that if at least some of the BEF was to be saved the Navy would have to lift them from Dunkirk. There were an estimated 500,000 British and French soldiers within the perimeter, with, it appeared, little hope of rescue. Finally Operation Dynamo was ordered to be set in motion, at 6.57 p.m. on 26th May. It was hoped that some 45,000 troops might be rescued over the next two days. After that, any evacuation was thought to be impossible.

The Navy had only limited shipping to carry out this task; destroyers were the largest warships employed in this danger zone. It, therefore, commandeered whatever shipping that was available, be they cross-Channel ferries, coasters, motor vessels, paddle-steamers, anything in fact that could get to Dunkirk, pick up troops and bring them back to England.

It was obvious that this naval effort would be heavily opposed by the German Luftwaffe. Nobody yet even guessed that the Luftwaffe had been given the task of bombing the troops in the Dunkirk perimeter. To combat this and protect the rescue ships, the Royal Air Force would be needed.

The task fell to Fighter Command's 11 Group which covered the south and south-east corner of England, directly opposite Dunkirk. 11 Group was commanded by Air Vice-Marshal Keith Park, MC, DFC, a New Zealander, and a successful two-seater fighter pilot from the First World War. His squadrons would provide the umbrella above the ships and port (and later the beaches) at Dunkirk.

Keith Park later broke down the whole operation into four parts covering the period 10th May to 4th June:

1 Fighter cover on the left flank of the Allied armies during their rapid advance through the Low Countries from 10th to 20th May.
2 Fighter support for the Allied forces by 11 Group units working from advance bases in France during the period 10th to 12th May.
3 Fighter cover and support for the Allied forces during their withdrawal from the Low Countries.
4 Close fighter cover for the final withdrawal of the Allied army into Dunkirk and the evacuation of the forces from that port and beaches.

In Phase 1 five RAF fighter squadrons were moved into forward aerodromes in Kent. From here they flew offensive patrols along the Belgian and Dutch coasts to the limit of their range. These 11 Group squadrons encountered little opposition during the first phase.

Numbers 3, 79 and 501 Squadrons were detached from 11 Group in Phase 2, to advance bases in France, operating patrols under control of the Air Forces in France and the Air Component.

As the BEF met heavy opposition and were forced to retreat, Park increased fighter support. In addition to the seven home-based squadrons, three composite squadrons, each of two flights taken from different squadrons in England, were transferred each day to refuelling points in France from which they operated in conjunction with the BAFF, returning nightly to their home bases. This support was provided during 17th to 19th May, but when eventually it was found that refuelling facilities in France were inadequate, as well as the airfields subject to Luftwaffe attack, these units returned from patrols to forward aerodromes in Kent.

In Phase 3 from 20th May onwards, during the final, critical withdrawal into the Dunkirk pocket, 11 Group had to provide an increasing number of patrols over France as well as providing fighter escort to bombers and reconnaissance aeroplanes.

When Phase 4 began on 26th May, Park had a daily average of just sixteen squadrons available, retaining the remaining six squadrons in his Group – Blenheims and unarmed Spitfires – solely for home defence. The story which now follows is the fighting record of Phase 4 which began late on 26th May, lasting officially till 4th June. The BEF at Dunkirk were to ask long and hard the question, 'Where is the RAF?' What follows should provide the answer.

CHAPTER TWO

The Opening Rounds

Royal Air Force squadrons were operating over and around Dunkirk well before the time Operation Dynamo was put into effect. As far as individual units were concerned it was just air cover, no hint or suggestion of an evacuation had yet been made.

No 610 Squadron had flown to Biggin Hill from Prestwick on 10th May and flew a number of patrols on the 21st between Dover and Boulogne, and later over Calais. 610 was commanded by Squadron Leader Alexander Lumsden Franks, AFC, known affectionately as 'Bonzo'. He was a highly skilled pilot, ex-Cranwell, who had a marked effect on his auxiliary squadron. In the words of John Ellis, one of his flight commanders:

> '. . . a regular officer who took over the squadron in November
> 1938. He was a large, cheerful Irishman – a great character with
> a fund of marvellous Irish stories. It was a great loss to the
> squadron and the RAF when he was shot down over Dunkirk.'

Fifty-four Squadron from Hornchurch also flew patrols on the 21st, the first at 8.20 a.m. Flight Lieutenant James Leathart was leading one section out to sea from Dunkirk. Twenty-five minutes later Leathart, known as 'Prof' (because of his earlier academic ability), spotted a Heinkel 111 bomber flying north. His No 2 flew in close to make certain it was a German, and then the three Spitfires chased it through cloud. Leathart eventually closed in and got a two-second burst, causing some damage before it became totally lost in the clouds. At around 1 p.m., Pilot Officer Johnny Allen of the same squadron was ordered off alone to investigate another doubtful aircraft. Near the Belgian coast he suddenly ran into a large force of Ju88's, and attacked one, possibly destroying it.

With several squadrons in action in France and now flying daily patrols off the Belgian and Dutch coasts, new squadrons began to be called down from the north to reinforce 11 Group. 605 Squadron at

Wick was ordered to Hawkinge on the 21st following a warning to its Commanding Officer, Squadron Leader G.V. Perry, of the probable move at 10.15 that morning. 13 Group HQ confirmed the move at 12.30 and the first of fifteen Hurricanes was away at 3 p.m. All had arrived at Hawkinge by 9 p.m., the ground crews leaving by train at 3.30 p.m.

Sixty-four, 65 and 74 Squadrons all flew patrols off the Belgian coast, but it was 74 Squadron that got into action on their patrol which began shortly after 5.30 p.m. Led by Flight Lieutenant A.G. 'Sailor' Malan, who was shortly to become one of Fighter Command's most successful pilots, 74 patrolled off the North Foreland. Later Malan saw bursting AA shells towards Dunkirk and persuaded control to let him take a look. Flying towards the French coast they found two He111's which were attacked and probably destroyed.

Malan then spotted six Ju88's, one some way from the others. Sending Pilot Officer R.D. 'Bertie' Aubert after a straggler, Malan and his other section man, Flying Officer Johnny Freeborn, attacked the other five. Malan and Freeborn both destroyed one Ju88, but Aubert in chasing his target, which he too shot down, ran short of petrol and decided to force land on Berck-sur-Mer aerodrome. Leaving his Spitfire he went into Boulogne in search of petrol and upon returning encountered German tanks. The airfield had been abandoned and without petrol he had no way of getting away. He therefore made his way to Calais, flying back to England in a Blenheim two days later.

At approximately the same time as this action was in progress, 610 Squadron were again on patrol, their fifth of the day. Ordered to patrol Calais-Boulogne to give protection to shipping around Dunkirk, Squadron Leader Franks saw fourteen twin-engined aircraft approach Cap Gris Nez from the east. The squadron positioned itself for an attack from behind and Franks led Red Section down. The squadron leader opened fire, sending one aircraft down but then Yellow Leader saw that they were Blenheims and yelled a warning. To be fair, visibility was very poor and the light was failing with a thick haze forming, but the damage had been done – one RAF Blenheim had been shot down.

At 4.30 a.m. on 22nd May, 605 Squadron were called to readiness and took off to patrol Calais-Boulogne including a twenty mile sweep inland. No hostile aircraft were seen, but they did look down upon a burning oil tanker off Boulogne. 74 Squadron were also in the air early, Sailor Malan leading nine Spitfires at 5 a.m. Forty-five minutes later they spotted a Ju88 flying north-east. Malan, Pilot Officer P.C.F. Stevenson and Sergeant E.A. Mould shot it down into the sea.

Flight Lieutenant G.A.W. 'Gerry' Saunders led a flight of 65 Squadron on a patrol of Dunkirk-Calais shortly after 8.30. It was uneventful for all except Pilot Officer K.G. Hart. His Spitfire (K9920) developed engine trouble, forcing him to make a wheels-up landing at North Foreland. His engine burst into flames, but by skilful piloting, Ken Hart got down and clambered out unhurt although the aeroplane was burnt out.

RAF fighters were also flying well inland, covering the troops making for the coast. 605 Squadron flew a patrol to the south of Arras, Red Section being attacked by six Messerschmitt 109's. They shot down two pilots, Flying Officer G. Austin (N2349) and Sergeant Moffat (L2058). Yellow Section engaged three He111's but Pilot Officer C.F. 'Bunny' Currant's Hurricane was shot through the oil system. He force-landed, burnt his aircraft and returned to the squadron twenty-four hours later with a broken nose. Flying Officer G.F.W. Wright (L2120) was also hit by return fire from the Heinkels; his Hurricane last seen diving away with glycol streaming from it.

At about the same time, eight further aircraft of 605 formed a composite squadron with three aircraft of 79 Squadron to patrol Abbeville-Doullens-Arras. Heavy AA fire was met and Flight Lieutenant P.G. Leeson (L2121) failed to return.

Shortly after lunch 65 Squadron flew another patrol, over Calais-Boulogne. Gerry Saunders' Section attacked a Ju88, Pilot Officer Smart (K9908) knocking out its rear-gunner and starboard engine before losing it in cloud.

The pilots of 145 Squadron ran into thirty Stuka dive-bombers at 6.30 p.m., attacking them just as they commenced their dives. They shot down six and damaged two more.

There was further action that evening when Squadron Leader J. 'Baron' Worrall led eleven aircraft of his 32 Squadron together with 601 Squadron to Calais-Boulogne, followed by a sweep inland. At around 7.40 p.m., when near St Omer, the squadrons became engaged with eight Me109's and in the battle five or six were shot down by 32 Squadron.

*

The pace continued on the 23rd, a day that saw one of the more famous events of the pre-evacuation period. 74 Squadron mounted a patrol at 6 a.m. between Boulogne and Calais. Flying at 2,000 feet, the Commanding Officer, Squadron Leader F.L. White, noticed a low flying aircraft south of Calais, moving in and out of cloud. Investigating, he saw it was a Henschel 126, light observation aeroplane. White flew around the aircraft to be certain of its identity, then positioned his Section for an attack.

As he led them down, the German pilot dropped down to ground level and began a turn to the left. White's overtaking speed was too high so he attempted two deflection shots, one appearing to hit the Henschel's right wing-tip, the second splattering the fuselage. Breaking sharply to avoid a collision, he passed over the machine. Looking back he saw the 'plane crash and break up, it having been finished off by Flying Officer W.E.G. 'Tink' Measures. However, the German gunner had managed to get a hit in White's radiator, forcing him to make a landing on Calais Marck aerodrome. With German forces about to take Calais, Squadron Leader White's position was a little precarious.

It was decided to mount an air rescue mission, 54 Squadron being asked to fly and escort a two-seater Miles Master to Calais, land and return with 74's Commanding Officer. At 10.30 Leathart took off (in Master N7681), escorted by two of 54's Spitfires, flown by Pilot Officer Al Deere, a New Zealander (N3180) and Pilot Officer Johnny Allen (P9289).

The flight out, made at low-level, proved uneventful, Leathart landing without incident. With broken cloud over the area, Deere ordered Allen up above them while he circled the airfield. No sooner did Deere see the Master safely down and trundle towards a small hangar than Allen yelled a warning that Messerschmitts were in the vicinity and he was engaging. He was at 12,000 feet, the 109's at 9,000 feet.

Allen attacked the nearest 109 which went into a stall turn and dived into cloud. Allen followed, firing a five-second burst, going through more cloud. Emerging he saw the 109 diving, streaming smoke. Climbing again, he tried to draw the German fighters away from the aerodrome and found still more enemy aircraft above the cloud. Two 109's attacked him, Allen making a head-on run at them. The first 109 roared past him but the other tried a beam attack which failed. He then dog-fought several 109's managing to send two diving into cloud with smoke coming from their engines.

Meanwhile, Deere had dived down to warn Leathart of the danger, but the Master carried no radio, so Deere had to try to warn him by waggling the wings of his Spitfire. Below, the Master was taxi-ing out for take-off and as it did so, Deere saw a 109 dive through the clouds towards the two-seater. It flew right across Deere's nose. He opened fire, more in an attempt to put off the German pilot than to do any real damage and he succeeded. As Deere then hauled after the 109, he heard Allen above call for assistance. Deere acknowledged but finished off the 109 first, it crashing in a vertical dive from 3,000 feet into the water's edge.

> Two Spitfires were considered enough as the Germans were not in occupation of Calais-Marck and it was thought, and I think rightly, that the Master could fly out at low level, land, collect White and get off again. It was just fortuitous that the Germans

happened to be over Calais-Marck at that time and probably it was just the lone Spitfire above that attracted them. They didn't know the Master was there until one came down through the thin cloud and saw it. The 109 came down at the exact moment the Master was flying off; of course the Master was painted yellow so stood out against the ground. He didn't see me though.

Pilot Officer A.C. Deere, 54 Squadron

Climbing to help Allen, Deere ran into two Messerschmitts. He knocked pieces off one as the fight began and then he had a real scrap with the leader chasing it inland, but ran out of ammunition before he could nail him. Both RAF pilots then made for England, Allen nursing his Spitfire which had been damaged, back to Manston. Leathart and White had both scrambled from the Master when attacked and dived into a nearby ditch, watching the fight above before taking off to fly safely to England. They had witnessed three Me109's crash. Leathart subsequently received the DSO, Deere and Allen both being awarded the DFC.

The abiding thing was all the time training and not thinking about war, then war being inevitable and we went out not knowing what to expect and apart from one brush with a Heinkel in the cloud this was our first combat and indeed, it was the first recorded combat of a Spitfire with a 109. It was the thrill of the thing really; there was no sense of danger at that stage. So much so that I stayed behind the last 109 to see if I could, after I'd used up my ammunition. That shows you how really green one was, and it was only that sense told me I'd better get out of the place, because we'd got inland a bit by that time, and petrol was a factor – always a factor over France, that I'd better break off and get away. But it did convince me, although I couldn't convince the powers-that-be, that the Spitfire I was, except in certain parameters, superior to the Me109 – except in the dive really. Certainly in the sustained climb and in the turn it was. My squadron, of course, were equipped with the first constant-speed Rotal airscrew and no other squadrons had for we were doing trials on it, so it gave a false impression of the capability of the majority of the Spitfires at that time, which were two speed, either fine or coarse, whereas the constant speed airscrew changed its pitch as the revs. went up. You had this constant factor of the airscrew changing to suit the conditions of climb etc. But the big thing for me was that we shouldn't have any fear of the 109 in combat.

Pilot Officer A.C. Deere, 54 Squadron

Back at Hornchurch, 54 Squadron were joined that morning by 92 Squadron who flew in from Northolt. They flew their first patrol at around 8.30 a.m., ran into six Me109's, and claimed all six shot down. They lost one pilot, Pilot Officer B.H.G. 'Pat' Learmond (P9370) who went down in flames. Pilot Officer Anthony Bartley was on this first sortie:

> I watched Paddy's plane in front of me, and repeated his last instructions: 'Stick to my tail, and for God's sake keep a look out behind'. 'Look out, 109's', someone yelled on the intercom and almost simultaneously I saw it. It was grey and evil-looking with its large black crosses, and I could see the pilot crouched in his cockpit. So this was it . . . and as I started after him, I had time to wonder if he felt as I did; if he loved to roll and loop in the towering cumulus, and reach for the sun, high up and alone in the sky; I wondered how old he was and whether this was his first fight, as it was mine; and then, I wondered how soon he would spot me closing in on him. He suddenly turned in a tight circle, but I turned tighter, and we both knew that the Spitfire could out-turn a Messerschmitt. He was looking back at me as I pressed the trigger, and the tracer flickered over his wingtips. Then I heard the bullets thudding into me as his compatriot flashed past. I'd forgotten Paddy's warning to look behind. I was angry now, and I attacked again, but Paddy suddenly appeared in front of me. He hit the 109 with his first burst and an aileron flew off and fluttered earthwards like an autumn leaf. The aircraft twisted in its agony, and spewed out its pilot. His face was white, and his blond hair streamed grotesquely. He didn't pull his rip cord. My petrol gauge was showing next to zero, so I radioed Paddy I was going home. I saw the blazing wreck of a Spitfire and I darted seawards over the swarming beaches. It was Pat Learmond's – the squadron's first war casualty.
>
> *Pilot Officer A.C. Bartley, 92 Squadron*

*

Baron Worrall's 32 Squadron flew escort to a Blenheim reconnaissance aircraft in the early afternoon. Near Ypres shortly after 1 p.m., they engaged nineteen Me110's and twelve Me109's. Flight Lieutenant P.M. Brothers shot down a 110, and Flight Lieutenant Mike Crossley got two. Pilot Officer D.H. 'Grubby' Grice saw a Hurricane go down on fire, presumably Sergeant G.L. Nowell, who failed to return. Gareth Nowell, DFM and Bar, had previously flown with 87 Squadron in France, having shot down more than a dozen German aircraft during the Blitzkrieg. He had already been shot down with 87, and now again with 32. This time he was badly injured but managed to return to England before the final collapse.

No 11 Group were reinforced by a two-seater fighter squadron on the 23rd, 264, flying the new Boulton Paul Defiant, flying from Duxford to Manston. The Defiant was very different from any other RAF fighter, having a pilot with no front guns, but with an air gunner in a power-operated turret just behind him, with four Browning .303 machine guns. Looking very similar to a Hurricane at first glance, this was to give some surprises to attacking German fighters initially, but the Germans soon found the aeroplane's weak spot. When in action against German bombers, the Defiant pilot needed to position his aeroplane in such a way that his gunner could bring his guns to bear. This either meant flying alongside, rather like ships from Nelson's period, or by flying across and in front of the enemy target, the gunner firing as the Defiant went by. This was called the cross-over attack. As yet untried, the Defiants of 264 Squadron were to have their first action over Dunkirk and learn the skills of air-combat. They were eventually to find that they were no real match for a determined Luftwaffe with superior aeroplanes.

However, 264 flew their first patrol that same afternoon off Dunkirk, Calais and Boulogne. Seven twin-engined Me110's were seen but they climbed into cloud. One more daring 110 pilot glided down towards the Defiants hoping to break-up the squadron formation, followed shortly by the other six. Seeing the Defiants still in good order, the 110's climbed again and made off. 264 made a second patrol in the evening with two Hurricane squadrons but this proved uneventful.

Ninety-two Squadron flew another patrol that evening and ran into a whole swarm of Me110's. They claimed seventeen shot down but lost three pilots and another wounded. Tony Bartley later wrote:

> The squadron took off again after re-fuelling and re-arming and ran into trouble as soon as we hit the beaches. A swarm of Heinkels approached like a gaggle of geese. Above them in attendance, followed a cloud of 109's and 110's. I didn't know how Roger proposed to attack this armada, and I thought of Henry V at Agincourt. Perhaps because it was not far from us.
>
> Suddenly Roger's voice broke the RT silence, 'Paddy, take on the high cover. Bob and I will take the bombers. Over.' I scrambled for altitude after Paddy, and then suddenly we were in the middle of it. They came down at us like a swarm of angry bees. I ducked a stream of tracer and turned in behind an Me110. He had a shark's jaw painted on his nose. I aimed with eight guns.

He turned over and went straight down. I watched him hit the ground in a burst of flame. My first Hun . . . I felt sick. Then I was in the milling mass of aeroplanes, twisting, turning, climbing and diving in pursuit of one another. The sky was filled with tracer and smoke trails, and suddenly my port wing was drilled with holes. Paddy came up on my left with five Me110's on his tail. I attacked the 110's and another five attacked me. I crouched lower in my cockpit to make myself as small a target as possible. I heard Roger swearing on the radio as he plunged into the bomber force. None of his Section returned. John Gillies went with him, and Paul Klipsch was killed. Paddy was hit in the thigh and landed at Hawkinge, his cockpit awash with blood.[1]

Pilot Officer A.C. Bartley, 92 Squadron

The day's total for 92 was twenty-three Germans shot down for the loss of four pilots, one wounded and seven other Spitfires shot up.

By the end of the 23rd, the Germans were in Boulogne, a BEF counter-attack at Arras had failed, and British troops were now on half-rations. The defensive ring around Dunkirk was strengthened by two divisions on the 24th, the pocket now some fifty kilometres wide and 100 kilometres deep from the sea.

In the air on the 24th, the RAF continued to fly patrols over the area and inland despite rain showers, though they still had no real idea of where the BEF actually was on the ground, nor how serious was the situation. Enemy opposition continued intermittently, some RAF squadrons seeing no signs of hostile aircraft at all, others seeing the enemy only too well.

The Blenheims of 235 Squadron at Bircham Newton sent two aeroplanes as fighter escort to Hudsons on an attack on the German coast, the Blenheims piloted by Flight Lieutenant Cross and Pilot Officer Ryan. Some Me109's engaged them and Ryan with his crew, Sergeant Martin and LAC Smith, were shot down by two 109's, (L9259).[2]

The 'Tigers' of 74 Squadron were in action again on their first patrol of the day, Flight Lieutenant W.P.F. Treacy and his section shooting down a Hs126 observation 'plane.

Flight Lieutenant Bob Tuck, in temporary command of 92 Squadron, led a patrol at 8.30 a.m. The squadron again saw action, claiming seven

---

[1] Squadron Leader R.J. Bushell was flying Spitfire N3194. He was killed by Gestapo after the Great Escape from Stalag Luft III in 1944. Flying Officer J. Gillies – POW – (N3290), Sergeant P. Klipsch (P9373), Flight Lieutenant C.P. Green (N3167).

[2] Flight Lieutenant Cross was killed in a crash at Detling on 29th May 1940 when an engine failed on take-off.

German aircraft shot down. Tuck shot down two Dornier 17's but had his cockpit canopy blown off (N3249) after destroying the first. Despite this he attacked another Dornier and saw it crash into a wood. Tuck received a slight wound when a small duralumin nut was knocked from his rudder pedal when his Spitfire was hit, flew up and embedded in the inside of his thigh. Pilot Officer Harry Edwards – a Canadian, got a possible Me110, then had his windscreen shattered by a bullet.[1] Flying Officer Pete Casanove was hit and had to force-land his Spitfire (P9374) at Calais.

> From his POW camp, we heard from Pete Casanove, one of our boys, who was captured at Dunkirk, after being shot down. He tried to get on to three destroyers but was turned off each one. The Navy said that all the accommodation was reserved for the Army, and the Air Force could go f - - - themselves.
>
> Alan Deere, another of my friends, was in the same predicament, but he knocked the naval officer out and smuggled himself aboard. Since then he has shot down umpteen more Huns and been awarded the DFC!
>
> *Pilot Officer A.C. Bartley, 92 Squadron*[2]

Sailor Malan and 74 Squadron got some action on their mid-day patrol. Malan and his section shot down a Dornier 17 while Paddy Treacy and Pilot Officer D.H.T. Dowding (the son of Sir Hugh Dowding, Commander-in-Chief, Fighter Command) got another. 264 Squadron flew a patrol shortly after mid-day, one Me 110 being shot down by Flight Lieutenant E.H. Whitehouse and his gunner, Pilot Officer H. Scott (in L6972).

No 74 Squadron were again in combat in the mid-afternoon when patrolling Dover-Calais-Boulogne. They found three Vic formations of He111's: Sailor Malan destroyed one of the bombers, Sergeant W.M. Skinner damaged another and Johnny Freeborn probably destroyed an escorting Me109. However, they lost Pilot Officer Bertie Aubert who had only arrived back from his forced landing at Berck that morning, and Paddy Treacy who baled out. Sergeant E.A. 'Tony' Mould also went down and so did Flying Officer D.S. 'Sammy' Hoare who force landed at Calais Marck.

Treacy managed to get home on a boat via Dunkirk harbour and so did Tony Mould. There was no valiant rescue for Sammy Hoare, as had occurred for his Commanding Officer the previous day. Before his

---

[1] Pilot Officer H.D. Edwards was killed in action 11th September 1940.
[2] From a letter to his father dated June 1940.

Spitfire could be repaired he was captured by advancing enemy soldiers.

Tony Mould had climbed with the others to engage the Heinkel formation at 20,000 feet. As they went into the attack he fired his first burst, but was hit by return fire in his petrol tank which immediately caught fire. The whole cockpit filled with flames and as he was flying at high speed had some initial difficulty in sliding back the cockpit hood but eventually managed it and dived over the right-hand side and away. His parachute opened and he landed about five miles to the south-west of Bergues, in a field of young wheat. Some French infantry in the locality fired several shots at him, despite him standing up with his hands in the air. Then some British soldiers arrived and took him with them to their Headquarters. They were Grenadier Guards and were expecting a move at any moment so they took him to a mixed detail of soldiers a mile or so away. It was here that he saw a Hs126 shot down by some Spitfires. (65 Squadron's action, see later.)

Mould was then provided with transport which conveyed him to Bergues where at the Regional Headquarters he was advised to make his way to Dunkirk. Making his way, he arrived at Dunkirk and reported to the Naval Traffic Officer. Mould found about eight other assorted RAF people also waiting for transport back to England as well as some army officers and civilians. By this time it was past eight o'clock but it was almost twenty-four hours before a troopship left with him on it for England. While he was waiting, there were several raids on the dock area and during one, at around 7 a.m. on the morning of the 25th, a large oil tank was set on fire which burned furiously all day.

It had not been a good day for 74 Squadron. They had lost Aubert killed, Sammy Hoare prisoner, Pilot Officer J.C. Mungo-Park slightly wounded in the arm, while Treacy and Mould were shot down but safe.

The action witnessed by Tony Mould was when 65 Squadron put up three sections to patrol Calais-Dunkirk at 5.40 p.m. Flight Lieutenant G.A.W. Saunders (P9436) initially saw AA bursting, then spotted the Hs126 above to the left. As he climbed the observation plane turned practically towards him, Gerry Saunders firing a deflection burst whereupon the Henschel flicked into a vertical dive. Pilot Officer Tommy Smart (N3129) then engaged the 126 as its pilot hedge-hopped away, his second burst silencing fire from the rear-gunner. Flight Sergeant W.H. Franklyn (N3164) followed up these attacks and the 126 crashed in flames. This had been 65 Squadron's fourth patrol of the day and their only contact with the enemy.

Earlier, at 12.30 p.m., 54 Squadron had had the first two actions of the day. At 12,000 feet above Calais, they had met two large formations of He111's escorted by Me109 and Me110's. 54 attempted to engage but the 109's swooped down, preventing an organised attack. A series of dogfights ensued and they claimed nine German aircraft shot down plus four probables. It was 54's first real big fight and all aircraft returned safely. Sergeant J.W.B. Phillips shot down three 109's and possibly a fourth.

> Over Dunkirk at 10,000 feet we ran into a whole flock of Messerschmitts, which came charging down out of the clouds. They had obviously been sitting upstairs guarding some bombers hidden in the smoke below. They nearly caught us. I saw tracers going past my ears and actually heard the gun rattle from one on my tail and then he was gone. I followed him down, banging the throttle open and leaning on my stick but in the last smoke clouds hanging over Dunkirk I lost him.
>
> Up again I saw the rest of the squadron at about 6,000 feet. They were in a hell of a mix-up with Hun fighters and some Junkers 88's and I climbed up to join them. My radio was open and as I climbed I could hear a stream of occasionally comic backchat passing backwards and forwards between some of the other members of the squadron, occasionally punctuated with bursts of gunfire as they were popping off at Huns. Once, for instance, I heard a New Zealander calling and saying calmly, 'There's a Messerschmitt on your tail', and the reply, 'Okay, pal', and then I was in it too.
>
> Again there was that lovely feeling of the gluey controls and the target being slowly hauled into the sights. Then thumb down on the trigger again and the smooth shuddering of the machine as the eight-gun blast let go. This time the squirt I gave him must have cut him in two. His tail folded back on his wings and there was a great smoke and flash of flame as he went down.
>
> *Flight Lieutenant J.A. Leathart, 54 Squadron*[1]

At 4.37 p.m., the squadron was once again over Calais where they saw twelve Me109's. In the battle that followed, four were shot down, one pilot being seen to bale out. However, 54 lost two pilots; Flying Officer T.N. Linley (P9455) did not return, nor did Sergeant Phillips (P9388). Sergeant Phillips had led Green Section and spotted initially seven 109's and requested Leathart to take a look as they looked more like Curtiss Hawks. Leathart gave the OK and Phillips dived down. Seeing that they were in fact 109's, the section broke up the 109's. Phillips got behind one and fired at it as it went into cloud, but followed it through and

[1] From an article which appeared in *Life Magazine* in 1940 following an interview with James Leathart, a copy of which Air Commodore Leathart loaned to this author.

down until they were down to 500 feet and twenty to thirty miles inland. The 109 pilot then throttled back but Phillips too throttled back and gave the Messerschmitt a burst and it dived into the ground.

Phillips then spotted a convoy of seven to ten lorries and strafed them. Flying back towards Calais he was fired on by a Bofors gun which registered hits in his wings, oil sump and petrol tank. His cockpit filled with oil and the machine then caught fire. Phillips baled out, his parachute opening at 50 feet and on landing he smashed his leg. He tried to crawl but was taken prisoner by storm troopers.

The Hurricanes of 17 and 605 Squadrons, forming a composite unit, flew one of the first operations on the morning of the 25th, escorting six Blenheims over Gravelines on a reconnaissance sortie. When they had carried out this task, the fighters flew a sweep of Menin-Courtrai-Tournai for an hour. Pilot Officer Ian Muirhead of 605, spotted two Hs126's at 10,000 feet, destroying one of them.

Other squadrons flew patrols, but it was 92 Squadron who found the enemy towards the end of their stint over Dunkirk; at 1 p.m. Pilot Officer Harry Edwards, leading Yellow Section, saw AA fire and then two Do17's at 22,000 feet. One was heading out to sea, the other flying towards Holland. Chasing the one heading for the coast, Edwards ordered the standard Number One Fighter Command attack. Closing in, Edwards fired all his ammunition in three bursts. As he broke away he found that his two wingmen were not behind him. They had not heard his call and had not followed him.

Flight Lieutenant Bob Tuck and his section engaged another Do17 and following a long chase, it finally blew up when down below 4,000 feet. It had taken a surprising number of hits and had been almost turned into a flying sieve. As Tuck tried to finish it off, one of his pilots yelled, 'Go on, skip, throw your boots at it!'

> We mustered nine machines, and, on our patrol lines spotted a lone Dornier 17 bomber. We had a good look round, expecting a covey of fighters lurking about waiting for us to fall for their bait. However, the Do17 was unescorted, so there was an undisciplined scramble for first shot. I closed in second after Bob Tuck, and got in some useful bursts. The poor old bomber didn't stand an earthly, and by the time the fourth pilot had made his attack it was practically in pieces. We watched two men jump before it hit the water. One parachute did not open so I suppose he must have been too dead to pull the cord. We let the other man float down unharmed.
>
> *Pilot Officer A.C. Bartley, 92 Squadron*

That afternoon 92 Squadron flew to Duxford to rest and re-equip. A new Commanding Officer, Squadron Leader P.J. Sanders, arrived on the 27th to replace Roger Bushell. 92 would be back.

A composite formation of 17, 605 and 79 Squadrons (a total of twenty-one Hurricanes) covered more Blenheims over Calais shortly before mid-day, then turned to patrol Courtrai-Hazebrouck-Dunkirk.

South-east of Calais, Squadron Leader G.D. Emms, Pilot Officer D. Hanson and Pilot Officer Ken Manger attacked a Do17, forcing it to crash-land five miles from Ardres. Meanwhile the other two sections and the six pilots of 605 Squadron found juicier targets. Off Calais at 15,000 feet they ran into forty to fifty Ju87 Stukas.

Flight Lieutenant W.A. Toyne climbed his section up-sun and then attacked a group of five 87's. One he fired at spewed petrol and light smoke, then went down. Toyne then attacked two more which he damaged. Pilot Officer H.A.C. 'Birdy' Bird-Wilson climbed with the sun behind him and saw a Ju87 coming straight at him. He managed to get onto its tail and opened fire. The Stuka dived steeply, Birdy following. Closing the gap he fired another burst, the Stuka then pulled out but then went down again in a spin. Flying Officer W.J. Harper attacked another Ju87 and sent it into the sea. Similarly Flying Officer Meredith attacked another 87 which dived vertically into the sea. Sergeant Steward sent one down in a spin. Pilot Officer Whittaker was one of the Hurricanes left as top cover and as the scrap developed, he saw a Ju87 emerge from the battle. Diving on it, his first burst silenced the rear gunner and the 87 started down in a spin. He then turned onto three other Stukas, and knocked out the gunner of one of them as it rolled over onto its back. Whittaker closed again, only to find his guns empty.

Flight Lieutenant C.F.G. Adye patrolled up-sun and missed this action but he helped Squadron Leader G.D. Emms attack the Do17, which he last saw with white smoke streaming from its starboard engine, to be finished off by Emms as already related. Adye then almost ran head-on into a Hs126. He fired a five-second burst at point blank range and the observation 'plane burst into flames and crashed into a wood from 200 feet.

No 605 Squadron, meanwhile, also engaged the Ju87 formation and then they found another gaggle about to dive-bomb ships off Gravelines. Flying Officer G.R. Edge attacked the latter group, the leading Stuka turning to meet him head-on. Edge fired and the German broke away over him, but very close. Edge then chased another down until it fell crashing into a ploughed field. Turning for the coast he saw two more groups of Stukas and attacked the rear of one, putting a long burst into it from close range. The 87 began to pour out black smoke and the other Stukas formed a defensive circle, their combined fire forcing him away. Pilot Officer I.J. Muirhead claimed his second aircraft of the day by shooting down another Ju87, then made it three by downing a Ju87 from the second group they attacked.

The two squadrons had thus shot down five or six definitely with several more possibles as well as getting a Dornier and one Hs126. Neither squadron suffered any loss, only some Hurricanes slightly damaged by return fire.

Fighter Command did, however, lose two pilots and some aircraft during the day. 54 Squadron got into action in the mid-afternoon when escorting Fleet Air Arm Swordfish on a bombing raid over Gravelines and Calais. The Spitfires engaged formations of Me109's and Me110's which they eventually drove off, after inflicting casualties.

Flight Lieutenant Max Pearson leading Blue Section saw the 110's form a defensive circle, a manoeuvre that RAF pilots would see increasingly over the following weeks. Pearson turned onto the rear-most 110 and stuck to him. As his sights came on, he fired a three-second burst which shattered parts of the perspex cockpit covering and started the 110's port engine smoking. Another burst sent the Messerschmitt crashing into Gravelines on fire. Pearson noted a jagged red line painted around the nose of the 110.

'Prof' Leathart experienced radio failure and did not hear Pearson's warning of enemy aircraft and so his Number 3, Johnny Allen, led their Red Section after Pearson's Blue. Climbing into the fight, Allen saw two 110's attacking a Spitfire, so dived vertically on the rear one, firing a long burst at it. One of the 110's engines burst into flames and fell away out of control. Using the speed of his dive, Allen pulled up and shot at the other 110 which went down with both engines smoking.

Allen then felt his machine (N3188) hit by a cannon shell, exploding somewhere in his engine. Diving into nearby cloud he lost height, but within a very few minutes his engine stopped and then caught fire. Gliding towards some ships he then took to his parachute and came down in the Channel from where he was picked up by a British destroyer within ten minutes. To achieve his successful bale out he had unstrapped himself, locked open the cockpit hood, then put the Spitfire into a half-barrel role at 100 mph. When it went onto its back he pushed the stick forward and fell out without any difficulty.

> Allen suddenly said, 'Oh hell, my engine's packed up.' Then, 'I'm on fire.' There was a silence for a second or two and he said, 'Yippee! There's a destroyer downstairs. I'm baling out.' A second later I heard him mutter, 'But how?'
>
> It is as a matter of fact not easy to bale out of a Spitfire. The best way is to turn her over on her back and drop out through the

hood – if you can. That, we found out later, was exactly what he had done. He turned up in the mess three days afterwards wearing a naval sub-lieutenant's jacket and bell-bottomed trousers and carrying a sailor's kit bag over his shoulder.

Flight Lieutenant J.A. Leathart, 54 Squadron

Leathart, meantime, found the 110 circle and attacked one that came adrift. As he attacked he felt his Spitfire caught by a burst of fire from somewhere which seemed to rack it from stem to stern. He hit his head on the roof of the canopy and thought he'd been hit himself. Diving out of the battle he found everything in order and later discovered his machine totally undamaged, so he assumed he had passed close to an exploding AA shell.

Green Section had followed Red Section and seen the 110's too and were climbing preparatory to attack when they were attacked themselves by about a dozen Me109's. Pilot Officer Colin Gray, a New Zealander, fired a four-second burst at one as it passed and it went down. A few moments later he saw a parachute appear. The 109 had in fact dived past Sergeant John (Jock) Norwell who also gave it a burst and then the German baled out as flames began to stream from his fighter. Gray and Norwell shared the kill.

Gray was then hit by two bursts of fire, hitting both wings and practically shooting away his controls. Although difficult to control, he managed to fly it back to base, to find he'd also been hit by flak.

Pilot Officer George Gribble had his Spitfire (N3103) shot up which forced him to land on the beach near Dunkirk. He got back by ship, carrying his Spitfire's radio under his arm. Feeling that their radio equipment was still 'secret', he had taken it from the aeroplane and brought it back, despite the ship's captain trying to dissuade him from cluttering up space for equipment. Johnny Allen too returned, dressed in the uniform of a naval lieutenant. Sergeant Buckland (N3096) was not so fortunate and failed to return.

No 151 Squadron flew a patrol over France escorting Blenheims bombing installations around St Omer. In a turn, Pilot Officer Bushell collided with Flight Lieutenant F.A. Ives. Freddie Ives, the B Flight Commander, was forced down, crash-landing near Nieuport. It was a tragic accident, and luckily Ives survived this crash but as we shall see later, Ives was not destined to return to England.

*

The Defiants of 264 Squadron flew two patrols on the 25th, but found no sign of enemy aircraft. 56 Squadron escorted Blenheims to St Omer in the late afternoon without incident and 145 Squadron flew one of the last patrols of the day when they flew between Calais and incoming ammunition ships. Again no enemy aircraft were seen but although the soldiers fighting defensively in the Dunkirk pocket needed ammunition, this does show that, to the Air Force, if nobody else, ships were still apparently sailing for Dunkirk with supplies, and not necessarily for evacuation purposes.

However, time was now running out for the BEF. If any sort of number was to be rescued then the order to mount 'Dynamo' had to be given soon.

CHAPTER THREE

Sunday, 26th May 1940

The initial plan for Operation Dynamo was for naval and commandeered civilian ships to sail to and from Dunkirk harbour, bringing back the maximum number of soldiers until the Dunkirk perimeter fell. As this perimeter line now only measured approximately twelve miles inland from the sea, it seemed that any rearguard action must be limited, either through being overwhelmed or through eventual lack of ammunition.

As the time drew near for Dynamo, and with non-essential forces already being taken out of the port of Dunkirk, the Admiralty was anxious for air cover from the Royal Air Force. Not only for Dunkirk itself, but over the miles of sea from Dunkirk to Dover, Ramsgate or Folkestone.

The request for air cover was passed down from Dowding to Keith Park, AOC No 11 Group Fighter Command. The request was natural, but Park was to be hard-pressed to answer it. Fighter Command was well below strength and Park was to have on average only sixteen fighter squadrons with which to provide any form of air umbrella. In round figures this meant just 200 aeroplanes, provided all squadrons had good serviceability. Should the immediate conflict last any length of time, this serviceability must deteriorate. Heavy casualties too would begin to create gaps in the total of aeroplanes available.

Eleven Group knew all about serviceability and casualties already. Since the German offensive began on 10th May, an official figure of pilot losses in the group totalled fifty-four during 112 offensive patrols. Thirty of these losses had occurred in just six days – 20th to 25th May. Park was also to be handicapped by a directive from Air Ministry to provide continuous weak fighter patrols throughout the eighteen hours of daylight. Park objected to this order, forecasting that this would undoubtedly incur heavy casualties. It was obvious to him that his squadrons would be outnumbered. He had fought in the First World War and been outnumbered, but these lessons of World War I, like so many other lessons, had been forgotten.

Another factor in the forefront of Park's mind was the fact that Fighter Command generally had been trained to defend the British Isles, above the British Isles. Dunkirk was fifty miles from many of 11 Group's airfields. Fifty miles there and fifty miles back, mostly over water. A climb to operational height, the flights out and back, left a limited patrol time. There was no long range fuel tank at this stage of the war and no radar coverage that would prove a saviour during the subsequent battles over Britain.

But what did the pilots think? Over the last few days the war situation had changed dramatically. Though few knew for sure just how serious it all was, they were all keen to get into action.

> I don't think one had much time to think about the problems, we all hated flying over the sea on one engine.
> We didn't really have any previous experience on which to base a judgement of any sort, or reason to make any deduction.
> It was just that a fight was on and we were ready.
> *Pilot Officer Peter L. Parrott, 145 Squadron*

On this May Sunday, with the RAF squadrons still not knowing how serious the situation had become, operations began early.

The Hurricanes of 17 Squadron, one of the few squadrons to fly continuously throughout the Dunkirk campaign, were the first off on the 26th, twelve aircraft taking off at 4.40 a.m. to rendezvous over Biggin Hill with 79 Squadron. They flew to a point south of Lille where message bags were dropped. AA fire came up from Merville but no ground forces were seen.

Sweeping towards Calais, they crossed the coast and were again fired on by AA. Almost immediately six Me109's dived on them from behind. A dog-fight began, Red Section of 17 Squadron screaming round to engage the Germans. Pilot Officer D. Hanson's Hurricane was hit in the tail. Turning tightly, he saw a 109 diving near another Hurricane. Hanson attacked and the 109 pulled up to the right but the British pilot stayed with him, firing with his sights on. The 109 then dived vertically with grey smoke coming from the engine, but he then lost it when engaged by another 109.

B Flight of 17, crossed out above Dunkirk, led by Flight Lieutenant Toyne, finding a Dornier 17 and a Junkers 88. With petrol short, Toyne had to leave after firing just a quick burst, but Pilot Officer Bird-Wilson managed an effective shot at the 88. As he engaged a Spitfire and a Hurricane joined in and all three attacked. The bomber dived for the coast, very low and as Birdy watched, one of its engines caught fire shortly before it crashed into a field south-west of Gravelines.

Sergeant Wynne, who had become separated from the squadron, saw a German bomber and was about to attack when he glanced back to see another right behind him, with several Me110's behind it. Wynne wisely broke away and flew for home. Flight Lieutenant Adye, Pilot Officer's Whittaker and Ken Manger attacked the Dornier inland and although the rear-gunner was knocked out, the Dornier was not seen to crash before the Hurricanes broke off pursuit. 17 Squadron lost one pilot, Flight Sergeant Jones failing to get home.

In the sky at the same time was 54 Squadron led by 'Prof' Leathart, who had been given command of the squadron on this day. Three sections were providing cover for the unloading of ammunition ships at Dunkirk. When they arrived they spotted two Me110's, Leathart attacking one which dived straight into the sea. Flight Lieutenant Pearson led his section after the other 110 which tried to escape inland flying low, but the Spitfires kept with it. Pearson pursued it as far as Lille before breaking off the action by which time the 110 was flying very slowly with smoke coming from both engines.

Reforming his remaining five pilots off Calais, Leathart engaged German bombers attacking a British destroyer. Singling out one Ju88 on its own, Leathart shot it into the sea, then shot down another Me110 in flames to make a total of three destroyed to celebrate his promotion to squadron leader.

> The squadron ran into the biggest cloud of fighters that I'd seen so far. They were all Messerschmitt 109's and 110's with Ju88's and there must have been pretty nearly 100 of them. They seemed like a swarm of bees. We went in, however, and tore off a chunk each. My recollections of that show are a bit hazy because we were fighting upstairs and downstairs between 1,000 and 15,000 feet and I was blacking out fairly often in the pull-outs after diving after a Hun. But I'm certain I got three and the rest of the squadron wasn't doing too badly because at one time the air seemed to be full of burning aircraft.
>
> *Flight Lieutenant J.A. Leathart, 54 Squadron*

Pilot Officer Al Deere (N3180) was attacked by 110's in this action, but fought them and shot down two. However, as he watched the second one going down towards the sea, a 109 put a burst into his Spitfire, which left a gaping hole in one wing and punctured the tyre. Johnny Allen too was attacked by a 109. Tracer shells zipped over his cockpit and looking in his rear-view mirror he saw the 109 right behind him. Allen looped and rolled off the top, got behind the 109, firing as the 109 dived vertically.

Another of the 110's was put into the sea by Pilot Officer Desmond McMullan, Sergeant Tew probably got another, while Flight Lieutenant 'Wonky' Way crippled a Ju88.

Squadron Leader Desmond Cooke led his 65 Squadron over Dunkirk with 54 and also ran into action. He found four Vic formations of twenty Messerschmitt 110's, and a dog-fight developed. Cooke knocked out the starboard engine of one, Pilot Officer J.B.N. Nicholas smashing the port engine of another. Flying Officer George Proudman blasted another and saw it crash in flames. Pilot Officer Stan Grant destroyed another which fell in flames. Flight Lieutenant Saunders and his section, flying high cover, dived down and with Sergeant Kilner engaged a single Ju88. Saunders fired three bursts at port and starboard engines, followed by Kilner. They watched the 88 dive steeply with both motors smoking and although it levelled out lower down they felt it would not get far. Flying Officer Johnny Welford engaged six Me110's, broke them up and caused them to dive away. As he turned for home his Spitfire (P9437) was hit by AA fire. He was forced to abandon the machine but he was too low and his parachute did not have time to open properly.

These three squadrons all landed back between 6.15 and 6.45 a.m. having lost two pilots but claiming two Ju88's, eight Me110's, two Me109's plus five Me110's and one Do17 possibly destroyed.

Shortly after 7.30, 19 Squadron took off to patrol, arriving over Calais at 7.50. They had flown down to Hornchurch from Duxford the previous day. Twelve Spitfires had been flown in and two other pilots had arrived by road. Other than section leaders, the other names were drawn from a hat to see who must stay at home for the squadron's first patrol over Dunkirk.

The lucky twelve, led by the Commanding Officer, Squadron Leader G.D. Stephenson (N3040) looked down on a sight that became familiar to the RAF pilots, a huge cloud of black smoke. The Spitfires were at 18,000 feet, just below a layer of cloud. As they began to turn, twenty-one Ju87's suddenly appeared heading out to sea over Calais. 19 Squadron closed in behind them.

Perhaps thinking the Spitfires were their own 109 escort, the Stuka formation gave no sign of panic and flew on seemingly unconcerned. Indeed there was a large escort of about thirty Messerschmitt 109's which Green Section, under Flight Lieutenant G.E. Ball, spotted and engaged. Meantime, Flight Lieutenant Wilf Clouston, a New Zealander, led Blue Section into the Stukas. Coming up behind the far-left bomber, he fired from fifty yards and it turned slowly on its back to dive vertically into the sea. Clouston then fired at another 87 which caught fire and spiralled down towards the water. Flight Sergeant Harry Steere broke off one pass due to heavy cross-fire from the German rear-gunner but coming round again, attacked a Stuka he saw climbing out of the battle. His fire caused the Stuka to drop its port wing as it commenced to spiral down in flames.

Flight Lieutenant Brian Lane (N3040) engaged a Junkers, chasing it as it twisted and turned to avoid Lane's eight guns but it finally took enough hits to force it to fall away out of control. Then the Me109's intervened.

Eric Ball (L3198) now warned the squadron that 109's were about to attack which heralded the start of a terrific dog-fight. In this tussle, Ball, noting that there were never fewer than three 109's trying to work round behind him, fired at one and saw it go down with smoke coming from the engine. However, he was then hit and sustained wounds to his head and arm.

Sandy Lane saw a 109 flash by him and attack Pilot Officer Watty Watson. Lane yelled a warning but as he did so he saw the flash of an exploding cannon shell hit Watson's aircraft (N3237). It fell away smoking, but Watson succeeded in baling out. Lane himself was attacked and in a hectic scrap he possibly shot down one Messerschmitt.

Sergeant J.A. Potter in Lane's section saw another 109 attack Flight Sergeant G.C. Unwin, and fired, forcing the 109 pilot away. Becoming separated, Jack Potter found himself in a desperate fight, discovering that the 109's seemed to fight in pairs and that it was impossible to attack one without having a second on his tail. Eventually he found a lone 109 on the edge of the battle and attacked. The 109 climbed followed by Potter, but as it did a stall-turn to the left, the enemy pilot exposed the whole of the top of his fighter whilst flying at something like 100 mph. Potter took the golden opportunity and fired a long burst, seeing his bullets smash into the 109's cockpit. The Messerschmitt fell out of control and with no other aeroplanes about, Potter followed it down to watch it fall into the sea.

The squadron claimed five Ju87's and two 109's for certain, with another three 87's and three 109's as probably destroyed. It was their first real combat and they had done well. However, on the debit side they lost Watson missing and the Commanding Officer, Squadron Leader G.D. Stephenson (N3200). Pilot Officer M.D. Lyne confirmed seeing the Commanding Officer shoot down a Stuka but then Sergeant Potter saw his Spitfire in an apparently controlled glide over the French coast leaving a thin trail of blue smoke behind it. In addition, Flight Lieutenant Ball was slightly wounded as already stated. He later said that he thought he was dead, but when he saw tracer coming past him, came to the conclusion he must still be alive![1]

---

[1] Flight Lieutenant G.E. Ball, DFC, later flew in 242 Squadron under Squadron Leader D.R.S. Bader, but was taken prisoner in 1941.

While 19 Squadron was battling with these German aircraft 65 Squadron was taking off on their second patrol of the morning. Again led by Desmond Cooke they came on the scene to see 19 Squadron's dog-fights in progress.

George Proudman attacked a Ju87[1] straggling behind and shot it down in flames. He then engaged a 109, leaving it in a smoking dive. Tommy Smart attacked a 109 but his fire caused no visible damage. As it broke away, a 110 came down from above onto his tail. Smart broke into a steep right-hand bank, came down and round onto the 110's tail. The Messerschmitt took hits as it twisted vainly to avoid the Spitfire's eight guns, began to smoke and fell away.

Another 109 went into the sea after Flying Officer J.B.N. Nicholas hit it and Flight Sergeant Bill Franklyn destroyed another, his second confirmed kill of the day. Flying Officer K.G. Hart (K9921) tagged onto a small formation of 109's, destroyed one but was hit from behind and forced down. He crash-landed on the beach at Dunkirk without injury to himself, destroyed his aeroplane and, as he nonchalantly recorded in his combat report, '. . . after the usual formalities, returned to base by sea.'!

Thus in the space of a little over an hour, 19 and 65 Squadron had shot down twenty-four German aircraft (thirteen confirmed and eleven unconfirmed) for the loss of three Spitfires, two pilots missing, and another wounded.

The Hurricanes of 17 and 79 Squadrons arrived above Dunkirk around 10.30 for their third mission of the morning. By this time the Luftwaffe had departed, leaving the sky clear of their aircraft.

The weather was turning hazy now and was to deteriorate as the morning continued. With no signs of German aircraft, the composite formation flew up and down dutifully until 11.40, when they turned for home. As they did so, three Me109's came screaming out of some cloud and came in on their rear quarter, breaking up the British formation. Pilot Officer R.C. Whittaker pulled out of a turn to see a 109 being chased by a Hurricane, which in turn had a 109 on its tail. As he saw this, he saw the RAF plane catch fire and the pilot take to his parachute. Whittaker came down behind the victorious 109, which went into a stall-turn to the left. As it did so, Whittaker fired a five second burst at it and broke away. The 109 dropped into cloud and when Whittaker came below, he saw two circles of foam in the sea. The Hurricane in flames was piloted by Flight Lieutenant C.F.G. Adye who landed in the sea, but he did not survive.

---

[1] Recorded as a Hs126 dive-bomber.

*

Increasingly low cloud with rain curtailed RAF activities for the rest of the morning. Shortly after mid-day Squadron Leader Phil Hunter led his Defiant squadron on a patrol off Calais-Dunkirk, in order to prevent the Germans bombing a French ammunition convoy sailing to Dunkirk from Dover. Squadron Leader Hunter later spotted some German tanks and road transport near Calais and lost height to investigate but heavy AA fire forced them to regain height.

Flight Lieutenant Mike Crossley led a patrol of 32 Squadron, in company with nine fighters of 605 Squadron led by Squadron Leader Perry, over the same vicinity in the early afternoon but the sky remained clear of hostile aircraft. At about two o'clock, as he turned for home, he saw a Ju88 approaching from the east at the same level as himself.

At first he was not certain if it was, perhaps, a Blenheim – they did look alike from certain angles – so did not attack. When he saw that it was in fact a German it was too late but then he spotted another Junkers which flew right across him from right to left. The German pilot obviously saw him too for the 88 suddenly began to dive towards the smoke from the still burning oil tanks at Dunkirk. Closing in behind the 88, Crossley began firing, causing both of the German's engines to trail black and white smoke. The oil smoke proved too thin to hide the bomber but a Hurricane from 605 Squadron suddenly cut right across in front of Crossley, making him pull up to avoid a collision.

Pilots of 605 Squadron had also seen the 88's, counting four or five in all. They came in using the smoke to cover their approach as they made for the harbour. Pilot Officer T.P.M. Cooper-Slipper dived down on one Junkers chasing it through the smoke. As he emerged the other side, the 88 was in a turn and almost onto its back, then it went into more smoke. Diving through this he saw the 88 crash into the sea and vanish. Two other 88's were claimed hit by 605 pilots and Pilot Officer I.J. Muirhead (N2346) reported an attack on an Me110. Whether this was in fact another twin-engined Ju88 is not certain, but Muirhead followed his victim through the smoke, noticing return fire from the rear gunner cease after a long burst. The German machine dived towards Ostend. Muirhead followed and fired, but he now noticed fumes in his cockpit. As the chase and dive continued, his cockpit began to fill up with glycol and steam. He had felt no strikes on his Hurricane and assumed the damage to be light so decided to force-land at Steene aerodrome to effect a repair. Steene was about twenty miles along the coast but his Hurricane was too badly damaged and soon he could not even see the instrument panel for fumes. Deciding to jump before the machine caught fire, he slid back the hood, undid the harness and after rolling the Hurricane onto its back, fell away at a height of 1,000 feet.

Muirhead descended by parachute, saw his fighter crash, then he came under fire from the ground, holes appearing through his silken canopy. Spilling air from the 'chute, he crashed down through a tree without injury, but rifle-fire continued to be aimed in his direction.

Undoing the parachute harness, Muirhead dropped into a ditch, but the soldiers, who turned out to be Belgian, continued firing. The RAF pilot was rescued by a RAMC officer who sent him to Ostend by car but not before some members of the RASC told him that the German machine he was chasing, had crashed about a mile away.

Arriving at Ostend, Belgian Air Force HQ told him that a ship would be leaving for England that evening and to get to the harbour.

*

The Spitfire pilots of 19 Squadron were again in action in the mid-afternoon. Ten aircraft, led by Flight Lieutenant Lane (N3040), who had assumed temporary command following the loss of their Commanding Officer that morning, flew out shortly after 2.30 p.m.

The weather had improved with several broken layers of cloud, the lowest being at 9,000 feet. Approaching the French coast, Lane led the patrol about a thousand feet below this cloud in order to spot any German bombers that might be in the area. They patrolled for half an hour then from a gap above came eight Me109's. Lane could not see them at first but Flying Officer Gordon Sinclair, leading the look-out Section (Green), had them in sight. The Spitfires tried to get into a better position but then the 109's started to dive upon them from the rear, breaking up the RAF fighters. As Sinclair came out of a turn, he saw his Number Two spinning down. Sinclair attacked this 109 and had the satisfaction of seeing it spin down for several thousand feet. In the event his No 2 got back safely.

Flying Officer G.W. 'John' Petre saw a Spitfire behind a 109 and a 109 behind the Spitfire. Turning to assist, he was too late and watched the Spitfire roll slowly onto its back and dive. Petre fired at the 109 and it fell vertically towards the sea. Sandy Lane attacked another which also dived vertically for the sea, having flown right into Lane's fire. 19 Squadron lost Sergeant Irwin (P9305) while Pilot Officer Lyne (L1031) force-landed near Deal with a bullet through his knee.

*

Further patrols were flown during the afternoon but the Luftwaffe failed to appear. In the late afternoon it started to rain, and some patrols were called off. Only 145 Squadron – nine aircraft – found a He111 in the murk which was probably destroyed. It cost them a damaged Hurricane flown by Pilot Officer P.L. Parrott (P2589) who had to force-land near

Dover having been hit by return fire.

Roy Dutton was leading the squadron and somebody spotted an aircraft and we went off after it. I was flying No. 2 in the last section and was keeping a look-out and spotted another one off to our right which was up to the north of Dunkirk. So I called over the radio, then peeled off to go after it. I did a stern attack on it – it was a Heinkel 111 – and it very rudely shot back at me. I had just got one of its engines smoking when he put two bullets into me. One hit the wing and one hit the front water jacket on the Merlin and I immediately had a cockpit full of glycol steam so I turned round realising that the engine would run for a little while but not quite sure how long. It began to run rough, getting hot very quickly and the rest of the squadron caught me up when I was about ten or fifteen miles off the coast, having seen the trail of smoke. Somebody called up, 'Who is it, what's the matter with him?' I called that it was Peter Parrott and Roy Dutton said OK, come in on my wing.

I was very lucky for I was losing height and I was down to about 1,500 feet when I crossed the English coast and then the engine seized absolutely solid and the prop stopped. Ahead of me were three fields all in a row on the top of a hill, so I picked those. I went sailing over the first one, and then went over the second one so decided I had to get down so just pushed the stick forward and came to a standstill pretty quickly. Unfortunately there was a flock of sheep in the field and I knocked a few off. I got out and being a Sunday afternoon there were a lot of people out walking. There was a crowd around pretty quickly and a policeman came up pushing a bicycle so I said can you stand by this and where is the nearest telephone. He said the farmer's house down there about half a mile, and as he was saying this, he said, 'Oh! Here's the farmer coming now,' and the farmer drove up in a horse and trap. As he got down the first thing he said was, 'Who's going to pay for these sheep then?' So in a lordly tone I replied, 'The Air Ministry!' I then asked if I could use his telephone and he said, 'Yes, the 'ouse is down there!' which meant I had to walk which I did. By the time I walked down to the farmhouse, he was back at home, with his wife, having high tea, which looked pretty good to me. The phone was in the hall, on the wall, so I used that and then he said I could sit in the parlour which was on the other side of the hall. Eventually his wife did come over and asked if I'd like a cup of tea but I thought the hell with you, no thanks!

Pilot Officer Peter L. Parrott, 145 Squadron

This ended the air encounters for 26th May but with Operation Dynamo being ordered that evening, the fighter squadrons knew that more action was imminent.

Fighter Command, aware that intense air operations would be flown over the next day or so, prepared to meet the demand for additional or possibly replacement squadrons to support Park's 11 Group units. 616 Squadron at Leconfield was told to prepare for a move to Rochford the next day to relieve 74 Squadron. 610 (Auxiliary) Squadron at Biggin Hill moved to Biggin's satellite airfield at Gravesend, as recalled by its senior (Regular) Flight Commander, Flight Lieutenant John Ellis:

> We used the clubhouse as our officers' mess where the facilities were minimal so Flying Officer 'Peter' Keighley, who was a manager in Harrods before the war, arranged for them to run our Mess. A Harrods van arrived every morning with staff, food and drink for the day. So for those eight hectic days we lived well – fillet steak for lunch and lobster thermidor for dinner! It was well worth the cost as the novelty of the arrangement did quite a lot for morale as in that week we lost the CO and four other pilots and Peter Keighley who was picked up in the Channel.
>
> *Flight Lieutenant J. Ellis, 610 Squadron*

CHAPTER FOUR

Monday, 27th May 1940

As dawn brightened the sky over Dunkirk on the first morning of Operation Dynamo, so the fighter pilots in 11 Group stood ready. For those who had seen action already over the last few days, however briefly, more action was to follow. For those who would be joining the battle over the next week, many of whom had yet to even see their first enemy aircraft in the air despite eight months of war, realisation that there was indeed a war on would be swift. Sudden death awaited them over the Channel or the French coast. The war since 10th May had been so quick and furious that there had been no time to brief those yet to see action what it was really all about. Those who had been in the thick of the fighting in France were either still trying to survive against high odds, or were already dead.

The pilots in Fighter Command about to begin their fighting careers would have to learn the hard way. Experience would come and lessons would be learnt. For all of them there was to be a sudden awareness that all they had been taught over the last years of peace was almost completely inadequate for modern warfare.

Only a year or so earlier, the RAF had prepared for war in hurriedly camouflaged two-seat or single-seat biplanes against a very modern Luftwaffe. Since that crisis at the time of Munich, Fighter Command had been rapidly re-equipped with more modern aeroplanes – Hurricanes and Spitfires. Yet though modern in design the tactics and formation flying used were virtually obsolete. The 'book' trained pilots to fly in sections of three, a leader and two wingmen. Four such sections made up a squadron formation. However, the two wingmen were so intent on keeping station and watching their leader's tail that they had little chance of being able to watch the sky for signs of hostile aircraft. A change of tactics to flying in sections line astern failed to improve the flexibility of the sections, and although section leaders could see all round, the wingmen following were still not able to look freely about them.

Methods of attack were also in the 'book'. Number One attacks,

Number Two attacks, and so on. Each designed for a given situation, but as events were to prove, almost wholly useless in fast modern air combat.

The lucky ones learnt quickly – the others did not and ultimately paid the price.

*

On 'Day One' of Dynamo it was still the same squadrons who took off for Dunkirk who had been flying over the port in recent days. They were learning but the gaps in their ranks already bore witness to the aggressive actions of the Luftwaffe. Yet each patrol, each air battle, gave the survivors just that little bit more experience. And it wasn't always the long serving pilots, the flight or squadron commanders, senior NCO's, etc. who necessarily learnt quickly. Each pilot found out how to survive on his own.

At 4.30 a.m. nine battle-veterans of 54 Squadron took off from Hornchurch for Dunkirk. The black oily smoke columns made navigation to the French port not the slightest problem. Dunkirk seemed aflame. At this early stage of Dynamo, ships of the Royal Navy and other impressed vessels were sailing to Dunkirk harbour, to load soldiers from the dock-side or the harbour mole. Only later would rescue from the beaches near Dunkirk or nearby St Malo-les-Bains become necessary.

In the smoky atmosphere and grey clouds which shrouded the sky over the French coast, 54 Squadron encountered a single Ju88 bomber. Flight Lieutenant Max Pearson (N3030) gave chase, and was seen to dive into the smoke over Dunkirk but he was not seen again. Max Pearson had been an experienced pre-war fighter pilot in England and the Middle East, and had been keen to come to grips with the enemy. In the previous few days he had claimed three or four victories. Now he had gone; swiftly and completely.[1]

No 19 Squadron took off from Hornchurch at 5.45 a.m. as 213 Squadron took off to patrol with six Hurricanes of 242 Squadron. 19 patrolled between Calais and Dunkirk, 213 and 242 over Ostend-Zeebrugge, but the sky stayed empty of German aircraft.

At around 6.30 six aircraft of 17 Squadron flew to Hornchurch to await further orders. 65 Squadron, led by Squadron Leader Cooke (K9907), flew a patrol to Calais but few aircraft were seen and none engaged. Towards the end of their patrol they spotted some Dorniers. Cooke and Flight Sergeant R.R. McPherson (K9921) attacked from

---

[1] Max Pearson's brother was Squadron Leader H.M. 'Toby' Pearson who had commanded 54 Squadron from April 1938 to May 1940.

astern and emptied their machine-guns into one. It looked damaged as it disappeared in clouds. Oddly enough, in 65 Squadron's diary, mention is made of Pilot Officer Deere seeing the Dornier crash from his vantage point on Dunkirk beach. However, Al Deere was not on Dunkirk beach until the next day. He did see a Dornier crash on that day but it was not 65's Dornier of the 27th!

Flying Officer G. Proudman saw a Dornier, firing a long burst into it as it made for cloud. Smoke began to trail from its engines but Proudman's machine (N3128) was then hit by the rear-gunner and the British pilot received a wound in the left leg. The bullet entered the cockpit, went through the rudder bar, through his leg to finish up in his parachute pack.

> George Proudman was one of the stalwarts of the squadron; he used to smoke his pipe in the cockpit while climbing to gain height, a foolhardy thing to do but amusing at the time. Always the joker he kept our spirits up when things were looking black but we finally lost him early in July, I think, when the convoy attacks started in the first phase of the Battle of Britain. I was on a few days' leave at the time when the whole of Green Section failed to return. Had I been there I would probably not be writing this letter because I always flew in that section.
>
> *Pilot Officer S.B. Grant, 65 Squadron*

The Spitfire pilots of 74 Squadron meantime had left Hornchurch at eight minutes to eight o'clock. An hour later they were in action. Exploding AA fire drew their attention to the south of Dunkirk. Flying at between 2,000 and 15,000 feet because of the clouds, the black puffs stained the sky at 5,000 feet. Flight Lieutenant Sailor Malan (K9953) led the squadron around huge mounds of white cumulus cloud but could see no sign of hostile aircraft. Turning back towards Dunkirk, several Me109's could be seen flying above and behind the Spitfires. Malan, a thinking leader who had already discovered the dangers of prewar flying tactics, split his men into pairs, then pulled his Spitfire up towards a 109 directly above. Still in the climb, the South African, who was to be the RAF's top scorer in Europe for most of the war, fired from 100 yards range. The 109 dived, followed by Malan, and before the German reached the clouds below, heavy smoke poured out of the starboard side of the engine.

Johnny Freeborn and Paddy Stevenson paired themselves off and tackled the 109's. Keeping close behind Freeborn, Stevenson was able to attack one Messerschmitt that attempted to go for Freeborn. His fire sent the 109 down into the clouds in an 'obvious distressed condition'.

With Stevenson covering from behind, Freeborn was free to shoot down another 109. Warrant Office Ernie Mayne, a pilot older than most (he was forty years old and had flown in World War I) heard a yell, warning him that he had a 109 on his tail. Turning sharply with another Spitfire, he saw a 109 cross in front of him so pulled after it. He tried to snap-shoot but could not get the deflection right and so closed to fifty yards before firing. He was then so close he had to break quickly to avoid a collision but Pilot Officer H.M. Stephen, flying above, saw the 109 go down.

Stephen himself had engaged in company with Flight Lieutenant Paddy Treacy, covering Treacy as both engaged the 109's head-on. As the flight developed a 109 appeared on Stephen's right side and he broke as the German tried to pair-off with another Messerschmitt. The resulting position was one Me109, one Spitfire (Treacy), a second Me109 and then Stephen, all flying in line astern.

'Steve' Stephen fired what he described as a very easy deflection shot of three to four seconds which shot away the cockpit canopy and the windscreen section. The German pilot appeared to fall forward on his control column and the fighter curved down towards the ground. Moments later Stephen was circling the wreckage on the ground. Treacy meantime, fired a burst of eight seconds, setting his 109 on fire and then watched as it spun vertically into the ground.

This made it five Me109's destroyed and two probables for the 'Tiger' Squadron, for no loss. As the Spitfires turned for home, Malan and Stevenson engaged one of several Dorniers that had been in the vicinity of the air battle and damaged it. However, the rear-gunner got in a good burst at Stevenson's Spitfire (P1084), and hit the aircraft's radiator, which resulted in the cockpit filling with fumes. Stevenson gained height while he still had an engine, then glided down towards Dunkirk to make a wheels-up landing.

Removing the blind-flying panel, reflector gunsight and wireless set from the Spitfire, Paddy Stevenson set fire to the wreck and later reported to the RAF commander at Dunkirk. On the way he managed to salvage the blind-flying panel from Pilot Officer Gribbles' Spitfire (54 Squadron, forced down on 25th May) and arranged for its eight machine-guns and ammunition tanks to be removed. The RAF commander then organised transport and Stevenson was back with the squadron on the 31st.

Probably some of these Me109's engaged by 74 Squadron were also found by a patrol of Defiants of 264 Squadron. Led by Squadron Leader Philip Hunter, 264 flew from Manston in squadron formation and came into contact for the first time with the German Me109 fighter. Hunter spotted eight Messerschmitts and ordered his men into line astern. There appeared to be three Spitfires close behind the 109's, but Hunter edged into an attack position. With no front guns in the Defiant, all attacking movements had to be flown to allow the aircraft's rear-gunner to bring his four .303 machine-guns to bear. If the enemy attacked from behind, the defensive fire was simple. In any other manoeuvre the pilot had to bring the Defiant broadside onto a target or fly what was called a 'cross-over' pass whereby the pilot crossed over in front of an opponent, the gunner firing as they did so. It appeared that in this action of the 27th, the Defiants edged in to pass near to the front of the 109's.

Hunter's gunner, Leading Aircraftman F.H. King, opened fire with two bursts, hitting one 109 which burst into flames and dived earthwards. Pilot Officer R.W. Stokes and Leading Aircraftman Fairbrother with Pilot Officer M.H. Young and Leading Aircraftman Johnson engaged another 109 which fell away out of control, streaming smoke. The Defiants were to gain some successes over Dunkirk being often mistaken for Hurricanes. When 109 pilots learned how to combat them, they became almost totally useless in day combat.

*

While all this action was taking place, 17 and 605 Squadrons finally received orders to fly an escort mission to Blenheims on a raid on Courtrai. No enemy fighters were encountered and 605 headed towards Courtrai to fly a patrol. Owing to a strange set of courses flown by the Blenheims, 605 became split up. Then in the patrol area, some of 605 found six Dornier 17's five miles south-east of Dunkirk. These were engaged ineffectively. Flying Officer Norman Forbes (L2119) was seen to go down near Poperinghe shortly before this engagement and he was later reported to be in German hands.

*

All appeared quiet mid morning. At 11 a.m., 19 Squadron flew a patrol, Flight Sergeant Unwin shooting up a He111, while Sergeants Potter and Jennings put hits into a Do215. Some Me 110's made an attack but were evaded.

The Defiants of 264 had had a quick turn-round and were back in the air by 11.20 a.m. At 12.30, while at 17,000 feet over Dunkirk, twelve He111 bombers were seen at 6,000 to 7,000 feet, approaching in sections line astern from the west. Squadron Leader Hunter gave the order to engage and led three sections down from the sun, leaving one section above to provide cover. The attack split-up the Heinkels, some diving for cloud, others for sea level. Each section chased one Heinkel of those heading for the sea. They secured positions below and ahead of the bombers so that the gunners could fire up at them.

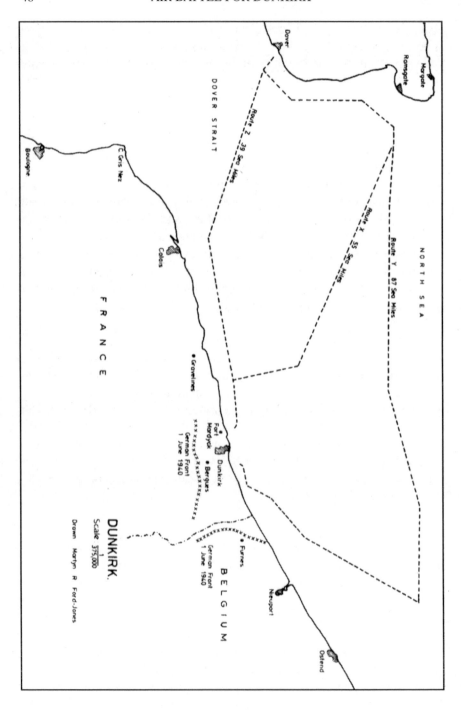

Hunter and Pilot Officer Young put themselves under the starboard and port wings respectively where their gunners opened up on the Heinkel above. It was peppered with their fire and headed towards the coast with both engines on fire. Flight Lieutenant E.H. Whitehouse got under one bomber only to be told by his gunner, Pilot Officer, H. Scott, that only his two lower guns were functioning. Whitehouse, therefore, closed to within twelve feet where Scott opened fire. As the Defiant broke away, the Heinkel's port engine caught fire and the aeroplane nosed downwards to the right of the Defiant, passing just in front of its right wing.

Two other Defiants flew cross-over attacks on another Heinkel; Flight Lieutenant Nick Cooke with his gunner Corporal Albert Lippett, and Pilot Officer D. Whitley and Leading Aircraftman Turner. Cooke's gunner raked the Heinkel, its engines starting to burn, while Whitley positioned his aircraft off to the right, his gunner blasting the bomber with 500 rounds, whereupon the Heinkel dived into the ground. The Defiants, again without loss, had shot down three bombers and possibly two others.

This action, fought between 12.30 and 12.45 p.m., heralded the start of three hours of intense aerial activity. The Luftwaffe was reducing the town and port of Dunkirk to rubble. On the western side of the perimeter, the French had been forced back to within five miles of the town. German artillery now dominated the town and at sea the Navy was forced to route rescue ships to sail through another route (Route Y), a northerly route and approach. This took the ships over 87 sea miles instead of a southerly 39 sea miles from Dover. A more direct, central route (Route X) had now to be swept of mines to give a 55-mile journey to the point of embarkation.

Nine Hurricanes of 145 Squadron were out on patrol at approximately this time, claimed at least two victories and lost three pilots, although no account of this is recorded in 11 Group's record of air actions. The Hurricanes encountered large numbers of Ju88's and Me110's, Pilot Officers A. Elson, P.H. O'C. Rainier and Sergeant A. Bailey failing to return. Two other Hurricanes were damaged. One of the two victories fell to Jas Storrar who claimed a Messerschmitt 110.

> I was billeted in one of the splendid houses down the road near Tangmere and they were empty of furniture and my bedroom was the drawing room, a very large room, empty except for one bed, one small table and my suitcase in another corner. We were flying two or three trips a day, coming back absolutely whacked and frightened; it was a pretty lonely room at night.
>
> When we were at Croydon before the shooting war began we

bought a Packard between three of us. Little did I know that it was going to be my own property and I would hold full share of it within a few days after the commencement of the Dunkirk period.

Pilot Officer J.E. Storrar, 145 Squadron

The Spitfires of 65 Squadron took to the sky for their second sortie of the day at 1 o'clock. Forty-five minutes later, Squadron Leader Cooke was north-east of Dunkirk when he saw a mixed formation of bombers approaching in sections of three and five. The German bomber pilots saw the Spitfires and their sections began to split up. Cooke followed one Dornier that was heading for cloud and chased it twenty miles inland, firing and pursuing through cloud to leave it finally damaged and with no return fire from its rear gunner.

Gerry Saunders led his Blue Section into three Dorniers which also split up. He and his Number 2 attacked, forcing it down trailing smoke. Two of the crew baled out as Saunders broke away. Pilot Officer Tommy Smart shot another down into the sea, then found another Dornier out to sea. After a chase he closed to find the bomber already crippled with its right-hand engine smoking. Smart attacked and the Dornier went into the water with both engines flaming. Sergeant N.T. Phillips became separated from his section and saw a Dornier being attacked by two Spitfires. He dived onto the German and after firing several bursts, last saw the bomber going into cloud with smoke streaming from its engines and fuselage.

Some Me110's then came on the scene but were engaged by Green Section led by Stan Grant. He saw one Messerschmitt above and slightly behind in a steep turn. Pulling round he managed to keep into the German's turn, firing all the while, knocking out the rear gunner. Grant then saw a 110 on his own tail and broke away, leaving his target with smoke pouring from one engine.

Half an hour later 601 Squadron still found between fifteen and twenty-five Me110's above Dunkirk. They were above the Hurricanes whose pilots pulled up to engage. Flying Officer G.W.S. 'Mouse' Cleaver blacked out trying to stay with his section leader; coming round he saw two 110's directly below him and chased them away into cloud. Below the 110's were some bombers, and Flying Officer W.P. Clyde went for them with his section. As they dived Billy Clyde ran into some 110's and a dog-fight began and he possibly shot one down. Then, with his ammunition gone he found two 110's on his tail and putting his aircraft into a steep right hand turn dived to 1,000 feet. He remained in the turn for about fifteen minutes, the 110's staying above and trying to get him, but failing. Meanwhile, Flying Officer Tom Hubbard got behind another 110 and succeeded in sending it down in flames.

Pilot Officer Johnnie McGrath saw some 110's form into a defensive circle above, then they began to dive at the Hurricanes. McGrath turned to meet them, exchanging shots with one which came at him head-on. The 110's fire went wide but the RAF pilot's aim was better. The Messerschmitt went down, hit the sea and sank. He then attacked a 110 circling above a Hurricane which was just above the water. McGrath dived from 6,000 feet, firing as the 110 turned to fire up at him. The 110's port engine spewed smoke and when McGrath turned, there was no sign of the German.

Two 110's were destroyed by Pilot Officer Peter Robinson, despite a 110 hitting his aircraft from behind in the initial clash. The first he sent crashing into the sea, then blew the wing off the second which also fell into the sea.

*

Squadron Leader James Leathart led 54 Squadron towards Dunkirk shortly after 2 p.m. Off Calais Prof Leathart spotted a lone Ju88 at 17,000 feet. Leading his section into the attack, Leathart saw the bomber begin to dive towards the sea. He opened fire, saw hits, then seeing several more Ju88's, broke off to engage them. Al Deere, his Number 2, continued the attack on the 88, and fired two bursts before he too went after another bomber. Johnny Allen, Number 3, then attacked and finished off the crippled Junkers.

As Leathart waded in, he thought a ship below them – the target for the 88's – looked like a hospital ship. As he came in, two bombers jettisoned their bombs and flew off. Leathart chased them, only to be led into flak fire from Calais. Deere, meantime, diving on another Ju88, noticed his airspeed was an indicated 460 miles per hour. He overtook his target so swiftly that he decided to use all his remaining ammunition in one long burst. It was on target. The bomber caught fire and crashed, wheels-up, in a field fifteen miles south-east of Calais, making two kills for 54.

The stalwarts of 17 Squadron (the only RAF squadron to see action over the entire period of the Dunkirk evacuation being on operations continually from 25th May to 3rd June) making another composite formation with 605 Squadron, flew out at 2.30, a total of fourteen Hurricanes. They were to patrol inland from Furness to St Omer, crossing into France to the east of Dunkirk. With 17 Squadron leading, the formation turned towards St Omer and almost immediately ran into six Dornier 17's flying in two three-man vic formations.

Flying Officer R.V. Meredith led his section to attack the leading vic, setting the port engine of the left-hand Dornier on fire. His Number 2, and 605 Squadron, confirmed seeing it go down.[1] Sergeant G.A. Steward damaged a second Dornier. 605 attacked the Dorniers also but the sudden appearance of about fifty Me110's and Me109's above took all the pilots' minds off the bombers. The Hurricanes, somewhat split-up, evaded the German fighters in the clouds. 605's pilots encountered small groups of 109's in and out of the cloud and lost two of their number. These were the Commanding Officer, Squadron Leader George Perry (P3423) and Flying Officer Pete Danielson (P3581).

It was a severe blow to the Auxiliary Squadron and the other pilots considered the losses entirely due to the policy of sending out small numbers of RAF fighters when it was clear by this stage that the Luftwaffe were employing three and even four times the number of fighters.

Since 605 received the call to move south on 21st May, it had lost six pilots, another taken prisoner, one had been injured and Pilot Officer Muirhead was still missing since the 26th. The squadron was withdrawn the next day, returning to Drem to reform.

As for Ian Muirhead, he had successfully arrived at Ostend and been allotted a place in the SS *Aboukir* after her cargo of food had been unloaded. It was here that he met Flight Lieutenant Freddy Ives of 151 Squadron who, it will be recalled, was forced down following a collision on 25th May. As Muirhead had been an NCO pilot with 151 Squadron before receiving his commission, meeting Ives was a welcome relief. There were several RAF people in Ostend, including Flying Officer Cogman who had baled out near Düsseldorf while on a bombing raid. He had evaded capture and walked, in uniform, through the German lines in a week. There was also a crew of a Wellington (L7793) from 37 Squadron based at RAF Feltwell. They had force-landed at Steene following hits from AA fire when bombing troop concentrations around Courtrai and Brussels on the night of 25/26th May. The captain was Squadron Leader A.R. Glencross; navigator, Pilot Officer Cameron; observer, Sergeant Parkhouse; gunner, Senior Aircraftman B.B. Stanhope; wireless operator LAC Dear. While waiting for the ship, Muirhead, Ives and Cogman repaired to the French Marine Mission about half a mile from the harbour.

Two fighter squadrons patrolled mid-afternoon of the 27th, 74 Tiger Squadron at 3.15 followed by 56 Squadron half an hour later. Both saw action.

The Tigers encountered Dorniers over Gravelines, Malan giving the 'Tally-ho!'. He had been ordered to patrol at a higher altitude, but by

---

[1] Flying Officer Richard Meredith was lost in action on 3rd June 1940.

four o'clock they had seen nothing. Being a thinking fighter pilot, Malan led his men down to a lower altitude and found the enemy. The South African claimed one probable, while Pilot Officer D.H. Dowding chased another Dornier inland. He pursued it for twenty miles but could only claim a 'damaged' before coming under intense AA fire. With one engine stopped, the Dornier had to be left.

Flight Lieutenant Tink Measures and Pilot Officer Pete St John shot down a Dornier which crashed east of Desvres, but they too came under accurate AA fire from German positions. The two pilots went into an aerobatic sequence above the gunners before heading for the coast.

Paddy Treacy and his flight joined in the battle, he and Steve Stephen chasing three Dorniers inland. Catching up with one near Fringes, Treacy started its port engine smoking. Trying desperately to hide in cloud, the two Spitfires continued to engage it, Stephen putting a long burst into the bomber's starboard engine. With both motors burning it went down.

Treacy, however, was in trouble. A hit from the German rear-gunner struck his Spitfire and the engine soon began to seize. There was also a strong smell of glycol. Looking down, he mistook burning Calais for Dunkirk but when he realised his mistake he turned north along the coast. Flying low and with no flying speed he was engaged by flak near Oye Plage. Taking avoiding action he crash-landed near Gravelines, being captured immediately. Later the Germans confirmed that the Dornier had crashed. He quickly escaped and tried to cross the Channel in a rowing boat but was attacked by two Me110's and recaptured by a German motor boat.[1] 74's score totalled four destroyed and two probables, but it was their last action over Dunkirk. They too were withdrawn from the battle, flying to Leconfield. Since 19th May they had lost four pilots (three subsequently reported prisoners) and another wounded. Stevenson was still missing but he got back on the 31st.

The Hurricanes of 56 Squadron patrolled more to the north, inland from Ostend, led by Squadron Leader 'Führer' Knowles. At 4.15p.m., near Ostend, they found ten He111's. Keeping one section as cover, Knowles led the other nine, picking off the left-hand Heinkel which crashed with one engine on fire. The other Heinkels were all dropping their bombs as quickly as they could as the Hurricanes snarled amongst them. Knowles, with Pilot Officer A.W. Baker, then crippled another Heinkel. Flight Lieutenant J.H. Coghlan (P3547) put a five-second burst into another, followed by two more of equal duration. The bomber's fuselage burst into flames and as it went down, Pilot Officer Fisher and Flying Officer Leonid Eriminsky[2] finished it off.

---

[1] Flight Lieutenant W.P.F. Treacy, DSO, later escaped his captors and returned to England via Spain early in 1941. Sadly he was killed in a collision over the Channel on 3rd April.
[2] Eriminsky, of Russian descent, was killed in a flying accident on 17th June 1940.

Pilot Officer Michael Maxwell (brother of Gerald Maxwell, MC, DFC, AFC, who gained twenty-seven victories as a fighter pilot in World War I with 56 Squadron) chased after another Heinkel and damaged it but was then hit by 'friendly' Belgian AA fire and had to bale out (P3478). Coming down he was surrounded by Belgian troops who thought he was a German or possibly a Fifth Columnist. As the only item of identification he had on him was a handkerchief, he was welcomed as an ally. Apparently they felt that only an Englishman would have nothing but a handkerchief on him! The AA battery that got him, also confirmed that his Heinkel had crashed and then assisted him in getting to the coast. They also confided that they had been shooting at aircraft all day but he was the first one they had hit! Put on a ship at Ostend he returned the next day, but not before his mother had been told of his loss. 56 lost another pilot, Flight Lieutenant R.H.A. Lee, being shot down into the sea (P3311). Dickie Lee already had a DSO and DFC on the way for his actions with 85 Squadron in France. After surviving his ducking in the sea, being picked up after an hour in the water, he rejoined 85 Squadron, only to die in the Battle of Britain.

The Hurricane pilots of 213 Squadron had their first taste of action over Dunkirk on the 27th, although half of the squadron had seen service in France earlier under Flight Lieutenant R.D.G. 'Widge' Wight. Their first two patrols of the day had found empty skies, but just before 5 p.m. when just inland from Dunkirk, Widge Wight spotted four Me 109's flying on a parallel course. Calling the sightings, he dived on them, but then saw another eight above. Continuing his dive he fired at one Messerschmitt, whose pilot half rolled when white smoke poured from his engine, then he jumped out. Pulling up, he attacked the top formation of 109's, opened up on one which did a diving turn and its pilot also took to his parachute.

The squadron adjutant, Flying Officer E.G. 'Tim' Winning, climbed after another 109 which flick-rolled into the smoke over Dunkirk. Although later he saw burning wreckage on the banks of a canal south of Bombourg, he was only credited with a probable. Pilot Officer H.D. Atkinson also got a possible, his target going down smoking over the same location.

*

The day's fighting above the evacuation had been intense and this continued into the early evening. Dorniers, Heinkels and Messerschmitts filled large parts of the sky over the harbour and six RAF squadrons got in amongst them between 7 and 8 p.m.

It was again 56 Squadron who got into the action at 7 o'clock; eight Hurricanes led by Knowles with 610 Squadron's Spitfires, the latter's first operational patrol since flying into Gravesend on the 26th. Since their unfortunate incident with the Blenheim on the 21st they had only flown one patrol.

The two squadrons met over Manston and flew for some time before sighting hostile aircraft at about 7 o'clock. 610 were at 18,000 feet, 56 with Hurricanes, in support at 20,000 feet.

Flying Officer E.B.B. Smith caught sight of a single Heinkel, and attacked but not before he closed in to identify it definitely as such. 610 were not going to be caught a second time! Satisfied of its nationality, Brian Smith opened fire, seeing pieces fly off the bomber and smoke trail from its starboard engine and then its wheels flopped down. Emptying his guns into the Heinkel, he saw one crewman bale out as he pulled away. Then he saw the Messerschmitts coming down.

> On our first patrol over Dunkirk on 27th May, we spotted a lone Heinkel 111 which A Flight attacked while I, with B Flight, kept a look-out for enemy fighters. The whole of A Flight had a go at the Heinkel but all except Brian Smith opened fire at too great a range. Flying Officer Smith eventually closed in and claimed it as destroyed but as we watched this my flight was set on out of the sun from a clear blue sky by a squadron of Me110's. For a few minutes the sky was full of aircraft milling around chasing each other. I pursued a 110 and had no difficulty in turning inside him. As soon as I opened fire the rear-gunner stopped firing and the aircraft rolled over and dived down vertically. Almost immediately I chased a second 110 and closed in to about three hundred yards. I hit him in the starboard engine which was on fire but had to break off when I saw in my mirror another 110 on my tail. By this time I was twenty miles or so inland from Dunkirk.
>
> We lost two pilots on this sortie, Flying Officer Medcalf and Sergeant Medway.
>
> *Flight Lieutenant J. Ellis, 610 Squadron*

Bonzo Franks, leading 610, engaged a 110 which was diving on another Spitfire, firing a seven second burst which caused the enemy machine to turn onto its back. Following it down he saw it crash into the sea. Above him the sky seemed full of 110's and Spitfires. As he climbed back up he saw another Spitfire being attacked by a 110 which broke away rapidly when Franks used up the rest of his ammunition on it.

One Spitfire pilot who had a 110 on his tail was that flown by Pilot Officer Peter Lamb. Breaking away he evaded finally by diving into the smoke pall over Dunkirk. Coming out again he saw two Ju88's ahead but three 110's coming at him forced him again to conceal himself in the smoke.

Flight Lieutenant A.T. Smith also had a 110 forced away from his tail, then proceeded to attack another which went into a spin on fire, then chased another down to 2,000 feet into the smoke above Calais. Oil covered his wings and cockpit and he doubted very much if it pulled out of its dive.

Altogether, 610 claimed three 110's definite, three more possibles, plus the Heinkel. The pilots felt certain the Heinkel had been a decoy for the 110's. Certainly a red Very light was fired by the bomber crew which brought the 110's down. They in turn shot down Medcalf and Medway and put a bullet through the Spitfire flown by Flying Officer G.M.T. Kerr.

The leader of Green Section, Flying Officer Johnny Kerr-Wilson, got into several actions during this patrol, fighting 110's and Ju88's that he found when going through the smoke. Later, on his own, he saw six Ju87 Stukas and drove them away from a ship they were about to dive-bomb. Returning to base, his engine ran out of fuel one mile short of the airfield although his fuel gauge showed 30 gallons. Luckily he was able to glide to the runway only to discover his starboard wheel had been hit. As soon as he touched down the wheel fell off, tipping the aeroplane up onto its nose.

The Hurricane pilots of 56 Squadron, meanwhile, flying higher up had run into several formations of 110's. Squadron Leader Knowles found ten at his unit's height and attacked. He singled out one as they split up and it burst into flames, then went down in a steep spiral. He sent another down in like fashion before breaking away when one of 610's Spitfires came straight for him. Johnny Coghlan climbed higher towards five 110's at 25,000 feet but they saw him and attacked from directly ahead. Coghlan broke underneath them and as he dived picked out one of the lower ten 110's and fired; then with three others still after him he broke away.

Sergeant George Smythe, flying in the rearguard section, saw a group of five 110's diving down out of the sun at the Commanding Officer. He and Flying Officer Fisher attacked but then he saw Fisher go down with glycol smoke streaming from his shattered radiator. Smythe then engaged with 110's sending one down with grey smoke coming from one engine but was then surrounded by tracer shells from rear-gunners of other 110's. His Hurricane was hit and he flew home losing petrol from a damaged fuel tank as well as other damage. Flying Officer Fisher, despite being wounded, got down safely and later returned to the squadron.

Three squadrons of Hurricanes patrolled at 7 p.m. until 8.25, together with the Spitfires of 19 Squadron. 79, 145 and 601 all engaged Me 110's, 19 Squadron finding Dornier bombers.

The Hurricanes, eighteen in number, formed a composite unit and in a sky clearing of cloud, yet filled with smoke, found a continuing presence of German Ju88's and twin-engined Messerschmitts.

No 145 Squadron, who had already lost three pilots in their earlier patrol of the day, lost a further three in this action, although they claimed two 110's confirmed and one probable. Pilot Officers D.N. Forde, E.C.J. Wakeham and J.H. Ashton were all shot down but all three later got back across the Channel to return to the squadron.

Two pilots of 601 failed to get back, slightly compensated for by four 110's shot down. Flying Officer Charles Lee-Steere was lost, but Flight Lieutenant Sir Archibald Hope, Bt, later returned.

I was leading 601 Squadron on 27th May and on our way to the Dunkirk area we were attacked by a number of Me 110's. In the ensuing dog-fight I received three cannon shells all, I think, either in the wing root or in the radiator. Be that as it may, it quickly became apparent that I could not keep the aircraft in the air. We were about five or six miles from the shore somewhere between Calais and Dunkirk, and there had been reports that morning that the Germans had reached the coast at Gravelines. I therefore made for the beach and flew east along it as far as I could. The beach was smooth sand without rocks or groins of any sort, so when the engine finally stopped I just made a simple belly landing. I got out of the aircraft and fired my revolver into the fuselage fuel tank and then threw in a match which ignited the petrol straight away. I crossed the beach and started climbing across some sand dunes where I met a French farmer coming towards me. I spoke virtually no French and my recollection is that he didn't speak any English. However, I think he understood that I wanted to go to the nearest British unit.

We continued across the dunes when there were two loud explosions behind us from my aircraft, which were I supposed the oxygen cylinders blowing up. We crossed a couple of fields and got into a van, and the Frenchman drove me a few miles to a place called Bergues where I found there was a brigade headquarters of the British Army. It was a small town and it had been bombed fairly recently. I went into the brigade headquarters and asked for transport to take me to Dunkirk whence I hoped to get a ship back to England. They promised to do what they could, and at that moment an air-raid alarm went. Being inexperienced in such matters I went out into the garden to see what was going on and saw a squadron of British fighters flying overhead at about 15,000 to 20,000 feet.

While I was watching them some of the Army called to me to come in and take shelter, and I said it was quite unnecessary because they were our fighters overhead. The Army then asked me how I could possibly know that they were our fighters. I replied that they were Hurricanes and they asked how I could know that. I said I could see that they had one white wing and one black wing and I happened to know (which was quite untrue) that there were no Spitfires operating that day therefore they must be Hurricanes. This reply astonished the Army who said that they did not know that all British fighters had the under surface of their wings on one side painted white and the other painted black. They said they had frequently seen aircraft with these markings and did not realise they were RAF. Many people will remember that at the time of Dunkirk there was a public outcry and much distress in the Army because they were not being protected by the RAF. The cry of the soldiers was 'Where is the RAF?' Various explanations were given, e.g. that the RAF was flying very high or was defending forward or behind the troops, but personally I think that at least part of the explanation must be that there had been an extraordinary failure by British Intelligence in that at a unit as important as a brigade headquarters no one knew the standard RAF markings.

In due course the Army found a vehicle that took me down to Dunkirk and dropped me somewhere near the docks. There was some desultory bombing going on and I asked at the dock gates when and where I could get a ship back to England. I was told to come back the following morning and it was suggested that I should go into the neighbouring sand dunes to spend the night. This I did and gradually found my way with large numbers of soldiers down to the beach where we sat all night. From time to time there were air-raids and one or two villas on the edge of the beach were set on fire. There was a naval captain wandering up and down the beach and we kept asking him when the ships would appear. He put his glass to his eye and said he could see them coming, but they never turned up. Later on in the war I met this same man again and he admitted to me that all he told us during that night was a complete fabrication.

At, I suppose, about four or five in the morning we were finally instructed to go down the mole. I found a wounded man lying on a stretcher and I collected a party of stretcher bearers and got them to carry him down towards the mole. Unfortunately he died on the way. In due course we went along the mole in a long procession and I was taken on board a destroyer, HMS *Wakeful*, which was subsequently sunk during the evacuation proper. The Navy treated me marvellously and in due course brought us back to Dover where I telephoned the squadron and they sent a Magister to Hawkinge to pick me up later on in the day. I still had my parachute with me which I had kept from my Hurricane.

Flight Lieutenant A. Hope, 601 Squadron

Sir Archibald later flew in the Battle of Britain, won the DFC and commanded 601 in August 1940. He had already seen action in France when flights from 3 and 601 Squadrons were based at Merville.

The Dorniers encountered by 19 Squadron were located near Dunkirk at around 8 p.m. The pilots had already been warned that there would be 'hell over Dunkirk this evening'. With the sea shining blue and gold in the setting sun and a deep blue sky above, all were excited at the prospect of action.

It came when bombs were seen erupting on the sea near an oil tanker lying offshore. AA fire located a single raider for the Spitfires. Flight Lieutenant Brian 'Sandy' Lane, thinking it might be a decoy, ordered Wilf Clouston to keep high cover while he took his section down. The German crew were alert and quickly turned their aeroplane inland and away. As Lane closed in he found it to be a single-engined Hs126. While he and his Number 2 Frankie Brinsden did everything to try and bring it down, its pilot brilliantly evaded the faster aircraft's attacks and soon they had to leave it, being many miles inland rather than over Dunkirk where they should have been. They both returned to the coast but the section's Number 3, Sergeant Grumpy Unwin, sitting in the sun, dived down onto the now unsuspecting Hs126 and shot it down into a field with its engine on fire.

I could see the other two were having little success against the Henschel, it was very low and slow. Suddenly Sandy told us to reform and I saw them break away. Finding myself with the sun behind me and seeing the German begin to fly straight and level, I realised that he'd been so busy with them that he'd not seen me. So I just dived down and got him on the first pass.

Flight Sergeant G.C. Unwin, 19 Squadron

Meanwhile Clouston had found a Dornier at 15,000 feet. It had dived, pursued by the Spitfires. Breaking away from his first attack, Clouston was followed in by Sergeant B. Jennings who fired from behind but blacked out in his pull-out and lost sight of the bomber. He saw a large splash in the sea but could not be sure if this was the Dornier or a bomb exploding.

Clouston climbed again and found another Dornier at 20,000 feet. He managed a surprise attack from the sun, hit the bomber in a stern attack, sending it down in flames and on its back.

*

The day ended with a patrol by 616 Squadron who had been ordered down from Leconfield to Rochford to replace 74 Squadron. They found an empty sky.

It had been a hectic and battle-filled day. The situation on the ground and at Dunkirk was still very confused but the RAF had been in considerable action. Eighteen of its fighter pilots had failed to return and two more had been wounded. About half of those missing eventually got back via Dunkirk but the fighter squadrons all knew they had been in a scrap.

On the credit side, claims for nearly fifty German aircraft had been made plus half that number as probables. The Luftwaffe too knew that they had been in a fight.

CHAPTER FIVE

Tuesday, 28th May 1940

The survival and return of many pilots shot down over Dunkirk was to become a feature of the whole campaign. Not only those that came down during the period 27th May-2nd June who got back but others who had been brought down earlier.

As 28th May began it is now known that several pilots were making it back towards the coast. One such was Pilot Officer B.J. Wicks of 56 Squadron. He had been on a patrol in the afternoon of 22nd May when the squadron engaged several Hs126 observation planes. Brian Wicks had shot down one, but in pursuing another at low level had been hit by ground fire. Covered in petrol from a damaged tank, he eventually had to force land in France.

Unhappily he found he was behind the German advance and with his clothes soaked in petrol he was not able to risk setting light to his Hurricane (N2431). At dusk, covered in mud and very wet from walking through marshland, he came upon a small cottage where the French family made him welcome. The next morning, he moved on and when later he met some Belgian refugees, they gave him not only some dungarees to help cover his uniform but also a car so that he could drive north towards the coast. Yet this was just the beginning of a whole series of adventures which lasted until 2nd June.

As the sky lightened on 28th May, the three Hornchurch squadrons were up and ready. Shortly after 4.30 a.m., 19, 54 and 65 Squadrons took to the air. It had become clear that the British squadrons flying on one unit strength were no match for the much larger fighter formations the Germans were using. Hornchurch was ordered to fly its squadrons as a wing.

The weather on this May morning was dull, with huge masses of thundery cloud covering the sky. It had been raining when the pilots had been awoken an hour earlier. 54 and 65 Squadrons were both reduced to eight serviceable Spitfires following the recent hard fighting. Both squadrons were due for rest and re-equipping and would fly north after this dawn patrol.

All our aircraft were damaged in one way or another and when, after one last sortie over the area on 28th May, we were withdrawn to Kirton in Lindsey to refurbish practically every aircraft had a bullet through the main spar which technically made them unfit to fly even in transit! Three days later I celebrated my twenty-first birthday and on 5th June we returned to Hornchurch but by this time it was all over bar the shouting.

Pilot Officer S.B. Grant, 65 Squadron

As they crossed the Channel, the cloudy weather made a wing effort almost impossible and indeed 54 Squadron soon became separated. When they arrived on their patrol line they spotted a lone Do17 looking for shipping targets in the early morning light. Al Deere was leading the eight Spitfires and ordering four to continue on, Deere chased after the bomber with the other section. It was obvious that the German crew had not seen the approaching danger as the Dornier continued down and away from the protectiveness of the cloud. The Spitfires got to within 500 yards before the German rear-gunner started to fire back at them, while his pilot banked towards the land.

Deere opened fire, seeing a flash of flame from the Dornier's port engine. As he steadied for another shot, the rear-gunner's fire hit his Spitfire (N3180). A fine spray of glycol quickly turned to white smoke, obscuring his forward vision. He had no chance of making it back to England so had to force-land quickly. Switching off his engine the New Zealander side-slipped towards the beach. With the hood back, Deere crunched onto the beach sending sand and water into the air and into his face, and also banged his forehead on the edge of the windscreen, knocking himself out.

Coming round, he was conscious of his hissing and burning Spitfire. Scrambling from the cockpit he moved some distance before dropping down to rest. Blood was pouring from a deep cut above his left eye, while oil and sand covered his face and neck. He had landed about three miles west of Nieuport, midway between Ostend and Dunkirk. Picked up by Belgian soldiers, he left his now blazing Spitfire and was later helped by a Belgian girl who washed his face and treated his forehead. Giving the lady his Mae West, he was advised to head for Ostend.

The rear gunner hit two of us I think. He certainly brought me down and he hit Desmond McMullen's Spitfire but he was a pretty effective shot that guy. The Spitfire, of course, was very vulnerable from a rear gunner because of the glycol header tank, which at that time wasn't armour-plated. That was the means of cooling your engine and if that went you'd had it.

Pilot Officer A.C. Deere, 54 Squadron

The squadron returned to Hornchurch. Except for the Dornier, which eventually crashed, no other enemy aircraft were encountered. Yet already there was another squadron airborne. 213 Squadron took off to escort six Blenheims to St Omer. This was accomplished without incident and then 213 swung round to fly a patrol between Gravelines and Nieuport. At 7.10 p.m. Flight Lieutenant Widge Wight spotted a Heinkel dropping bombs and flew to engage. The bomber slowed suddenly causing Wight to overshoot but Sergeant Sammy Butterfield put some bullets into it before it disappeared.

Five minutes later Wight saw six Me109's diving towards them. Engaging, he selected one and his fire caused a blaze near the tail before it snapped off, sending the rest of the fighter down just south of Middlekerke. Pilot Officer W.M. 'Bill' Sizer went after a 109 that flew across in front of him then slid in behind it. As he chased it inland, the 109 began to trail smoke and rolled over. Passing over it, Sizer looked back and down to see the Messerschmitt crash into a wood.

Widge Wight later reported experiencing return cannon fire from a backwards firing gun on the 109. Several pilots reported this phenomenon over Dunkirk when engaged with 109's but it was obviously puffs of smoke discharged from the engine's supercharger when the 109 pilot endeavoured to put on speed when attacked.

The 109's fighting with 213 evened the score by shooting down two Hurricanes. Tim Winning, the adjutant, failed to get home and Sergeant Boyd went into the sea but was picked up safely. 213 was to be in action later on this dull morning.

These early patrols were relieved just after 7 a.m. by 242 and 611 Squadrons. 611 based at Digby were brought south to Martlesham at dawn to join the battle. On their arrival at Martlesham the landing area was partly obscured by mist which caused Pilot Officer C.H. MacFie to swerve on landing to avoid another aircraft and he turned his Spitfire (N3055) up onto its nose. Neither squadron saw any sign of hostile aircraft; Flight Lieutenant K.M. Stoddart of 611 had an early return to Manston with engine trouble.

When we were first ordered to Dunkirk I was up over the North Sea, about 3 a.m. looking for enemy aircraft. I was ordered to land at Digby where I was then told to get my squadron down to Martlesham Heath. We set off, if memory is right, about 5 a.m. and landed singly in a ground mist through which it was very difficult to see the ground. Pilot Officer MacFie didn't and tipped into a sandbank.

We were expected to join up with other squadrons which I think on this occasion did not arrive and we went on our own. I can't really distinguish between this trip and others at this distance in time. The task was to patrol the beaches at 5,000 or 6,000 feet and attack anything we saw. On this occasion, I believe we saw nothing and after droning about at minimum revs to conserve petrol, returned home. I recall we had to take out our VHF radios and replace them with the old TR9 sets which were 'out of sight, out of sound' quality. Perhaps we were kidding the Hun that we had nothing so modern as VHF. We also had to take out the DeWilde ammunition from our gun belts, later called Incendiary Mk 6 bullets. There was some argument that these bullets might be considered 'explosive' which was contrary to some warfare rules.

I was always concerned that I would stay over Dunkirk too long and drop the lot of us in the Channel through lack of petrol. This reminds me of the occasion when take-off had been delayed awaiting other squadrons to join us. We drank tea and more tea and then more tea. When I was leading my mob of hooligans home, I was seized with an irresistible desire to pee. For hygienic and sartorial reasons but above all lest I be charged with wetting myself through fright, which well might have been true, I undid my Sutton Harness, then my parachute, then my overalls, then my flies. Fishing about for a bit of anatomy which on a cold morning before breakfast was not easy to find, I then let fly. Meantime my brother officers had been led through several steep dives and a half roll or two. Barrie Heath wondering if I was ill or had been wounded, called out, 'What are you doing?''Having a pee! Roger. Out.'Someone replied, 'I'll bet.'

Squadron Leader J.E. McComb, 611 Squadron

Early on in the evacuation we were sent out from Digby via Martlesham to patrol the beaches at about 24,000 feet. We were briefed by Stanford Tuck at Martlesham who had just returned and who said that virtually the whole place was a shambles and we would have to do the best we could. I remember flying across the sea in fairly close 'vic' formation with Sergeant Sadler and myself weaving in the rear 'vic'. Jimmy McComb, who was leading the squadron, suddenly disappeared from sight inside his cockpit and after a delay, his number two called up and said, 'Where are you Jimmy?'He replied very quickly by saying, 'I am having a pee, you bloody fool.' Nobody wanted to fly his aircraft after that!

Flying Officer B. Heath, 611 Squadron

A further Hornchurch 'Wing' show was put on at 9 a.m., 19, 65 and 616 flying out with a total of twenty-nine Spitfires, led by Des Cooke of 65 Squadron. Again cloud caused the large group to become somewhat separated. 616 in their first real action, got entangled with a huge formation of Me109s, and when 19 Squadron saw them as they flew through a valley of towering cloud, there was a terrific dog-fight going on, 616 fighting for their lives. Despite its being their first action, the pilots had already decided to fight in pairs, which they did as soon as the 109s were met.

This was certainly an innovation, and one that was to prove successful in the months to come. It should be remembered that the peacetime air force had been trained to expect only long range enemy bombers flying from a distant Germany without short range fighter escort. Given those circumstances then the peacetime thinking would have been fairly acceptable and the fighter pilots, flying around nicely in their vics of three, in daylight and over their own familiar sectors of southern England, would have easily met the enemy. But suddenly all the circumstances had changed. They were flying many miles from home, over water, and having to contend with very aggressive German fighters and bombers, flying not from German bases, but from those recently captured from the French and Belgians.

Pilot Officer Ken Holden kept with his Number 1 and got into fights with two 109's, each time evading their deadly fire. Then, coming out of a shuddering turn he found himself right in front of a 109. When he opened fire, his second burst caused black smoke to come from the engine, then the Messerschmitt spun down into the smoke. Flying Officer G. Moberly, leading Green Section, engaged 109's as they swept across in front of him. Sighting on one he fired and the 109's right wing folded up and the machine dived straight down. Moberly was then attacked from underneath but blacked out as he pulled hard to evade. Pilot Officer E.W.S. Scott as Green Two also fired at a 109 ahead of him; it turned onto its back and dived smoking. Then he was set upon from behind and his Spitfire caught hits in both wings, but he half rolled away from the danger.

The squadron got away fairly lightly from this action, only Sergeant M. Ridley receiving a slight head wound. His Spitfire, and that of Squadron Leader M. Robinson, were seriously damaged, the latter having to crash-land at Manston.

Coming onto the scene of battle, 19 Squadron waded in. Flight Lieutenant Sandy Lane went for a 109 although he could see another in his rear-view mirror. He fired a burst but found his guns firing slowly as his compressed air bottle was leaking. He tried again but the 109 turned towards him, its fire passing just underneath his wing. The two fighters circled but with his guns now useless he broke off the action. Flight

Sergeant Harry Steere got a 109 in flames and Grumpy Unwin made a stern attack on another, sending it spinning down from 8,000 to 3,000 feet. Steere was a bit shaken when he got home, confiding to Lane that he'd seen his 109 pilot caught half in and half out of his cockpit as the fighter fell in flames.

No 65 Squadron, in the lead but much lower down, came out of the cloud base to find nine Do17's. Squadron Leader Cooke closed in using full boost and despite heavy crossfire continued to attack, sending one Dornier into cloud badly damaged. The French later confirmed seeing two Dorniers crash inland. Flight Sergeant Franklyn and Sergeant J.R. Kilner similarly damaged another and this too was believed to have crashed on the beach. Tommy Smart's Spitfire (P9435) was hit in the glycol tank, forcing him to land on the beach also, but he got back two days later aboard a destroyer.

> I remember Tommy being shot down. He turned up in the squadron either later that evening or the following day little the worse for wear. You might be amused to know that in October 1942 I took over the Takali Wing in Malta and Tommy came out at that moment to command one of the squadrons, No 229. We did many a merry op together fighter bombing and strafing the airfields in Sicily. He was killed later in the war.
>
> *Pilot Officer S.B. Grant, 65 Squadron*

At 10 o'clock 213 Squadron were back in the air patrolling the beaches. It was now obvious to the Germans that there was a large scale evacuation in progress from Dunkirk harbour and in consequence the Luftwaffe sent large numbers of aircraft to the area as well as out over the sea. In this way they hoped to smash the harbour sufficiently to make the loading of troops impossible as well as sinking ships coming to and exiting from the port.

In the company of 213 came the mostly Canadian-manned 242 Squadron, while flying as top cover was 229 Squadron. The Commanding Officer of 229 was Harold Maguire, a former seaplane pilot of considerable experience. He recalls the excellent ground support given to the squadrons at Biggin and the regular intelligence provided at briefings. They knew exactly how serious the situation was for the BEF. He also remembers Edwardes Jones – 'E-J' – of 213 who usually led the Biggin squadrons. E-J would look for trouble all the time which led to some anxious moments with one eye on fuel gauges. Maguire recollects worrying more about not getting home than meeting the enemy. Biggin Hill were now mounting patrols in wing strength – this patrol totalled thirty-two fighters.

Owing to cloud and smoke, it was again impossible for the three squadrons to fly and fight together. They soon became separated and some of them patrolled above cloud layers while others decided to reduce height and fly beneath them.

Squadron Leader Harold Maguire, leading his 229 Squadron, was the first to come into contact with enemy aircraft at 10.40, three miles north-east of Dunkirk. They met AA fire which seemed to be directed at both British and German aircraft impartially. Through this barrage came twelve Do215's with another loose in the box. Maguire attacked the loose one, knocking out its rear-gunner with his first burst. The bomber dived, obviously in difficulty but the pilot regained control lower down. Pilot Officer G.M. Simpson, a New Zealander from Christchurch, attacked a Dornier and in a chase through and down into the clouds used all his ammunition without result. In desperation he then tried to force the Dornier onto the ground by repeatedly diving at it but failed.

Brother New Zealander Pilot Officer Vic Verity, something of a sheep expert who spent his off-duty time touring local farms to look at the sheep, chased another down to the ground but he had no more success than Geoff Simpson and lost the bomber low down. Flight Lieutenant F.N. Clouston, yet another New Zealander, also forced a Dornier down, knocking out the rear-gunner but achieving no definite result. The only confirmed success by 229 Squadron came shortly after this action when Sergeant J.C. Harrison who had broken away to identify a light plane – it turned out to be a Lysander – saw a dogfight above. Flying towards it he saw a 109 come out of the fight right in front of him. Harrison fired and the 109 half rolled and dived earthwards. Pulling the emergency boost, Harrison followed it down, still firing, and watched it crash into the ground.

The mostly Canadian pilots of 242 Squadron found considerable cloud over Ostend and, as they descended through it, Flight Lieutenant Don Miller's section became separated. They spotted a Ju88, chased it, but lost it in cloud. Miller then saw a dozen Me109's in loose formation and took his men into the attack. He went for the leader, fired a five-second burst and it appeared to fall away out of control. As three 109's then came in behind him, Miller, seeing the sky full of Messerschmitts, lost control in cloud and was down to 500 feet before levelling out.

As the Canadians had gone down on the twelve Me109's they had in fact been bounced in turn by about sixty more. Two Hurricanes were hit, Pilot Officer Dale Jones being killed, Pilot Officer Arthur Deacon being forced to attempt a crash-landing. Deacon was hit in a turn, hot oil pouring back into his face from a shattered oil line. Cutting his engine, he slid back the hood, jettisoned the side flap and tried to make the beach. As he did so, he pulled back the stick but went straight in. He was badly gashed on the face and had a leg wound and the next thing he remembered was coming round in the garden of a hospital where his injuries were seen to. Hearing that Belgium had capitulated he got into some civilian clothes and after wandering around Ostend, Middlekerke and Dunkirk eventually found himself in Antwerp. The American Legation refused to help him and shortly afterwards he was taken prisoner.

One pilot shot down one of the attacking 109's in flames, then escaped into cloud. Although not mentioned in his combat report, he then saw an aircraft in the cloud and fired. This proved to be Willie McKnight, whose machine was damaged – its sump pump was blown off. McKnight had just shot a 109 into the sea when it happened and in his subsequent combat report, said he had been shot up by a 109, thereby protecting his friend. Apparently on landing, McKnight had confronted the pilot angrily but then burst into laughter about the whole incident.

Meanwhile 213 Squadron were engaged by 109's, but the RAF pilots saw them coming and turned to fight. Flight Lieutenant Widge Wight attacked one sending it down smoking then later joined up with the Commanding Officer, Squadron Leader J.H. Edwardes Jones and headed for base. Wight then saw some eighty aircraft which initially he thought were Blenheims and Spitfires but on close inspection turned out to be Ju88's and Me109's. Edwardes Jones and Wight turned to engage and fought with four Me109's, Wight catching one in a stall-turn and emptied his guns into it. The 109 dived away and with no ammunition and low on fuel turned for home.

Edwardes Jones, circling tightly with six 109's, heard Wight call that he was turning for base. Still turning he finally got one 109 in his sights and pressed the button only to find his guns still on 'safe'. Moments later the 109 had disappeared.

Pilot Officer Harry Atkinson climbed with other pilots to engage the 109's, and attacked one which then dived. He then headed after one making for France, zoomed up underneath it and fired. Smoke poured from its engine and it crashed eight miles into the German lines. (Atkinson also reported being fired on by a rear-firing cannon in the action.) Sergeant J.A. Lichman also claimed a 109 down, but by far the busiest pilot in 213 Squadron this morning was Sergeant Butterfield. In the dog-fight a 109 sailed in front of his Hurricane, then started to climb. Butterfield fired and the 109 burst into flames and went down. A second 109 claimed the RAF pilot's attention and its port wing folded up. As he pulled up from this kill a Ju88 flew in front of him. He attacked this and it half rolled into the sea. He was then hit by a cannon shell, and an Me110 flew past him. He turned behind the German, and his first burst set its starboard engine on fire; then it too turned over and hit the sea.

Seeing a large formation of Messerschmitts above, Butterfield headed for home but three came screaming down at him. Pulling the plug, he twisted and turned to avoid their fire, but his machine was hit several times. Two shells smashed his instrument panel, three more hit the fighter underneath, then the engine stopped. Flames began to lick at the wing roots as his machine dropped. At 400 feet he had no chance to bale out conventionally so with the last of his forward speed, pulled up, slid back the hood, crouched on the seat and as the Hurricane stalled, dived out to the left and took a header off the wing. As he was still under attack he delayed opening his parachute until about 200 feet above the sea. Seconds later he was in the water, to be rescued shortly afterwards by the paddle steamer *Sundown* and deposited ashore at Margate.

All three squadrons suffered losses by the Luftwaffe in this prolonged battle in the last hour of the morning. 229 lost Sergeant Hillman, 242 lost Deacon and Jones. Sergeant Hillman had been with Squadron Leader Maguire when they found themselves out of ammunition, low on fuel and being chased over the sea by a very determined Me110 pilot. With little choice of options, Maguire told Hillman that they had better evade and get down as quickly as they could. Maguire rolled onto his back, pulled back the stick and dived for the sea. The 110 pilot was good. He followed their manoeuvre and apparently shot down Hillman. (As well as Butterfield down but safe, 213 lost Sergeant J.A. Lichman, who was also rescued from the sea wounded in the arm and Pilot Officer G.G. Stone. His body was picked up from the water and buried at sea by the Navy.)

These were not the last losses of the 28th. At 11.35, ten Defiants of 264 Squadron left Manston led by Phil Hunter. Early in their patrol they encountered thirty Me109's ten miles out to sea. Hunter ordered his men into line astern and to keep close together in a circle. Almost at once a 109 came in, only to be shot down by Hunter's rear-gunner, Leading Aircraftman King. Shortly afterwards another came down, King sending this down in flames also. However, the 109's managed to pick off some of the two-seaters.

The Defiants began to split up under the German attack. Sergeant Roland Thorn, with Leading Aircraftman Barker, was last in the circle. Their machine was hit on the wings and tail, but Barker sent down one 109 out of control. Pilot Officer M.H. Young's gunner hit another Messerschmitt which fell away on fire and hit the sea. A total of six 109's was claimed, but three Defiants went down. Squadron Leader Hunter at one stage seeing several aircraft going down in flames, also a number of parachutes drifting down. The three missing were Flight Lieutenant Whitehouse/Pilot Officer H. Scott, Pilot Officer A. McLeod/Pilot Officer Hatfield, Sergeant Daisley/Leading Aircraftman Revill.

*

Dunkirk for the RAF was primarily a fighter battle but several non-fighter aircraft were involved in fighter actions. 220 Squadron operated Lockheed Hudson twin-engined-maritime reconnaissance aircraft with a crew of four. It carried seven .303 machine guns, two for the pilot, two for the rear-gunner, one for a ventral position and sometimes two in beam positions.

Flying Officer Hilton Aubrey Haarhoff was a 27-year-old South African rear-gunner in the squadron, who kept a diary of the more important happenings of his air force life. On 28th May 1940 he wrote:

> Proceeded to Bircham Newton once more – the whole squadron was sent there as 'there was something on'! We were all called at 03.30 hours and told to get off with all possible speed. I flew down with Harold Sheahan, another South African, as Selley was not leaving till later in the morning. Arrived at Bircham Newton, we had breakfast and were told we were at 'quick available', and that we might be doing a trip to the other side to act as protective escort to shipping which was evacuating the BEF from Dunkirk. At about 8.30 we were sent for and on reporting to 'ops' we were informed that we were to maintain a patrol of three Hudsons in battle flight between Dunkirk and Dover. Sheahan was to lead. the first with Selley and Jouault in the supporting aircraft. I was to fly with Selley.
>
> We took off at 9.45 and it was not long before we reached Dover and there we set course for Dunkirk – the visibility was none too good and tons of low cloud obscured the sky. There was a variety of medium sized ships both going to and coming from the Dunkirk side, and frequent destroyers fussing to and fro. The ships which were coming from the east were moderately loaded, mainly transport and guns.
>
> When we reached Dunkirk the place was a hive of activity. We could see the distant flash of guns and bomb bursts inland, but as our beat was over the sea we were not able to go much closer. On one circuit, we ventured over the beach and immediately the ack-ack opened up at us – pretty accurate too, and what's more they were either our own or Allied guns. However, we took violent avoiding action and the guns ceased suddenly, apparently as we had been identified.
>
> Our patrol was between Dunkirk and Dover and we set off for the English side and I timed it at about forty minutes for the round trip. When we got back to Dunkirk for the second time we

caught sight of a flight of Ju88's and they had just let go their eggs – we went straight for them but they nipped into the cloud and I hope our 'Fighter boys' who were patrolling above were able to do their stuff. We continued our runs in each direction, occasionally coming down very low when we passed an interesting looking ship to break the monotony.

Whenever we did this the troops on the ships would give us a wave and grin as we sped past. Selley, who was an exhibitionist, always delighted in any thing of this nature, and he was invariably a bit nearer the water or the ship than any of the others. However, I was bucked whenever such occurred as I felt an extreme pride in our Navy, so I did not mind at all, though I know Sergeant Fletcher, our navigator, did not like it at all.

The time passed all too quickly which was not surprising with so much to see and also the fact that one was continually on the *qui vive* for Jerry aircraft, but due to the heavy low cloud their activities against the ships were somewhat restricted, though a considerable amount of aerial activity seemed to be going on all the while further inland. There the cloud was small in quantities and the ack-ack bursts could be seen as flashes of black with white puffs following. Other than the Ju88's which we sighted earlier we saw no further Jerry aircraft. Once when nearing a destroyer we could see that their pom-poms were manned and firing into the cloud – we signalled and asked what the bother was about and reply came back 'possible enemy aircraft'.

The cloud was at about 1,000 feet as we broke up and went into the layer but it extended considerably, so having gone up a further 2,000 feet Selley decided to come down and we joined Sheahan who had remained behind to act as protection. Not long afterwards Jouault likewise rejoined the Flight, after having searched fruitlessly. I think those 'Matlows'were getting in a bit of firing practice. Eventually 16.00 hours came and our relief flight – they met us on the Dunkirk side and we returned to the English side together, two flights of three aircraft, flying about ¼ mile apart, with the ships making a centre line. For some unknown reason I thought that that picture was symbolic, and it impressed me very much. We said *au revoir* to Dawnton and his battle flight at Dover, and set course for Bircham, where we landed very tired and exceedingly hungry, not having had any food since breakfast.

Flying Officer H.A. Haarhoff, 220 Squadron

The weather, though fair, had not been good and around mid-day it rained. It had the effect of keeping the Luftwaffe away in the afternoon but those who did sneak in had plenty of cover. Fighter patrols were still flown but there were no encounters of note in the afternoon and evening and certainly no combat victories.

On the ground the evacuation of troops had been slow from the harbour. So slow that it was decided to begin to take-off soldiers from the nearby beaches. The port had been bombed almost continually and was a shambles. Large ships would continue to take men off the mole but others would begin to lay off-shore and be supplied with soldiers from the beaches by relays of small boats. All over southern England, rivers, ports and canals had been scoured for any small boats capable of crossing the Channel to carry out this mammoth task. More often than not their owners or crewmen stayed with their boats, not only sailing them to Dover, Ramsgate or the Thames Estuary, but volunteering to take them to the French coast and rescue the troops under fire. This, together with a sea which remained remarkably calm, became the real miracle of Dunkirk.

*

On the ground Pilot Officer Al Deere was beginning to realise just how serious the situation in Dunkirk really was. Forced down on his squadron's dawn patrol, and with a nasty gash to his forehead, he had the choice of making for Ostend or Dunkirk. He chose Ostend which was, in the event, chancy. The Germans would soon enter the Belgian port of Ostend. It was only now that he learned for the first time that the British Army was really evacuating and not withdrawing to regroup.

As he reached a main road, the heavy flow of refugees was so great that he had little choice than to change his direction and head towards Dunkirk. Via a crowded civilian bus, a 'liberated' bicycle, and on foot he eventually reached the outskirts of Dunkirk and found some British soldiers. An enquiry to them about his getting back to England left him in little doubt that nobody knew anything and it was every man for himself.

Driving a short way with the soldiers, he reached Dunkirk. Nearby a gun was firing at an aircraft that was obviously damaged and trying to make a forced landing. He yelled for them to stop and couldn't they see it was a British aeroplane? But after days of air attack it was obviously a case of shoot first, question it later.

As he waited for a promised destroyer, it began to drizzle which kept the sky clear of enemy aircraft for a short while. Helped by a Navy commander, he was eventually escorted to the mole, where they weaved their way through the lines of soldiers. In the confusion caused by a crippled Ju88 being chased by a Spitfire flying overhead he lost contact with his Navy man and made his way again towards the destroyer. He was suddenly halted by an angry and irate army major who in no uncertain terms told him to take his proper turn.

'I am an RAF officer,' said Deere, although with a ground sheet over his shoulders, and a bandaged head he could have been anything.

'I don't give a damn who you are,' retorted the major, 'get in line with the rest.'

'All I am trying to do is get back as quickly as possible in order to rejoin my squadron which is operating over here.'

'For all the good you chaps seem to be doing over here you might just as well stay on the ground.'

'You have absolutely no say over what I do, and can go to hell!' countered Deere angrily; he then marched smartly past a very shaken and startled major but the delay cost him a place on the destroyer which even now was beginning to move away from the mole.

Later he got aboard another destroyer and was escorted to the wardroom. A stony silence greeted him and when he enquired the reason was again met with the question of what were the RAF doing? For Deere who had flown in action for several days, fought numerous enemy aircraft and shot down five of them, it was particularly galling.

The destroyer then came under air attack and when shortly afterwards he was asked to come up on deck to help with aircraft identification (the gunners had just been firing at a Blenheim) he was happy to oblige.

While Deere was making his way home, the remainder of 54 Squadron flew north to Catterick to recoup after ten strenuous days in action. The squadron had claimed thirty-one destroyed plus eighteen probables. They had lost four pilots and seven aircraft, with several other Spitfires damaged.

Back in the air the sky remained cloudy and dull. 610 Squadron flew out at 2.15 p.m., and later at 6.20.

> The next day – 28th May, we carried out two patrols but visibility was very poor and we saw no enemy aircraft. We flew low over the beaches from time to time to give the Army a bit of encouragement and show them we were about. We also saw the roads all along the coast packed with civilian evacuees riding in horse drawn carts, pushing prams and pulling hand carts.
>
> *Flight Lieutenant J. Ellis, 610 Squadron*

At 7 o'clock, 220 Squadron operated a further patrol as recorded in Hilton Haarhoff's diary:

> We were off by seven o'clock and made straight for the Dutch coast, where we were warned numerous Jerries were likely to be

seen. We kept a close formation and everyone was wide awake against surprise attacks. Selley flew on Sheahan's left, and as I was the only officer airgunner, it had been arranged that if we were attacked by fighters we were to change position with Sheahan, so that I could act as fire controller. As we flew down the Dutch coast there was little activity to be seen, and on drawing near to the land, a battery of guns opened fire on us. I'm quite sure they were long range shore batteries, because one of the shells went off quite a hundred yards from our flight, and yet we had a violent shaking, in addition to which our aircraft, being nearest, got peppered with pieces of shrapnel, though nobody was hit. When the first explosion occurred Sheahan at once put his nose down and turned and we followed suit and soon threw the guns off. They fired at us for quite a time but their aim was in all cases far too high.

As we approached the Belgian border we could see in the distance an object on the water, which turned out to be an upturned table on which was lying three men and a bicycle. One was wounded as we could see the white of bandages. While Sheahan remained behind, Selley and Jouault flew off to fetch help and we sighted an armed trawler which we diverted towards the spot, about ten miles distant. As the trawler was making its way to the table, Selley flew to and fro, and eventually we saw the men being taken off, though the cycle and table were left to fend for themselves! Jouault had returned by this time, and as it was getting dusk and the visibility was poor we decided to return to base and landed at Bircham absolutely dog-tired. Our aircraft had sustained a dozen holes, Sheahan's had four and Jouault's one. These were all from the one shell which burst near us – I hate to think what might have been the result, if it had burst any closer!

Flying Officer H.A. Haarhoff, 220 Squadron

No 213 Squadron flew the last patrol of the day, led by Squadron Leader Humphrey Edwardes Jones, at 7.45 p.m., lasting till 9.40 when he headed his Hurricanes back to Biggin Hill.

In the main, during the 28th, the Luftwaffe had contented themselves with bombing the town and port of Dunkirk. Compared with what was to come it was still on a small scale. This was due in part to an increase in RAF air cover, weather and the heavy pall of smoke that covered the area for most of the day.

Royal Air Force fighters claimed twenty-two German aircraft with another half a dozen or so possibles. Fourteen RAF pilots had been shot down (plus three Defiant gunners), but five pilots returned although one of these was wounded. Another pilot was also wounded during the day. The Germans admitted a loss of twenty-three aircraft.

On the sea the little ships were entering the battle. With more and more surface vessels off Dunkirk and the French coast, the Luftwaffe would be out for their blood the next day. Fighter Command's 11 Group fighter pilots were in for another hard day's fighting. It had been another full and tiring day, but worse was still to come.

In Ostend, Pilot Officer Ian Muirhead had spent the whole day waiting for nightfall when his assigned ship, the *Aboukir*, was due to sail. The harbour had been subjected to bombing raids all through the day and he and Flight Lieutenant Ives had been continually asked where the RAF were and why they were not patrolling target areas. The two fighter pilots had seen several patrols of British fighters throughout the day but each time they had flown back towards England so German bombers appeared. As the day progressed, they also saw that Me109's preceded the bombers by several minutes and would circle, obviously making sure that no RAF aircraft were in the vicinity. From their vantage point the two men also witnessed several low-flying Luftwaffe aeroplanes machine-gunning refugees who seemed to be wandering hopelessly all over the small country roads inland from the harbour town.

At 10 p.m. that night the *Aboukir* finally set off downstream towards the sea. As they left a flare was dropped over the mouth of the canal, obviously as a signal as they were expecting further air raids. Muirhead and Ives overhauled and then manned a Lewis machine gun on the wheelhouse deck. In the darkness they were shadowed by at least one enemy aircraft which continued to drop flares from around 2,000 feet. Four such flares were dropped, each burning for about fifteen minutes. Finally two torpedoes came at them, one passing astern, the other going under the boat. Shortly afterwards they saw what appeared to be a submarine but was actually an E-boat. There followed a violent explosion, and Muirhead found himself entangled in wire beneath the surface of the sea. Freeing himself he found a large piece of wood to cling to. Then he saw the roof of the tank-house float by and pulled himself on this. Looking towards the boat all he could see was its stern pointing vertically out of the water, its propeller still turning, then it sank out of sight.

He was joined on the 'raft' by two airmen of 37 Squadron, Senior Aircraftman B.B. Stanhope and Leading Aircraftman G.A. Dear. He also found his legs to be completely useless. Meanwhile the German E-boat was circling around and in the light of a flare was shooting people who were struggling in the water. Muirhead told his two companions to slip into the water and use the sturdy roof as protection from the bullets. After some time the boat moved off and all was silent.

At daybreak there were several small, scattered groups of survivors. Several ships, including two coastal motor-boats were nearby. They were eventually rescued by a destroyer, Muirhead and his two companions having meantime pulled the *Aboukir*'s second mate out of the sea. Aboard HMS *Grenade*, Muirhead had his severely bruised legs treated and then he was put to sleep. In a very detailed report made out later by Muirhead he recorded that of the 230 RAF, Army and refugees on the *Aboukir*, only thirty-two survived, ten being RAF, but he was the only officer. Flight Lieutenant Ives was not rescued. Transferred to HMS *Greyhound*, the survivors were later landed at Dover.

Muirhead later wrote to his former squadron, 151, recording the gallant end of Freddie Ives. His calming influence had helped to keep the morale of women and children refugees high, despite language difficulties, while on shore he had helped with the wounded.[1]

[1] Ian Muirhead, DFC was killed in action on 15th October 1940.

CHAPTER SIX

Wednesday, 29th May 1940

As far as air action was concerned, the 29th began slowly. The message was now getting round that whenever possible, squadrons should not operate alone but in wing formations. This helped in part to combat the larger German formations but, with 11 Group's limited fighter force, reduced the total air coverage it could provide.

The dawn patrols were provided by the Hornchurch squadrons, 19, 41, 222 and 616 Squadrons flying out at 4.15 a.m. They arrived over Dunkirk at 4.45 with 19 and 222 flying high cover on watch for fighters, while 41 and 616 flew at medium height to deal with bombers. Rendezvousing over Manston, the four squadrons flew out but failed to find any sign of the Luftwaffe.

As the day continued, with the weather cloudy and overcast, the skies seemed ominously clear of German aeroplanes. So bad was the weather that on the first patrol, 41 Squadron had to land at Biggin Hill rather than Hornchurch. Pilot Officer J.W. Broadhurst of 222 Squadron, failing to locate Hornchurch in the poor visibility, ran out of petrol and had to force-land with his wheels up (P9376).

A further four squadrons (17, 145, 245 and 601) flew patrols around breakfast time but still no enemy aircraft appeared. Baron von Richthofen's 8th Flieger Corps was keen to get into the air but with the cloud base so low it would be impossible for his Stukas to make any kind of effective attack. Göring was sending him a constant stream of criticism but he and everyone else had to wait for the weather to improve and for the cloud ceiling to rise. The whole morning passed but then suddenly the Luftwaffe was there, and to meet them were just two Hurricane squadrons, 17 and 245, with a total of eighteen aeroplanes. It was just on one o'clock and the skies had cleared.

Anti-aircraft heralded the Germans' arrival to the south of Dunkirk. 17 Squadron were at 15,000 feet just off the French coast and through the bursting shells came twenty to thirty Dornier 215's.[1] They were in

---

[1] There is very little difference between Do215 and the more likely Do17. In this story the author has kept to the types referred to by the pilots.

open formation with Me110's above, but they began to split up upon sighting the Hurricanes. While 245 kept an eye on the Messerschmitts, 17 engaged the bombers. Squadron Leader Geoffrey Emms attacked one and his first five-second burst smashed into the port engine, causing a stream of petrol to stream back. It broke formation and began to lose height but Emms left it to attack another Dornier.

Pilot Officer Ken Manger followed a Hurricane on an attack upon a Dornier, continuing the attack from 200 yards. The bomber's port engine caught fire, the machine turned over onto its back and dived. Manger went after a second Dornier, setting its starboard engine alight. The engine broke up with bits and pieces flying off, then the Dornier headed down. Manger followed it through the cloud to see it crash into a field ten miles south of Calais.

Meanwhile some of the 110's had come down. Pilot Officer 'Birdy' Bird-Wilson followed his section leader in an attack on six of them, but the Messerschmitts flew into their usual defensive circle. Attacking the circle, Birdy's fire forced one 110 to break away upwards. As the British pilot pulled round in a turn he saw a 110 go down in a spiral dive but lost sight of it after watching it for 5,000 feet. Pilot Officer Hanson also got a shot at this 110 but then he was hit. A cannon shell smashed through his port wing, a bullet splintered his map case, while a splinter hit his right leg.

The other Hurricane squadron got in amongst the scattering Dorniers, shot down one and possibly a second.

Following this first clash of what was to turn out to be a very busy afternoon, 56 and 151 Squadrons flew out from Manston at two o'clock, carrying out a patrol at 29,000 feet. Near the end of the patrol Squadron Leader Teddy Donaldson, leading 151, saw five Me110's flying east towards Dunkirk and engaged. 56 were supposed to cover 151 but for some reason they flew off in another direction. Suddenly Donaldson found himself alone and in a desperate dog-fight with four 110's. Flying as hard as he knew how, he fought desperately for five minutes, the 110's outclimbing and out-turning his Hurricane at that height. Eventually two 110's got on his tail with the other two flying either side of him. The sky was clear of any protective cloud so Donaldson had no choice but to throw his fighter about the sky, firing at the 110's whenever he could. Finally with no way out, Donaldson rolled onto his back and allowed the engine to cut out.

In consequence, black smoke poured out of the exhausts together with petrol and glycol pouring out of the vents. Then he pulled over into a dive from 23,000 feet to the sea. The 110's thought they had got him and did not follow. In the terrific pull-out at sea level, the Hurricane's belly was split open, but he escaped to fight again, landing back at

Manston with only five gallons of fuel left. One 110 was, however, shot down, hit by Pilot Officer Blomley (P3304), being seen to crash near the French coast.

The Hurricanes of 56 Squadron had seen the 110's – they had made a head-on pass at them. Sergeant George Smythe fired a quick burst at them as they passed and a brief scrap developed. Smythe, seeking a target, looked down and saw some Ju87's about to make an attack on a ship outside the harbour. Smythe dived straight down in pursuit forcing the Stuka pilots to drop their bombs wildly into the sea and he had the impression that the last Stuka fell into the harbour. But flying at over 400 miles per hour and only being 200 feet above the sea he could not be certain. Nevertheless, he was certain of the next 87 he fired at: it went in just to the west of the harbour, seen and confirmed by Pilot Officer K.C. Dryden and Sergeant Baker. Dryden in particular was in the process of making a forced landing on the beach having been hit in the dog-fight, but saw the Stuka crash. He later returned by boat. 56 lost another pilot in this scattered tussle, Sergeant J.M. Elliott failing to make it home.

The Defiants of 264 Squadron were also in on the action, twelve aeroplanes flying lower down specifically on the look-out for bombers while 56, 151 and also eight Hurricanes of 213 watched out for the fighters.

While the fight was going on above, six Me109's dived down towards the Defiants. Squadron Leader Hunter and his gunner saw them coming and Hunter kept his planes flying in sections line-astern. His gunner engaged the leading Messerschmitt as it came in from the sun, opening fire at 300 yards. It continued in for another 200 yards, then burst into flames. Another 109 flew overhead, was fired at by Pilot Officer Terry Welsh's gunner, LAC Hayden, and it fell seawards. Pilot Officer M.H. Young's rear-man sent another 109 down smoking and Flight Lieutenant N.G. Cooke and Corporal Lippett set fire to another which had closed in behind another Defiant.

Whether or not this latter Defiant was that flown by Pilot Officer D.H.S. Kay is not certain, but his machine (L6957) was hit. His starboard aileron was torn to shreds and the hydraulics knocked out. Kay put the aeroplane into a dive and flew home, only to discover that his 31-year-old Canadian gunner, Leading Aircraftman E.J. Jones (promoted to sergeant after his loss), had baled out and was missing. His turret had been hit but he would have been safer to stay put. His body was later washed ashore on the French coast and buried in Dunkirk cemetery. Pilot Officer E.G. Barwell, with Pilot Officer J.E.M. Williams in the back turret, saw a 109 go down on Kay. Fire from Williams sent it into the sea, but this was probably the same 109 fired at by Cooke and Lippett. The rear-gunners in the Defiants were beginning to run into problems faced by air gunners throughout the war. If more than one fired at an aircraft and the target went down, then, of course, each would claim it was their fire that did the damage. This was understandable, but it made it difficult to sort out who got what.

No sooner had this 109 attack been beaten off than the Defiants ran into more enemy aircraft. Phil Hunter saw an He111 approaching to bomb the beaches from 300 feet. He put his Defiant into a dive from the direction of the sun, but then he saw a large formation of Stukas approaching Calais from behind them; before the Defiants could engage, the dive bombers' escort of Me110's came in. Yelling at his pilots to form line-astern, he led them out to sea, his rear-gunner shooting one 110 into the sea in flames.

Then the 110's were chasing amongst the Defiants, as Hunter led the main formation down to sea level in a spiral dive, pre-arranged in case of a determined attack. Sergeant Thorn and Leading Aircraftman Barker shot down a Messerschmitt; Terry Welsh was in trouble with a power loss and as a 110 came down on him, his gunner, Hayden, told him to dive to the sea. Pulling the boost cut-out, the engine picked up and Welsh went into a steep diving spiral, Hayden firing as they went. Hayden then reported his guns out of action but he managed to clear stoppages in three and shot down a 110 into the sea. Pilot Officer Young's gunner also got hits on a 110 and it too dived into the sea. In total, 264 claimed eight 109's, nine 110's and one Stuka.

Meantime, the third Hurricane Squadron, 213, was in amongst the German bombers and fighters. Near Nieuport the eight British pilots saw six Heinkel bombers at 15,000 feet which was about 4,000 feet above them. They climbed up and Pilot Officer H.D. Atkinson attacked a straggler. It was a straggler because it had already been shot at by Squadron Leader Edwardes Jones as he had fired into the formation, knocking bits from three of them. Atkinson's target was already smoking slightly and following his first pass the Heinkel's port engine was pouring out black smoke, a flicker of flame and with the propeller idling. It was then that some 109's appeared and without ammunition, Atkinson turned away.

Other pilots fired at the bombers, Flight Sergeant C. Grayson crippled one, and Sergeant Llewellyn another. Llewellyn then engaged the 109's and shot down two. Flight Sergeant Grayson, unable to maintain position behind his victim, turned to give cover to the Defiants when he saw the Stuka formation below. He dived behind the rearmost dive-bomber to fire a four-second burst. Smoke appeared from his target, followed by a red glow from the front cockpit. It dived steeply but Grayson was already emptying his guns towards another Stuka. Pilot Officer Billy Gray likewise attacked the Stukas, sending one down smoking into the smoke and mist over Dunkirk.

Four more fighter squadrons (forty-two Spitfires and Hurricanes) took over the air umbrella shortly before five o'clock, 64, 229, 242 and 610. All became engaged in a sky now full of Messerschmitts. It was to prove a costly hour for the British flyers.

Squadron Leader Bonzo Franks led 610 Squadron at 25,000 feet, the squadron having decided to work in pairs if engaged. However, Flight Lieutenant Andrew Smith experienced icing trouble and had to leave the patrol, at 5.35, escorted home by Pilot Officer 'Peter' Keighley. The RAF were reduced now to just forty aircraft and would soon find themselves vastly outnumbered, for lurking in the clouds were a large number of German fighters. Because of the cloud they were able to sneak in below the top cover squadron.

Flying lower down around 10,000 feet, 229 and 242 Squadrons met the Germans first. Two Me109 formations came at them, totalling approximately forty-five fighters. As 229 Squadron turned to engage the first gaggle, Squadron Leader Maguire fired an eight-second burst into one and saw it go down vertically; then 109's were coming down on them. As he broke, Maguire looked down and saw a circle on the water where the 109 had presumably gone in.

The Messerschmitts hit 229 badly, as they split up and began to dog-fight. Pilot Officer A.R. Smith saw a 109 on the tail of a Hurricane, fired and watched it dive vertically. Pilot Officer Vernon Bright turned inside a 109, fired and saw it fall away. As he pulled up he saw another 109 dive past him and crash into the sea.

Pilot Officer R. Clifford Brown latched onto a 109 and chased it down to sea level, snapping off bursts as he went. The 109 pulled up just above the water but another burst from the Hurricane sent it into the Channel. Brown just managed himself to pull out when a 109 attacked him, and was saved by another Hurricane.

For 229 it was a defeat by the more numerous Messerschmitts. Five Hurricanes were shot down, only two pilots managing to bale out, one being Pilot Officer Anthony Linney. One of those lost was Flight Lieutenant Falcon Clouston whose body was later washed up on the island of Borkum. Clouston's brother was Squadron Leader A.E. Clouston, a test pilot at Farnborough, but more famous for his pre-war record breaking flights to the Cape, Australia and New Zealand in a DH 'Comet'.

> My brother was holidaying with us when the balloon went up and we never met again unfortunately. My next news of him was from his squadron commander, Maguire, who very decently flew over from Biggin Hill to tell me he was missing after a squadron

sortie over Dunkirk. I collected my brother's belongings from his station a little later. The Germans later informed the authorities that his body had been washed up on the island of Borkum and buried there.

Squadron Leader A.E. Clouston, Test Pilot, Farnborough

At least twenty Messerschmitts attacked 242 Squadron from above and from both flanks. Flight Lieutenant George Plinston, a British flight commander, who had only arrived on the squadron the previous day (he had seen action in France with 607 Squadron), went after a 109 that was behind Yellow One and shot it down. Stan Turner (Yellow One) got into a terrific fight with several 109's, but succeeded in sending two down badly hit before finally getting away from his opponents.

Willie McKnight saw 229 being engaged below and was about to help when the 109's hit 242. He and another Hurricane went after a 109 but then another 109 got behind the other Hurricane. McKnight turned sharply towards the 109, opening fire at point-blank range. The Messerschmitt rolled onto its side and fell straight into the sea. The Canadian swung round after another 109 flying behind a Hurricane. His first burst produced smoke before the 109 dived towards the shore. Pilot Officer Bob Grassick found a 109 below him and as it came into his sights he fired three bursts until smoke streamed from it. Going down with it, he watched it go into the sea. He then chased another which appeared to have already been badly shot up but he was unable to finish it off. McKnight, meantime, found a lone Do17 above him and attacked. His first burst knocked out its port engine and another burst produced smoke before the bomber crashed 91 miles to the east of Dunkirk. No 242 were lucky to suffer no losses although several Hurricanes were damaged. George Plinston landed at Manston with his coolant temperature up to 135 degrees. Johnny Latta, having chased one Messerschmitt into the low mist, was hit by a burst from another, that damaged his undercarriage. One wheel dropped down and he had to land with only one wheel down, but made it with little other damage except a crunched wing.

The two covering Spitfire squadrons were so heavily engaged themselves they had little chance to help the Hurricanes below.

Three of 64's pilots were shot down, one being the commanding officer, Squadron Leader E.G. Rogers (L1052). Flight Sergeant C. Flynn attacked one Messerschmitt but this ended when a bullet hit his Spitfire (K9813). This entered the side of his cockpit and knocked out all his electrics. He saw the 109 start to smoke and dive but had to leave it to its fate. Flight Lieutenant D.B. Hobson damaged another 109, the rest of the squadron damaging several others.

Meanwhile 610 Squadron were also in trouble.

> On our first patrol on 29th May, we were bounced by a squadron
> of Me109's. We broke up and I told my Number Two, Sergeant
> Jenkins, to keep a look out behind me while I chased a Me109
> flying straight and level in front of me. He obviously hadn't seen
> me so I closed in and finished him off. He dived down on fire and
> didn't bale out. On returning to the coast I saw a Spitfire attack
> and shoot down another Me109. I joined up with this Spitfire
> which turned out to be Jenkins.
>
> *Flight Lieutenant J. Ellis, 610 Squadron*

Squadron Leader Franks got a 109 (P9452), Flying Officer G.L.
Chambers, Pilot Officer S.C. Norris and John Ellis getting others. They
lost two – Flying Officer G.M.T. Kerr and Flying Officer J. Kerr-
Wilson. Kerr was flying with Franks and Chambers, Graham Chambers
seeing twelve Me109's attacking from behind when a warning was
called over the radio. He climbed into the sun, looking back to see a
terrific dog-fight starting. Turning round he went after a 109 that had
just broken from the tail of a Spitfire. The 109 pulled into a tight turn
but was hit by a seven-second burst of .303 bullets and it went straight
down. Stan Norris had a 109 on his tail with cannon shells flashing past
him. After a tussle he got on the 109's tail, and gave it a two-second
burst as it pulled into a climbing turn. The 109 twisted into a spin with
engine full on and went down gyrating wildly.

As the four squadrons finally disentangled themselves from the
Messerschmitts, the pilots all knew they had been in a fight. While
several pilots brought back bullet-ridden aeroplanes, ten of their number
– one quarter of their force – did not get back. It was to prove the
blackest half hour of the Dunkirk battle in the air.

*

Now the weather had cleared, the Luftwaffe had briefed a force of dive-
bombers to attack the ships off Dunkirk. The task fell to the 2nd Stuka
Wing, commanded by Major Oscar Dinort, himself based at Beaulieu. It
was their first chance at attacking shipping targets since war began.

These Stukas began to arrive over the target area just after five
o'clock, covered by Theo Osterkamp's 1st Fighter Wing. It had been
these Me109's that had so vigorously engaged the four RAF fighter
squadrons. So well did they engage the Spitfires and Hurricanes that
Dinort's Stukas had practically a free hand against British destroyers
and troop carrying vessels.

More Stukas and also Ju88's came in as early evening approached.

They too were escorted by Me109 and Me110 fighters, but four RAF units, totalling forty-four Spitfires, Hurricanes and Defiants, were there to meet them. 56 and 151 were the Hurricane squadrons from Manston flying a high patrol, 264 Squadron's Defiants below them. The pilots of 610 Squadron, who had only landed from the earlier sortie at around 6 p.m., were quickly turned round, refuelled, re-armed and were away again by 7.30, led by Bonzo Franks. 213 and 242 Squadrons were also in the air. There were only six from 242, reduced to five as Pilot Officer Jim Howitt crashed on take-off, sustaining injuries which led to his eventual release from the RAF. Howitt may have scored a kill in the squadron's earlier air battle but his crash prevented him completing a combat report and subsequent claim investigation. Another pilot returned with engine trouble, the remaining four seeing no sign of the fighting which embroiled the other units.

The actions began as soon as the British squadrons reached the French coast. He111's, Ju88's and Stukas were all milling about above the ships and harbour. Squadron Leader Hunter led his Defiants towards them, covered initially by his Hurricane escort, but once the engagement commenced he personally saw no further sign of the Hurricanes.

Squadron Leader Teddy Donaldson (P3305), leading 151 Squadron, spotted a Ju88 on its own and with Pilot Officer J.R. Hamar (P3301), dived to attack.[1] They believed it was a decoy for no sooner did they begin to open fire than they saw a number of Me109's coming at them. The Junkers, however, was hit and fell away into clouds with smoke pouring from it and with large pieces having been blasted from it.

Flying Officer Ken Newton and Pilot Officer Ronald Courtney saw the 109's above.

> The squadron had taken off from Manston – I believe it was in the afternoon – and I was flying Number Two in a section led by Flying Officer Ken Newton, a New Zealander. I think the Number Three in the section was Pilot Officer C.O. Wright, a South African. Over Dunkirk we saw a number of 109's well above us. Ken Newton asked the commanding officer if we could break away to engage them and we climbed up towards them. I was about to attack one of the 109's and was shot down by another behind me which I had not seen. The aircraft was badly damaged and I was wounded in the back of the neck and in the right leg. It was difficult to see because of the glycol and petrol which had been spraying into the cockpit and eventually I had to

[1] Jack Hamar DFC was killed in a flying accident on 28th July 1940.

bale out. I was picked up by a corvette, HMS *Shearwater*, and
taken to Ramsgate hospital.

Pilot Officer R. Courtney, 151 Squadron

Newton was also shot down, baled out and was later picked up from the
Channel by a hospital ship bound for Dunkirk. It returned with him the
following day.[1] Newton later told his squadron that after he saw
Courtney go down with smoke pouring out of his aircraft, he saw red
and shot down the offending 109. Then he was hit by others but got
away by rolling his machine over and over as though he was finished.
As he was not followed and seeing a hospital ship below, he glided
down, then baled out at 3,000 feet. After only ten minutes in the water
he was picked up by the ship and taken to Dunkirk. The ship was
bombed and machine-gunned all night in Dunkirk harbour while
picking up wounded soldiers.

Flying Officer Eriminsky and Flight Sergeant Taffy Higginson of 56
Squadron each shot down Me109's in their squadron action, Sergeant
Baker damaging an He111 he found below him. The experienced Taffy
Higginson saw the 109's wheeling round to engage 56, and turned to
engage them himself. Sliding in he began to fire a deflection shot,
ending up right behind the Messerschmitt. It began to draw away from
him but then the burst took effect and the 109 slowed down. It then fell
away in an uncontrolled spin, smoke pouring from it, finally to crash in
flames.[2]

As the Hurricanes fought it out, the Defiants engaged the enemy.
After seeing a lone Me110, which flew off, Phil Hunter saw large
numbers of Ju87's streaming in towards Dunkirk from various
directions. Immediately they saw the Defiants, the Stuka pilots began to
dive. It was no use chasing them down, so Hunter dived to low level to
catch them when they began to pull out of the dive. When they finally
clashed several Stukas were seen to drop their bombs hastily and the
Defiant gunners began to pick targets. Hunter went after one, his gunner
hammering it from 100 yards. The Stuka, mortally hit, burst into flames
and dived into the sea.

A running fight developed above the waves with the dive bombers.
Barwell and Williams put one into the sea in flames then closed up
below two others, Williams blazing away at one which dropped its
bombs then crashed in flames, although it was also being fired at by
another Defiant. A third 87 caught fire under Williams' guns and

[1] Flying Officer K.E. Newton was killed in action on 28th June 1940.
[2] Taffy Higginson had already seen action in France with a flight of 56 Squadron during the
Blitzkrieg. He was later to win the DFC and DFM. He was shot down over France in 1941 and
escaped to return to England.

crashed. Flight Lieutenant Nick Cooke, Pilot Officer Kay and Pilot Officer Whitley got amongst the Stukas. Cooke and Kay flying below them allowing their gunners the opportunity of firing up at them. In this way Cooke claimed no less than five shot down, Kay flying with a new gunner, LAC Cox, damaging another. Whitley carried out an overtaking attack on a Stuka and his gunner set it alight and it went down. Two Stukas then attacked their Defiant, putting several shots through its starboard wing and holing the petrol tank. Whitley banked away to join the others engaging more Stukas attacking the harbour area. The Defiant crews again attacked the dive-bombers as they pulled out of their dives. Whitley and his gunner shot one Stuka down in flames, then sent another, their third kill, crashing onto the beach.

It was a massacre. Pilot Officer Young and his rear man shot down two Stukas, Terry Welsh got two more, Sergeant Thorn another plus two more damaged; Pilot Officer Stokes got one crashed.

No sooner was this fight over than the Defiants went after some Ju88's, one being shot to pieces by the combined fire of several gunners, another being severely damaged, if not definitely destroyed. In total, the Defiants put in claims for eighteen Ju87's and one Ju88 destroyed, one 88 and two 87's probably so. They suffered no losses, only some Defiants damaged, Sergeant Thorne crash-landed back at Manston with a leaking fuel tank and on one wheel. Yet despite these actions many of the Stukas got through and sank a number of ships.

Sergeant R.T. Llewellyn was the only pilot in 213 Squadron to score a victory when he shot down an He111 which fell away with black smoke pouring from it.

> I happened to be at Duxford when Philip Hunter and his two-seater fighters landed back from a highly successful interception over Dunkirk. They were all cock-a-hoop and I tried to warn them that the Hun must have mistaken them for Hurricanes and would not make the same mistake twice!
>
> Meanwhile at my base at Wittering the squadrons were operating over Dunkirk using Martlesham as a forward base. No Spitfires could be used unless they had been fitted with armour plate and self sealing fuel tanks and at Wittering this really meant Hurricanes only.
>
> *Wing Commander H. Broadhurst, Station Commander,*
> *Wittering*

Up above these actions the Spitfire pilots of 610 Squadron had been reduced in number when Pilot Officer Norris had to return home with a rough engine, to be followed by Flying Officer B.G. Lamb with a leaking oxygen bottle. They were then engaged by Messerschmitts and claimed two possibly shot down. The squadron suffered two losses, its commanding officer, Bonzo Franks (N3177 DW-T), and Sergeant P.D. Jenkins, the latter being brought down by naval AA fire.

> In the late afternoon of the same day we flew another patrol over Dunkirk. We had only just arrived over the beaches at 12,000 feet when we were fired on either from Royal Navy ships or from AA guns on shore. Sergeant Jenkins, again my Number Two, was immediately hit in his port wing, half of which was blown off. The aircraft went down inverted and I saw Jenkins bale out. As he was drifting out to sea I decided to follow him down. He landed in the sea about two miles from a destroyer which I flew over at nought feet towards the parachute in the sea. The only response of the destroyer was to open fire on me with Bofors guns. So I had to withdraw and leave Jenkins to his fate. He was never seen again.
>
> As Jenkins was an outstanding pilot it was particularly tragic he should be lost in this way. At this stage of the war, the Army and Navy did not know the difference between a Spitfire and a Ju87!
>
> Squadron Leader Franks was missing after this sortie. No one saw him go down but later on we heard his body had been washed up on one of the small islands along the Dutch coast where he is buried.
>
> Flight Lieutenant Tom Smith, one of the original Auxiliary officers, was appointed the commanding officer. This was a mistake as although he was a very good officer, he had insufficient flying experience to lead his squadron in the air so I took over this responsibility for the next twelve months. I was in fact appointed commanding officer in July 1940 when Squadron Leader Smith was killed.
>
> *Flight Lieutenant J. Ellis, 610 Squadron*

May 29th ended with sixteen pilots missing, with three more wounded. In addition one Defiant gunner was lost. However, four of the missing pilots later turned up.

Claims against the Luftwaffe were many: over sixty destroyed and around two dozen more damaged or possibly destroyed. The Defiant squadron appeared to be the heroes of the day with thirty-five German aircraft claimed destroyed plus three probables. Undoubtedly a good deal of confusion and overclaiming by the gunners and pilots occurred but such was the nature of the air battles that it was inevitable. It would occur throughout the war on both sides. The Germans themselves claimed sixty-eight kills on the 29th, admitting the loss of eighteen aircraft.

*

The day had not only been fought by Fighter Command. At twelve minutes past three o'clock Avro Anson aircraft of 48 and 500 Squadron had flown patrols over the Channel and been attacked by Me109's. Pilot Officer Allington and his crew, Pilot Officer Wharry and Aircraftmen Harding and Dilnutt (48 Squadron), were attacked by nine Messerschmitts off Zeebrugge. LAC Leslie Dilnutt, as air gunner, claimed one Me109 shot down and two others damaged before the Anson (OY-X) was damaged by the enemy's fire power. LAC L.S. Dilnutt was awarded the DFM for his air gunnery. Allington managed to pancake onto the sea and later all the crew were rescued by a drifter and landed safely at Ramsgate.

A second Anson (500 Squadron's MK-L N5065) was also shot down into the sea, this crew too being rescued. They ran into Me109's, whose gunfire shattered the Anson's fuel tanks. With Corporal Richard Rogers radioing a May-Day call, the pilot, Sergeant Hoskins, brought the aeroplane down in another successful pancake onto the sea. After some time in the water the four-man crew was picked up by a returning tug, filled with soldiers, many badly wounded and shocked. Corporal Rogers himself suffered a broken collar bone and arm in the crash.

Hudson aircraft of 220 Squadron had also been active on what they termed 'Sands Patrols' – battle flights whose object was to protect shipping and attack any low flying dive-bombers they might find.

Three Hudsons had been sent out on each patrol and on one operation, the Hudson crew had directed HMS *Killang* to a raft carrying three wounded soldiers.

A feature of the evacuation of the 29th was the shift of rescue ships to the beaches as the harbour of Dunkirk continued to be heavily bombed and shelled, plus the need to speed up the rate of the evacuation. Rescue ships would sail in as near as possible while their own small boats plus the myriad of small ships taken across the Channel by their civilian owners, plied to and fro from ship to shore, others taking soldiers all the way back to England. The scene in the late afternoon of this day was recorded in Hilton Haarhoff's diary as seen from the turret of his Hudson.

> Our flight was not required for duty till the early afternoon and we took off at 14.00 hours for the Dover-Dunkirk patrol. The weather was warmish, but still very cloudy and with bad

visibility and we carried out the same trips between the two coasts as on the previous day. The volume of shipping had increased somewhat, and more men crowded on the decks were now to be seen. Most of the embarkations had up to now taken place from within the docks and the destroyers, Channel boats and other medium-sized craft made their way to quay-sides, whence the troops simply poured aboard, but not before the wounded had been seen to first. After the afternoon sun had started to dip, we noticed that there were numerous small craft now forming part of the endless stream towards Dunkirk. There were life-boats, yachts, and countless small pleasure craft – most of the latter towing something smaller or being towed in a long string behind a largish motor, or steam vessel. As night drew on barges towed by tugs appeared amongst the motley throng.

Just as it was getting dark the first of the small craft reached the other side, and the promenade and beaches of Dunkirk were now packed with troops. Those of the boats which were of shallow draught went into the beaches and the men waded out and clambered aboard. When a boat could not get in very far it sent out its dinghy which ferried the men over. In some cases one could see men hanging on to the side of a boat and swimming. We even saw a couple of chappies making their way out to a boat by means of a life belt in which they sat and paddled themselves! During the whole of our patrol, there had been no enemy air activity over our 'beat' or the beaches, but enemy dive-bombers, mostly Ju88's had been bombing Dunkirk docks considerably, and several buildings were smoking and burning. As we were near the end of our endurance we broke off our patrol at 19.15 hours, and reached Bircham safely, but with little fuel to spare. We made for food and bed as soon as possible.

Flying Officer H. A. Haarhoff, 220 Squadron

CHAPTER SEVEN

Thursday, 30th May 1940

In marked contrast to the previous day or even the previous few days, 30th May was very quiet as far as the air forces on both sides were concerned.

The weather in the early hours promised a reasonable if cloudy day but this changed somewhat around dawn, especially over Dunkirk. Fog and sea mist rolled in, mingling with the smoke from Dunkirk itself making it almost impossible for high level bombing by the Luftwaffe, and totally impossible for dive-bombing by either Ju87's or Ju88's. This was hardly credited further inland from Dunkirk, as the weather there was warm and sunny. Twice Richthofen's Stukas took off and twice they were forced to return with their bombs.

Earlier Hilton Haarhoff, with his crew of 220 Squadron, had flown an operation to the north of the Dunkirk area. While it could be said only to be indirectly in support of the evacuation, it is interesting as his diary records:

> It seems we were not to be allowed to catch up on our 'shut-eye' as at 1 a.m. we, Selley, self and crew, were called out to the 'Ops' room and told that we were to carry out an early morning recco of the Dutch coast – this patrol was known as the 'Cross-over' as it involved flying to the Dutch coast, then turning up the coast and flying over the islands as far as Sylt, then turn back as far as Ameland, and then northwards to Sylt once more, completing the run down to the Dutch-Belgian border and then home. We got off the deck at 2 a.m. and were not long in reaching Holland. Being so early in the day things were very quiet, but as the dawn approached we could see that it was going to be a nice day and there was a nice amount of cloud cover. We flew up the Dutch coast, coming down to take photographs whenever anything of interest appeared.
>
> On one occasion we photographed a Jerry transport machine which had been used to land troops in Holland, probably only the day before, while the invasion of Holland was in progress. The

tides had covered the undercarriage of the Junkers transport with sand and it looked very battered and very much u/s.

Our course carried us over several of the islands bordering the coast and when we reached Terschelling we sighted several flak ships, which fired coloured lights on our approach, but we flew on as far as Sylt and then turned back. Nowhere was there any signs of life. As we drew near the flak ships for the second time they opened fire on us, and we could see that they were under way. Their fire was quite accurate but Selley put them off by taking violent avoiding action. He called me up on the RT and said we'd bomb the b – as they started it! He opened the bomb doors and getting just below the cloud level at 1,500 feet he endeavoured to get into position above the biggest ship – a neat light-grey grain-boat – but just as he was about to release a bomb, the target turned off to one side. So Selley made another approach and another, and in each case just as he was ready to let things go, the flak-ship altered course – it seemed as if the man at the wheel could see every movement that Selley made in the cabin, so well timed were his evasive tactics. At this time as we were attempting to drop our bombs the three flak-ships were letting us have it whenever we came anywhere near. This little game had been going on for about fifteen minutes which we certainly were enjoying, when as Selley was making his fourth run-up on the target, I spotted three Me109's about 1,000 yards distant and on the water.

As I saw them, they commenced their climb towards us and I could see the tracers as the pilots tested their guns – no doubt they were smacking their lips too! The 109's were in a line abreast formation and fairly tightly packed. At first I thought it was a mirage due to the early morning light and over the RT told Selley so, but when I saw the tracers I realised that it was no mirage and that those boys meant some business! Almost in a shout I told Selley to get going as the 109's were about to attack – what happened then was done in split seconds.

I opened fire and Selley opened the throttles, and I felt our aircraft lurch forward and start climbing towards the cloud. As we were originally making an approach our route took us over the flak-ship which was firing like h – at us. We passed directly over the ship and I could see pom-pom tracer on all sides of us. The 109's were now at about 400 yards range and I could see their shots going below our tail – their aim was slightly off. I was firing as much as I could, when suddenly the Jerries turned off to starboard, the two aircraft on the right nearly colliding with each other! They had spotted the tracer coming up from the flak-ship

and did not want to fly over it as we were doing!! They made a
sweeping turn and then came in on our starboard quarter, but their
detour had broken their formation as they were all over the place,
and had also cost them some time, because the range was now
about 800 yards and before they could reduce this by much, we
had entered the friendly clouds! We changed course several times
and Selley slowed down to cruising and we were able to take
stock of ourselves.

Selley, Fletcher, Richardson and self were all unharmed and on
inspecting the aircraft we could see no damage at all! We laughed
heartily over the way the 109's had been fooled and needless to
say we called them some nice succulent names for upsetting our
game of 'cat and mouse' with the flak-ship. We decided that it
would be foolish to attempt to bomb the flak ships again as the
109's would inevitably remain in the vicinity. We decided to
continue our patrol along the coast, and came down beneath the
cloud then about 750 feet. Very shortly we came in sight of
Willemsoord, and decided to take some photographs. We hovered
over the town and harbour for quite twenty minutes and all
seemed quiet. We had managed to get some shots at the shipping
in the docks and Selley in his usual spirits decided to awaken the
inhabitants by zooming over the steeple! He dived down to about
250 feet and just then about twenty guns opened up at us – things
fairly burst wide open and I thought we'd been hit in a hundred
places! It did not take us long to nip back into the cloud!! Selley
called us up and said he had decided to bomb the place as they
had fired on us. We had seen about a dozen flying-boats in one
basin and these were to be our target. Selley climbed up to 2,000
feet and through a gap in the cloud got his bearings and started a
dive which would take him over the flying boats. He planned to
release his bombs as soon as he got a bead on the target. It was a
rather risky method of bombing with a view to hitting the flying-
boats but as we came out of the clouds we could see the target
just to our left and below us. Selley swung the Hudson and
pressed the teat, the height being about 600 feet. We started
climbing once more and the guns opened fire again, but did not
hit us. The explosion of the bombs we had dropped – three two-
fifty pounders – shook our aircraft quite forcibly. We did a circle
and came back to inspect the damage and saw that our bombs
were slightly off the target, having hit a building on the dock side,
but the flying-boats had received their share too. Several of these
were burning furiously and others were sinking and lying
overturned. That corner of the docks represented chaos and we

were satisfied that we had taught them a lesson, i.e. not to fire on British aircraft! After leaving Willemsoord we completed the rest of the patrol without further incident and landed at our base in time for a late breakfast – and then sleep!

Flying Officer H.A. Haarhof, 220 Squadron

An Anson aeroplane of 500 Squadron took off to fly a patrol at 9.28 a.m., piloted by Pilot Officer Wheelwright but it failed to return.

The squadrons had as usual been called well before dawn and No 616 Squadron were all at readiness by eight o'clock and were then put on thirty minutes availability. With the weather so bad, Flight Lieutenant Denys Gillam was sent off to fly a weather test and on landing back at Rochford had one leg of his Spitfire's undercarriage collapse, fortunately without injury to himself.

We had several casualties and as a very green squadron fatigue and losses were not understood. I remember one particular pilot, as he went to his aircraft, breaking down. Our medical officer went across and gave him a terrific punch and few well chosen words and we had no further trouble.

Flight Lieutenant D.E. Gillam, 616 Squadron

Despite the poor weather, Fighter Command flew patrols to the French coast but all reported bad weather and no enemy aircraft in sight. It was not until one o'clock that the first clash came when 245 Squadron were on patrol.

Visibility was bad and eventually the patrol had to be abandoned but not before a brief encounter with Luftwaffe bombers. At ten minutes past one, Pilot Officer H.S. Southwell sighted several Dorniers and Red Section attacked. Southwell put a burst of fire into one Dornier, noting the rear-gunner ceasing to return fire. Then the Dornier's starboard engine began to trail smoke and the aircraft went down in a long spiral. Flight Lieutenant J.A. Thomson also got hits on this bomber, reporting both its engines smoking, then he went after another one. As he opened fire, a single bullet from the Dornier hit his windscreen, then another hit his cockpit, grazing his thigh as it passed through. Before it left, the bullet hit the throttle lever, jamming it full open. Thomson, unable to see ahead because of the damaged windscreen, returned to base. Pilot Officer D. Pennington also went for the first Dornier as it went down, his burst knocking pieces from its tail and fuselage. They finally lost it in cloud at 4,000 feet badly damaged.

Six of 245 Squadron's aircraft landed at Kenley when the patrol was washed-out, the other three all having to force-land along the south coast, each aircraft being rendered unserviceable.

An hour later, four squadrons flew out, led by Squadron Leader Edwardes Jones, with his 213 Squadron. Humphrey Edwardes Jones recalls that when 11 Group began finally to fly in wing strength formations they had several early problems. Apart from the ludicrous situation of nobody knowing how the other squadrons in the 'wing' operated, there had obviously been no kind of training in flying with such a formation. It had to be a case of learning as they went along. He also recalls that he usually split his squadrons up once he had got them all to Dunkirk and then they patrolled independently. Some of the squadrons could not even cloud climb and when forced to do so would invariably lose formation. There seemed very little organisation on how the 'wings' should operate. Once he discovered that due to losses in one squadron, a flying officer would be leading not only his own squadron, but the wing, Edwardes Jones soon changed that! It appeared that it was a case of it being that squadron's turn to lead and nobody in authority had checked to see if they had a suitable leader.

It was now quite hectic for 11 Group's squadrons. Humphrey Edwardes Jones remembers being up well before 4 a.m. each day and sometimes flying as many as four patrols. The day ended at dusk, but with debriefing, a decent meal and checking on his aeroplane serviceability, it was about midnight before he got to bed.

On this patrol it was only 213 Squadron who located the enemy, shortly after 3 p.m., in the shape of one Dornier 17. Flight Lieutenant Widge Wight found it at 5,000 feet, one mile to the east of Dunkirk, 213 being at 15,000 feet. AA bursts attracted their attention to it. Edwardes Jones ordered Wight and his Blue Section to investigate, Widge diving down with the sun behind him. His first burst caused an explosion halfway along the Dornier's fuselage which was seen by Edwardes Jones who was still 10,000 feet above. Bits flew off and it appeared not to be under proper control afterwards. The bomber's port engine also caught fire intermittently. Wight closed right in to see the Dornier simply riddled with holes and no return fire came from the top gunner. The section made further attacks until the Dornier disappeared in cloud at 1,000 feet.

These were the only actions of the day. By the same token, RAF losses were nil due to enemy action although one pilot was killed. This was a member of 609 Squadron.

The Auxiliary boys of 609 had been moved south from Scotland on 18th May, being stationed at Northolt, no doubt as part of Fighter Command's reserves. Here a week later they began to receive armour plating for their Spitfires, items not needed while in Scotland which was way out of range for German fighters. Northolt's Station Commander, Group Captain S.F. Vincent, received the message for 609 to stand-by for action on the evening of the 29th. All were anxious. Like many before them, 609's pilots were about to see action for the first time. Training was over, their war was about to begin.

Early on the 30th came the call to stand-by for a patrol off the French coast. Hardly good weatherwise to start war flying in earnest. They took off from Northolt at mid-day, flying to Biggin Hill where their fuel tanks were topped up. Taking off in the wing led by 213 Squadron, 609 patrolled for an hour at 15,000 feet, seeing well below them the solid layer of haze and fog which prevented Luftwaffe attacks. Yet it was this valuable cover for the evacuation that proved the danger for 609 when it became time to return home. Owing to a delay in making rendezvous with the wing at the beginning of the patrol, 609's Spitfires were now very low on fuel. Yellow Section lost its way. Flying Officer Frankie Howell (N3203) managed to get down at Rochford but Flying Officers Joe Dawson and John Dundas had to force-land at Frinton-on-Sea; Dundas damaged a wing of his Spitfire (L1063). Red Two, Flying Officer Desmond Ayre (L1086) ran out of fuel near Harwich, spun in and crashed in the grounds of an explosives works at Oakley. He was killed instantly. The rest of 609 managed to get down at Manston with dry petrol tanks. Hardly an auspicious start for their war in the south.

*

Around 4 p.m., Flight Lieutenant John Ellis of 610 Squadron led a four-squadron wing-formation, with 64, 229, 242 Squadrons.

> On 30th May I led a formation of four Spitfire squadrons on an offensive patrol over Dunkirk. The other three squadrons were from Hornchurch and North Weald. Weather conditions were not good with poor visibility. We saw some Me110's but before we could attack them they disappeared into cloud. In the afternoon of the same day we again patrolled Dunkirk with the same four Spitfire squadrons but it was so hazy we could hardly see the coast. As usual we encountered heavy Ack-Ack fire from our own forces but we saw no enemy aircraft.
>
> *Flight Lieutenant J. Ellis, 610 Squadron*

Further patrols were flown right up to 7.30 that evening but the weather was impossible. The day had seen two Dorniers badly damaged, one Anson missing and one Spitfire and its pilot lost.

Below the cloud, mist, haze, fog and smoke the evacuation had carried on. With little or no hindrance from the Luftwaffe, nearly 54,000 Allied soldiers had been off-lifted from the harbour and beaches, the best day so far. To date over 126,000 had been brought away far exceeding the planners' wildest hopes of just four days earlier.

CHAPTER EIGHT

Friday, 31st May 1940

In spite of the relative calm in the air on the 30th, a message was received at Air Ministry from the Commander-in-Chief of the BEF, Lord Gort, VC, DSO, MVO, MC, commending the efforts of the RAF. The message, with another from the Chief of the Air Staff, when printed was sent to all Commands. Dated 30th May 1940, copies were distributed to squadrons involved directly or indirectly with air operations over Dunkirk. It showed that while many soldiers on the beaches or in the French harbour town were beginning to question the presence of the RAF, their Commander-in-Chief knew of the activities above and around his gallant force.

MESSAGES ADDRESSED TO COMMANDER-IN-CHIEF, BOMBER COMMAND, FROM LORD GORT AND FROM THE CHIEF OF THE AIR STAFF, ON 30th MAY 1940.

Message from Lord Gort:
Extremely grateful for valuable work of RAF. Presence and action of fighters is of first importance in preventing embarkation being interrupted and is having most heartening effect on troops.

Message from Chief of the Air Staff:
I wish to express to you my warmest congratulations on the successes achieved by all Units during the critical period of the last forty-eight hours and my profound appreciation of the effort which you have been able to sustain. The messages from Lord Gort and VA Dover[1] will show you clearly how vital a factor air support is during the continuance of the present operation, and I count on all ranks to continue to do their utmost to help the Navy and the Army, who are fighting most gallantly under conditions of extreme difficulty.

[1] Vice Admiral Dover, Bertram Ramsay.

Top left: Pilot Officer Tony Bartley, 92 Squadron.

Top right: Flight Lieutenant Bob Stanford Tuck, 92 Squadron.

Bottom: Pilots of 54 Squadron just prior to Dunkirk. Seated: (l to r) Flight Lieutenant James 'Prof' Leathart, Flying Officer A W A Bayne, Flight Lieutenant M C Pearson. Standing: Pilot Officer Colin Gray (NZ), Pilot Officer Bob Blake and Pilot Officer George Gribble. Gribble landed on the beach at Dunkirk on 25 May.

Top: Pictured later in the war as successful
fighter pilots, the two New Zealand aces with
54 Squadron, Al Deere and Colin Gray.

Bottom left: Flight Lieutenant Max Pearson,
54 Squadron, missing 27 May 1940.

Bottom right: Pilot Officer Peter Parrott,
145 Squadron.

Top: Little ships and big ships off Dunkirk.

Bottom: 74 Squadron. Seated: Bertie Aubert, KIA 24 May, S/Ldr F L White, rescued from Calais by 54 Sqn; A H Smith, W E G 'Tink' Measures, Sammy Hoare, PoW 24 May;

Standing: Don Cobden, Paddy Treacy – evaded after being shot down 27 May, Ernie Mayne, F/Sgt Llewellyn, John Mungo-Park (WIA 24 May), Johnny Freeborn, Tony Mould, brought down on the 24th.

Top left: Flight Lieutenant John Ellis, 610 Squadron.

Top right: H M Stephen and A G 'Sailor' Malan of 74 Squadron, with Malan's dog 'Peter'.

Bottom: 19 Squadron: (l to r) Brian Lane, Sgt Jack Potter, Sgt Jimmy Jennings, P/O Ray Aeberhardt, F/Sgt George Unwin, F/Sgt Harry Steere, F/O Frank Brindsen, F/O Walter Lawson, F/O Len Haines, P/O Arthur Vokes, F/L Wilf Clouston, F/O Thomas.

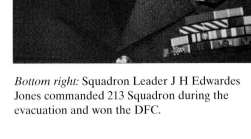

Top: The Boulton Paul Defiant which gave the Luftwaffe a surprise when flown by 264 Squadron over Dunkirk, although short-lived.

Bottom left: Sir Archibald Hope, 601 Squadron, force landed on the beach of Dunkirk on 27 May and came home on a destroyer.

Bottom right: Squadron Leader J H Edwardes Jones commanded 213 Squadron during the evacuation and won the DFC.

Top left: Squadron Leader Hector McGregor was about to take over 213 Squadron; he was shot down on 31 May and baled out, but got home.

Top right: Sergeant G A Steward, 17 Squadron, later won the DFM but was killed in 1941.

Bottom: B Flight 222 Squadron: Standing: Roy Morant, J M C Carpenter, H L Whitbread, G Massey-Sharpe, J W Broadhurst, F/Lt A I Robinson. Sitting: Sgts R B Johnson, I Hutchinson, L J White, E I Lewis and J I Johnson. Morant, Massey-Sharpe and White were all shot down on 1 June, Morant being the only survivor. Whitbread, Lewis, Broadhurst and both Johnsons were all to die in the Battle of Britain.

Top: Pilot Officers G Massey-Sharpe and John Broadhurst, 222 Squadron.

Above: Squadron Leader A L Franks AFC and Flight Lieutenant A T Smith, 610 Squadron. Alexander Franks was killed on 29 May, and Smith was to die in the Battle of Britain while commanding the Squadron.

Left: Flight Lieutenant Denys Gillam AFC, 616 Squadron.

Top left: Pilot Officer James Storrar, 145 Squadron.

Top right: Dunkirk beaches.

Middle: Pilot Officer G G A Davies, 222 Squadron. Hit by flak on 31 May he landed on the beaches, destroyed his Spitfire and returned by sea.

Bottom: Flight Sergeant George Unwin and Sergeant Jack Potter, 19 Squadron. Potter ditched in the Channel on 1 June and was rescued by a French fishing boat.

Top left: Flying Officer Johnny Bell, 616 Squadron, ditched on 1 June too, rescued by a minesweeper.

Top right: Pilot Officer Roy Morant, 222 Squadron, shot down 1 June to crash-land on the beaches, returning on a cross-Channel steamer.

Middle: The burning oil refinery at Dunkirk. Its smoke could be seen for miles.

Bottom: Roy Morant's Spitfire, P9377, which he set fire to on the beach at Dunkirk.

Top left: Squadron Leader George Lott, OC 43 Squadron.

Top right: Pilot Officer Nigel Weir, like so many young fighter pilots, scored his first victory over Dunkirk.

Above: 41 Squadron: Front row: F/O W J M Scott, F/O Bill Legard, W/C G Carter (Stn Cdr Catterick), S/L H R L Hood, F/L E N Ryder, F/O Stevens (Adj), F/O D R Gamblen. Middle: P/O R J Boret, F/Sgt Durrant, P/O J N MacKenzie, P/O O B Morrogh-Ryan, P/O G W Cory, F/O A D J Lovell, F/O W Stapleton, P/O R W Wallens; Rear: Sgt E V Darling, Sgt R C Ford, F/Sgt J W Sayers, Sgt I E Howitt, Sgt R A Carr-Lewty.

Right: Flying Officer Richard Selley, a South African pilot who flew ops in a Hudson of 220 Squadron and won the DFC over Dunkirk.

Top: A Hudson of 220 Squadron off burning Dunkirk.

Above: Lockheed Hudson of 206 Squadron.

Far left: Flying Officer H A Haarhoff also won the DFC at Dunkirk, as air gunner in Selley's crew.

Left: Squadron Leader J 'Baron' Worrall, OC 32 Squadron (as a later AVM).

Top left: Squadron Leader J McComb, OC 611 Squadron in 1940.

Top right: Three pilots of 65 Squadron, from the left, Stan Grant, Tommy Smart and Gerry Saunders. Smart had to land on the beach at Dunkirk on 28 May.

Bottom: 611 Squadron just prior to Dunkirk. Kneeling: Ralph Crompton, Ken Stoddart, Jack Leader, F/L A J Banham. Standing: Barrie Heath, F/L Hamilton, F/O Mitchell (at rear), Sidney Bazley, Colin MacFie, James McComb, –?-, Sgt Mather, F/Sgt Sadler, (rear) Sneezy Brown and Dirty Watkins.

Top: The remains of a Ju88 shot down at Dunkirk.

Middle left: Pilot Officer J N MacKenzie, New Zealander, with 41 Squadron.

Middle right: Pilot Officer H A C 'Birdy' Bird-Wilson, 17 Squadron, flew over Dunkirk and then went back into France in June, then fought in the Battle of Britain.

Left: Some of 17 Squadron: F/O W J Harper, P/O R C Whittaker, Hunter, F/O R V Meredith, F/O J Jefferies and P/O K Manger. Richard Meredith was killed on 3 June and Richard Whittaker was lost over France four days later. Ken Manger died in the Battle of Britain.

Top: Pilot Officer Howard Hill, 92 Squadron, pointing to some of the battle damage to Allan Wright's Spitfire after combat on 2 June. Hill died in the Battle of Britain.

Above: Allan Wright with his Spitfire N3250 on 2 June. Already the ground crew are patching the bullet holes put there by a Messerschmitt 109 that morning, after he had shot down another.

Right: The burning port of Dunkirk. There was little need to navigate to the harbour town – the smoke led the way.

The 'men in black' re-arm a Me110 fighter.

Top: Armourers help turn round a Hurricane in quick time during the Dunkirk period.

Above: On German airfields groundcrews bomb-up the deadly Ju87 Stuka dive-bombers.

Left: The aftermath. The debris of war at La Plage, Dunkirk, the evacuation over.

In Dunkirk, orders had now been received from the Admiralty that HM Government's policy was that not only British, but French troops too would be afforded equal opportunities to be evacuated in British ships and boats. This would increase the total number of soldiers expected by the Navy and elongate the period required to pick up all the troops now crowded into the narrow Dunkirk pocket. Ramsay had himself been campaigning for such a decision although he knew it would increase the dangers for the rescuers, and take several more days to complete the task.

The rate of the evacuation of troops was increasing steadily however. Over 194,600 would be taken off on the 31st including nearly 15,000 Frenchmen. More ships were called for in order to implement the final evacuation plan during the night of 31st May/1st June. In the event this 'final' plan was postponed for two more days.

On the night of 30/31st May, heavy artillery shelling was directed at Dunkirk, and Luftwaffe bombers laid mines during the dark hours. At dawn the shelling increased. The wind increased shortly after sun-rise resulting in several whalers being capsized. Yet the miracle of the Dunkirk evacuation, the comparatively calm state of the normally blustery Channel sea, continued to aid the Navy's task. The first part of the morning of the 31st was one of the very few occasions the sea did not remain calm.

The weather above, however, though cloudy, was fair. The usual dawn fighter patrols were sent out around 4.30 a.m. but few, if any, enemy aircraft were seen. Number 41 Squadron's diary indicates a combat on their early patrol but another record indicates this encounter to be later in the morning. Squadron Leader H.W. 'Tubby' Mermagen led his 222 Squadron out at 4.34 a.m., one of the pilots being Pilot Officer G.G.A. Davies.

> We took off in the early morning, myself flying No 3 to Tubby Mermagen and had done a few sweeps up and down just off Dunkirk. It was overcast with the cloud base at around 10,000 feet. We were on our way westwards again and just as we approached Dunkirk we flew through some anti-aircraft fire – black things appeared here and there. I was on Mermagen's left-hand side and he pulled up into cloud to get out of the AA fire and as we were going up through the cloud, my engine just coughed and spluttered, then faded and I went down. We had been told the previous day by a Hurricane pilot that if you had to land on the beach at Dunkirk with wheels down one could do so as it was very hard sand. So I decided to do that and I landed just opposite Fort West, Mardyke, on the beach. No problem at all except I was shot at on the way down by Fort West. The French had a 75 mm

gun and because, they said later, they didn't know what I was and believed I was a Stuka because I had my wheels down, and the only aeroplane with wheels down were Stukas. The reason I also decided to land wheels-down was that I thought that I might be able to fix it.

Upon inspection, however, there were some shrapnel holes on the under side of the engine and a fuel leak of some sort. I taxied up to the dunes as the engine was still going sufficiently for me to taxi though very little power. Some French Army soldiers appeared from nowhere and I asked if I could see their officer. As I could speak French this was no problem. They seemed very suspicious of me and in fact led me away at the point of the bayonet to Fort West. When I got there I found it was inhabited by a crew of a French destroyer which had been sunk. They were the survivors and had taken over the Fort. Fort West was being shelled periodically and it was very noisy – most disconcerting. I went to see the Captain and asked if he could do something about getting me to Dunkirk. They had a car and I also wanted to know what to do with the aircraft as I didn't know what the position was as many of us didn't realise the BEF were completely surrounded. At squadron level, certainly at pilot officer level, we had no real idea of the situation in or around Dunkirk. I went into Dunkirk in this car, which was a hazardous trip to say the least of it. We went past a big oil refinery and it had obviously suffered as the oil from the tanks was running across the road which was very dangerous to get across in the car although the French sailor didn't seem to mind.

We went into Dunkirk which was in a horrible mess. The thing that struck me was the smell, it smelled of death, of dead horses; rubbish all over the place. He took me to a place called the Bastione Trente Deux which was in the old part of Dunkirk, quite close to the docks where there was a naval captain in charge of the evacuation, poor chap! I went to see him and told him what had happened and what should I do with the aeroplane and he said burn it and get back the best way you can. So I went outside only to find the car gone. This didn't surprise me as we were being shelled every now and again and one had to lay down. Then I found the driver and he said he'd found another car – a better one! We got back to the Fort and I asked the Frenchman if they could not fire a shell from their '75' into the Spitfire which they could see from the Fort but they declined.

So I went down to the beach and rescued my parachute and helmet but forgot about the Mae West. In retrospect I should have taken the Mae West and left the other stuff. I tried to put a hole in the petrol tank with my revolver but no-way would that work. It was an old Colt .45 with lead slugs and there was a reinforced piece around the tank, fairly thick, and all it was doing was putting dents in it. The French soldiers standing around had rifles so I asked one if I could borrow his rifle which he did and with the first shot the Spitfire went bang and that was that – burnt up. I went back to the Fort where they gave me something to eat and a cup of the most appalling coffee, and then back into Dunkirk with the same driver.

At the harbour I saw at the end of the mole what looked like a minesweeper and a paddle-steamer, so I went out along the mole, and halfway along I wished I hadn't. There were some dead bodies lying about and I discovered the Germans were strafing from time to time. Fortunately they only came down once when I was there. I think it was a Ju88 which dropped some bombs in the middle of the harbour and the gunner was having a good old go. As I was going along the mole a soldier was coming back with a young German chap and was most annoyed because they would not allow him to take him back to England. I asked him what he was going to do with him and he said, take him back and let him go! As I got to the end of the mole, the minesweeper had disappeared but the paddle-steamer was still taking on people. I was among about only six who were actually on the mole and although a sailor said they were full he finally waved us all on. We left about six o'clock and got into either Margate or Ramsgate in the early hours of the morning in a sort of convoy. We were bombed a couple of times and we picked up quite a few people out of the water, all covered in oil but they were all right. At Margate we were all put on a train and not told where we were going. I tried to explain, when we got to London, to one of the Army RTO, that I wanted to get back to my unit at Hornchurch, but he wasn't having any and herded me back on the train. At Birmingham I managed to slip out of the gate of the station and I saw an RAF flag – it was a recruiting office. I went in and the recruiting officer seemed very suspicious of me; I was unshaven, a bit ragged and was carrying my parachute. I explained who I was and eventually convinced him to get through to my unit, then he gave me a train ticket and back I went. I eventually got back to Hornchurch about tea-time.

Pilot Officer G.G.A. Davies, 222 Squadron

From the distinct lack of Luftwaffe activity in the morning, it would suggest that the Germans were leaving the field free for their artillery. Not only were Dunkirk and La Panne under direct assault but so too were the rescue ships out to sea.

The first part of the day was clear of air combat and it was not until shortly before 11 a.m. that the action started. Ten Spitfires of 222 Squadron (their second patrol of the day) broke formation over Dunkirk due to layers of cloud. Pilot Officer Tim Vigors spotted a He111 between two cloud layers. Attacking it he saw a large flash from the port engine as it rolled onto its back before it disappeared in cloud. It was during this same patrol time that 41 Squadron was credited with one Me109 destroyed (Flight Lieutenant J.T. Webster R6635) and one He111 destroyed (Webster and Pilot Officer A.D.J. Lovell, P9429).

The mid-day patrols were flown by 17, 145 and 245 Squadrons; a total of twenty-nine Hurricanes. Bristol Blenheims of 107 Squadron had flown out to bomb German artillery positions and were engaged by Me109's. 17 and 145 Squadrons saw the encounter and sections dived to the rescue. Pilot Officer Ken Manger saw six 109's off Nieuport and closed in. As he did so, three 109's broke away and flew south, and one was seen to fall under the return fire from the Blenheim gunners. The other two turned to face 17 Squadron. Manger got in a deflection shot at one, set its engine on fire and saw it go down to hit the ground a few miles to the west of Nieuport. The other 109 attacked Manger but the British pilot turned to face it and it dived into some cloud.

The pilots of 145 Squadron dived down after the three fleeing 109's and shot down two. Flight Lieutenant Roy Dutton got one into the sea and shared the other with Flying Officer Mike Newling. Flying high overhead was 245 Squadron. They lost Pilot Officer K.B. McGlashan (N2702) who failed to return, thought to have gone down over the French coast. He got back the following day.

> One thing that got in my craw was that we got up before light and as soon as it was light, took off and flew up to Hawkinge, then flew over to Dunkirk. We came back and in the Mess was an admin officer having his two boiled eggs and reading the *Daily Mirror*, passing the comment -'And how's the war today, old boy?' I didn't feel it was a very apt remark at that time.
>
> I knew that it was a catastrophe for the Army, and towards the end when they were using the small boats etc., and the thing that struck us was the pall of smoke from the oil tanks at Dunkirk. When the wind blew towards the English coast it was apparent what was there. When the Dunkirk show was all over we went one day into Bognor and even then were aware of smoke blowing in from Dunkirk. We never went down very low because it didn't

matter who we were we got shot at. The people on the ground whenever they saw an aeroplane, thought it was a Jerry and let fly. Understandably, for there were not very many of us. Therefore, we usually stayed between 8 and 10,000 feet to stay out of range of light flak.

At that stage we were in Vics, and if anyone yelled, '109's!' there were twelve Hurricanes travelling in opposite directions as fast as possible, or looking round rapidly. We kept by the book, in Vics, right through Dunkirk and the Battle of Britain and in August, 145 Squadron was virtually destroyed and had to be reformed at Drem.

Pilot Officer J.E. Storrar, 145 Squadron

As these units disengaged a new squadron joined in the fighting. 111 Squadron from North Weald. They had seen considerable action over France during the retreat and had then been rested. They flew south from Digby to fly operations from North Weald on the 31st. The commanding officer was Squadron Leader John Thompson who recalls:

We had already seen quite a bit of action in France from 12th May when we went over daily from Northolt to various airfields in Northern France until that became impossible. We then, in conjunction with other fighter squadrons, flew sweeps over France and escorted bombers attacking targets in Northern France.

So, I had already had some experience of leading my chaps on operations before the Dunkirk show took place.

We had not at that stage of the war, in my opinion, developed an effective method of flying our aircraft in a suitable battle formation which would allow us to attack quickly and together and which would also provide us with the all-round cover needed, particularly behind. We were still flying our aircraft in Vics of three, not too close, but, on reflection, not open enough. This meant that we were not manoeuvrable enough and, in the face of German fighters this was a serious handicap. In view of the intensity of the operations, it was not possible to develop and work up a suitable formation until the battle was over. We had to make do with what we had. I always felt, even to some extent in the Battle of Britain, that our formations were not entirely suitable for the task in hand. It was a part of our pre-war training which was neglected, or shall I say, was perhaps not given enough thought. It was not until I got to Malta in 1942 as wing leader of a Spitfire wing that I flew what we called finger 4 formations. This was the best to be developed and which was to be the basic battle formation of the day fighter throughout the rest of the war.

Squadron Leader J.M. Thompson, 111 Squadron

On this their first Dunkirk patrol, they saw no sign of German aircraft, and landed at Hawkinge at 3.25 p.m. Nevertheless, other squadrons in the air at this time did see the Germans. Twelve Defiants flew out, protected by ten Hurricanes of 213 Squadron with top cover of eleven Spitfires of 609 Squadron.

A new commanding officer had arrived to take over 213, Squadron Leader H.D. McGregor, DSO, from New Zealand. McGregor had been in the RAF since 1928 and had commanded No 33 Squadron in the Middle East, being awarded his DSO while leading his unit in Palestine before the war. He was thirty years old. Humphrey Edwardes Jones remained in full command of 213 Squadron, being reluctant to hand over his unit until the Dunkirk show was over. In any event, he knew the form, whereas McGregor was new to operations and had only flown Spitfires, not Hurricanes. Yet he was understandably keen to fly sorties over Dunkirk, though Edwardes Jones was apprehensive. Finally, however, Edwardes Jones relented, got McGregor to fly some circuits in a Hurricane, and then allowed him to fly, though only as a wingman to the senior flight commander, Widge Wight.

On this afternoon patrol, Wight led 213, Edwardes Jones needing to catch up on some paperwork. McGregor did not have his own flying helmet or parachute so borrowed Edwardes Jones' but on the strict understanding that he return them!

The Spitfires of 609 flew as top cover at 20,000 feet, 213 Squadron at 15,000 feet while the Defiants of 264 flew below at 10,000 feet.

Almost as soon as the formations crossed the French coast at 2.20 p.m., the Defiant crews picked up a large formation of Me109's, estimated about seventy in number. There were also about a score of Heinkel bombers approaching from the south-east. Squadron Leader Hunter led his Defiants towards them but the bomber pilots hurriedly turned tail, some jettisoning their bombs into the sea. Then the 109's were coming down diving from the sun. Hunter ordered his squadron into a defensive circle. One Messerschmitt came in close and Hunter's gunner, LAC F.H. King, caught it with a burst and it spun down into the sea.

Other 109's came in, firing into the Defiants' circle. Pilot Officer Young positioned himself so his gunner could get a shot at a 109 that came into range and it fell away. As it dived Young saw the pilot take to his parachute. Immediately afterwards, his gunner, LAC Johnson, yelled out that another Defiant was coming up rather close. A second later there was a loud crash and Young went through the shattering experience of having his machine fall to pieces about him. He shouted to Johnson to get out but found that the radio had failed. Moments later he jumped and was falling in space.

The other Defiant (L6961) was flown by Pilot Officer Whitley with LAC Turner in the rear turret. Their Defiant was badly damaged in the collision, Whitley being forced to crash land near Dunkirk. The Messerschmitts also knocked out the Defiant crewed by Pilot Officer Hickman and LAC Fidler (L6968), both men baling out. As Squadron Leader Hunter turned in the circle – or what was left of it, he counted some eight parachutes in the air, also seeing one Defiant – possibly Young's – completely break up, its wing floating down on its own.

In addition to the Defiant men, and at least one German pilot, the other parachutes were probably some of 213 Squadron's pilots. 213 were heavily engaged and Flying Officer Robinson (AK-G) baled out. Flying Officer W.N. Gray (AK-D) and Sergeant Boyd (in A) were also shot down and may have parachuted inland from Dunkirk into German-held territory. Pilot Officer W.M. Sizer's Hurricane (P) was set on fire after he shot down a 109, but he managed to crash land south of Dunkirk, to return later by sea. Flight Lieutenant Wight bagged two 109's, Sergeant P.P. Norris got another while Sergeant Butterfield destroyed one and possibly a second. The other casualty was Squadron Leader McGregor, the new commanding officer designate, who also had to float down into the sea under a parachute, or more accurately, Edwardes Jones' parachute. To add to his discomfort, he landed in the middle of a minefield!

Pilot Officer E.G. Barwell, and his gunner, leading Green Section of 264, saw Hickman's rear man shoot down a 109, then watched as their Defiant fell away with smoke and petrol streaming from it. A moment later Barwell's gunner yelled a warning that German fighters were astern of them. Tracer shells flashed past their cockpit, Barwell pulling into a steep turn to the right. As the 109 curved after them, the gunner nailed it with a burst from his four guns. It caught fire and fell into the sea.

The battle ended with eight victories to the Defiants and Hurricanes, but with three Defiants and five Hurricanes down the scores were even.

Meanwhile, 609's Spitfires above were down to ten aircraft when one of the flight commander's machines failed to start while another Spitfire had to return with engine trouble. The squadron was suffering somewhat by not having effective leadership, sections more often operating separately in consequence. They failed to get into the main fight. One section saw a Heinkel way below them and dived at it, Flying Officer I.B.N. Russell disabling one of its engines. His section leader, however, was not seen again, Flight Lieutenant Dudley 'Presser' Persse-Joynt failing to return. Flying Officer Dawson of Yellow Section also found a Heinkel and probably destroyed it after a full-throttle dive.

When the surviving pilots of 213 landed, Edwardes Jones was in his office, writing letters to the next-of-kin of recent casualties. Widge Wight came into the office looking ashen, tired and totally crashed out. He explained to his commanding officer that the squadron had been in one hell of a fight, that four or five pilots were missing, including the new commanding officer!

In the sea, Squadron Leader McGregor of 213 Squadron was finally rescued from the minefield and the water. So intent was he on returning the borrowed helmet and parachute, that he held firmly onto the former and tied the latter to his wrist.

When a destroyer sailed up and members of the crew tried to pull him on board he was unable to let it go and he nearly had his arm wrenched off when he was hauled out. Only then did he untie it.

He did, however, bring back the flying helmet which Edwardes Jones continued to use despite it being damaged by sea water.

At first the rescued McGregor was taken to Dunkirk and put ashore for a while. For the first time, he, like other flyers placed in unfamiliar surroundings, was to experience the appalling noise of battle and hear the roar of aero engines and stuttering machine guns and the heavier thump of cannons from an air battle high above. These sounds were ordinarily screened from aircrew, drowned by the noise of their own engines. He eventually got back by ship to command 213 Squadron in the Battle of Britain.[1]

As the afternoon progressed it became clear that the Luftwaffe were sending their bombers into the battle area every half-hour. From intercepted signals it was discovered that it was the ships that were the priority targets, not Dunkirk itself. But so effective was the RAF's umbrella that only one ship was sunk by direct air attack.

The subsequent relieving squadrons also found the Luftwaffe. Eighteen Spitfires and eighteen Hurricanes of 64, 610, 229 and 242 Squadrons were on station by shortly after 4.30 p.m. They arrived off Dunkirk with 229 at 8,000 feet, 242 at 12,000 feet, 610 at 20,000 feet and 64 at 22,000 feet. In 242 Squadron's orders, they were also to try to locate a reported observation balloon south of Nieuport whose crew were directing artillery fire onto British positions.

Squadron Leader Harold Maguire was leading the composite squadrons of his own 229 and 242 on this 'medium altitude anti-bomber

---

[1] Later Air Marshal Sir Hector McGregor, KCB, CBE, DSO, Commander-in-Chief, Fighter Command, 1959-1962. He died on 11th April 1973.

sweep'. At ten minutes past 5 o'clock, puffs of AA fire indicated the presence of German aeroplanes and then he could see numerous twin-engined bombers heading for the shipping. Maguire led the formation into the attack, and engaged a Ju88, forcing it to jettison its bombs. It finally fled eastwards after Maguire put several good bursts into it. Pilot Officer Geoff Simpson damaged a Do17, one of two he found just above the water. Pilot Officer Vernon Bright saw a Ju87 doing a low diving attack on a cargo ship but as he chased it, either Navy guns or another aeroplane's fire sent it down in flames into the sea. He was then engaged by two Me110's but one was shot down by another aircraft, and after a dogfight he sent the other 110 down out of control but did not see it crash.

Pilot Officer V.B.S. Verity was probably the one to shoot the 110 off Bright's tail. He saw his burst of .303 smash into a 110's perspex hood, whereupon it dived into the sea. He fought another one and had his starboard aileron shot off which put his Hurricane into an inverted spin. After trying in vain to right the aircraft, he baled out. Sergeant D.F. Edgehill had four Me110's attack him and in the tussle he claimed two shot down in flames, the second one after his own machine had been hit and himself wounded. Diving to sea level, he headed home chased by 110's but got away. He felt himself becoming weaker and weaker and only just made base but crashed on his approach. The next thing he remembered was waking up in hospital. He did not return to the squadron until 1941.

Flight Lieutenant George Plinston was leading 242 and also saw the bombers as they approached from the south. Singling out a Ju88 which was starting a dive, he followed it down. Being unable to catch it he pursued it as it levelled out, then closing the gap, opened fire. It began smoking and headed for the French coast, its rear gun silent. Pilot Officer D.G. McQueen (P2767) shot up one Dornier and then saw a Ju88, possibly that attacked by Plinston, going down apparently out of control. Pilot Officer M.K. Stansfeld (P3268) went for an escorting Me110, its starboard engine disintegrating under his fire. As he banked round he saw the Messerschmitt crash onto the beach.

Willie McKnight as always was in the thick of the action. Having lagged behind somewhat, he began to climb to gain a better position before diving into the fight. He attacked the leading 110, and his fire caused it to swerve into a second 110, both falling in flames.

The two Spitfire squadrons above were also engaged with 110's, Pilot Officer H.P.F. Patten (N3230) claiming one, Flying Officer D.M. Taylor (N3273) another. Flight Lieutenant Henstock damaged another while Pilot Officer J.J. O'Meara shot down a 109. Flying Officer H.J. Woodward and his section leader attacked a Do17, but then his leader left him to it. Woodward chased it for some distance, being thrown about in the bomber's slipstream, but set both its engines on fire. Another Spitfire made a pass on it, but then Woodward followed it down to sea level, still on fire. He was then forced away by the unwelcome attention of three Me109's, shaking them off by flying steep turns at very low level, then scooting for home on the deck. The squadron lost Sergeant Hatch (K9813) and had two Spitfires damaged.

Blue Section of 610 Squadron attacked seven Me 110's they found flying in line astern. John Ellis, leading the squadron, had already seen the huge dog-fight going on well below between 229, 242 and the German aircraft and was planning his approach when he found the higher 110's. Ellis caught them up, collecting return fire from the last 110 as he closed in. This ceased abruptly when he opened fire from 300 yards. He then fired long bursts at each engine, then emptied his guns into the front cockpit. White smoke belched from each motor, as the 110 went into a bunt and headed down.

Pilot Officer P. Litchfield followed Ellis into the attack but his engine faltered and he had to push his nose down. As he did so he saw some 110's ahead, and fired at one at the end of the formation without visible results, although he was later credited with its possible destruction. The other two sections of the squadron were then attacked by six Me109's which shot down Flying Officer G.L. Chambers (N3274) and Flying Officer 'Peter' Keighley (L1013 DW-E).

> On this sortie Flying Officer Lambert Chambers was killed, and Pilot Officer Keighley baled out over the Channel but was rescued by a lifeboat on its way to Dunkirk so it was 24 hours before we knew he was safe.
>
> *Flight Lieutenant J. Ellis, 610 Squadron*

Keighley did in fact manage to get his crippled Spitfire two-thirds the way back across the Channel before its engine packed up, forcing him to bale out from 3,000 feet. He was eventually rescued and put ashore at Ramsgate.

It was proving a busy evening. Squadron Leader John Thompson led 111 Squadron over the Channel for the second time that day at 6.40 p.m. They met considerable numbers of Luftwaffe aircraft, although strangely their claims did not find their way into 11 Group's combat record. The squadron acted as top cover to the Defiants of 264 and the Spitfires of 609 Squadron. Also out on patrol were 229 and 242 Squadrons, two further sections of this latter unit later flying out to once again try to locate the German observation balloon south of Nieuport.

Squadron Leader Philip Hunter of 264 Squadron had previously arranged with the two covering squadrons that 111 Squadron should follow the formation in line astern, while 609 should shadow 264 some 3,000 feet above.

At around 7.30 p.m. Thompson, at 27,000 feet three miles to the north of Dunkirk, saw a large number of He111's two thousand feet below, escorted by a number of Me109's above. Keeping his position, he saw 264 and 609 engage the bombers. 609 was now led by Flying Officer I.B.N. Russell who had already seen considerable action in France with 607 Squadron. Known as 'Hack', Russell was an American who had flown with the RAF in the 1930's on a short service commission. Later he flew as an airline pilot in the USA, returning to Britain when the war began. 609 waded straight in, attacking the bombers and Hunter and his two-seaters also engaged.

Hack Russell and his No 2, Pilot Officer C.N. 'Teeny' Overton, simultaneously made beam attacks from opposite sides on one Heinkel, which had broken formation, and sent it into the sea in flames. Number Three in the section, Sergeant G.C. Bennett, followed the burning bomber down but was pounced on by one of several Me109 fighters that were now coming down from above. Russell saw the danger, swerved towards the Messerschmitt and fired. Half of the 109's port wing was sliced off and the fighter went into the sea.

Another 109 came down on Overton and after a terrific dog-fight Overton managed to get the German in his sights long enough to get in a burst. The 109 went into the water pouring out smoke.

The other two squadron sections were going for the Heinkels when a Ju88 and a Do17, both on a bombing run over the ships, were seen under them. Flying Officer Frankie Howell and his wingman went after the Junkers, Flying Officer Peter Drummond-Hay the Dornier. The Dornier was hit by all three Spitfires, its rear gunner was silenced and both engines were hit. Pilot Officer J.R. Buchanan, the section's Number Three, then got a 109, one of three which came down head-on. He then dived on a Heinkel sending it home on one engine, wheels down and bombs jettisoned.

Yet the 109's did have some success. Flying Officer J.C. 'Pinky' Gilbert disappeared and was not seen again, while Sergeant Bennett's Spitfire was forced down onto the sea. Russell, who had saved the Sergeant's life by knocking down Bennett's assailant, escorted him back towards England but his machine failed to make the coast. Bennett flopped down three miles out, Russell flying to Dover from where he guided the minesweeper *Playboy* to his rescue.

Squadron Leader Phil Hunter put his Defiants into an attacking position against the Heinkels. Four Defiant gunners opened fire and a

Heinkel fell into the sea on fire. Hunter's gunner, LAC King, then fired at the leader of three Heinkels which dived right into the sea. Pilot Officers Barwell and Williams, who had been in action during the day's earlier scrap, were also heavily involved on this patrol. They too had dived towards the main engagement when suddenly a Heinkel came over the top of them. Barwell ordered Williams to open fire which the gunner did. Bullets could be seen entering the Heinkel, mostly around the underside of the pilot's cabin. A moment later the bomber nosed forward and dived slowly towards the sea. At about 1,000 feet above the water two parachutes appeared but that was all before the Heinkel crashed leaving only a plume of spray.

The two men then chased after the main Heinkel formation, swooping under one which Williams hit with a burst. Then their own aeroplane began to fill with steam, the radiator having been hit by return fire. Barwell throttled back but then he saw another Vic formation of Heinkels. He flew into the attack, Williams hammering a 30-round burst into one before Barwell felt obliged to break away and head for the Kent coast, keeping engine revs down in order to maintain his height of 7,500 feet.

However, they found themselves gradually losing height and it was soon clear that they would have to go into the sea. Barwell saw two Navy destroyers, guided his Defiant between them and pancaked onto the sea about five miles from Dover. As it hit, the Defiant broke up, Williams being knocked unconscious in the crash. Barwell, coming to the surface, saw Williams upside down, pulled him right way up and supported him until one of the destroyers scooped them out of the water; Williams regained consciousness as it did so.

Pilot Officer G. Hackwood and LAC Lillie, also engaged in the shooting down of the first Heinkel, likewise found another above them at only fifty yards range. Little's fire exploded the port engine which caught fire, then the bomber was circling down towards the sea.

Barwell and Williams, though safe, were not the only casualties. Flight Lieutenant Nick Cooke and Corporal Albert Lippett, both recently decorated, failed to return and Pilot Officer R.M. Stokes with LAC Fairbrother were hit. Fairbrother was wounded and ordered to bale out, Stokes managing to struggle back to Manston where he crash-landed. Cooke and Lippett's loss was a grave blow to the squadron. A valuable flight commander and determined pilot, he and Lippett had been credited with at least ten victories in twenty days, including five and two shared just two days before their own loss.

High above these general actions, Thompson and 111 Squadron kept their height, watching the equally high flying Me109 escort. These made no move to help their bombers below while 111 Squadron stayed high. While both formations circled, Thompson gradually climbed towards them but when just 1,000 feet below, three 109's broke away and dived on the Hurricanes, the leader opening fire with cannon and machine-gun fire.

> I remember on one occasion we were attacked from close range head-on by 109's, and, although we were not hit, our ability to react was impaired. It was the first time I had seen a 109 at close range. They flashed past just above our heads. They seemed to come from nowhere and were gone in an instant.
>
> *Squadron Leader J.M. Thompson, 111 Squadron*

After this pass, the Hurricanes then engaged the main 109 formation, Thompson being engaged by two of them. They came from behind and above and he watched their bursts as they approached from 1,000 yards. When they had closed in to 500 yards, Thompson pulled up and did a sharp turn to the left. One Messerschmitt fired at him with full deflection but its shells fell astern. Thompson chased it round, succeeded in diving on it vertically, putting a five-second burst into the German from 100 yards.

In the general engagement that followed six or seven 109's were claimed as shot down while Sergeant W.L. Dymond (P2884) shot up two Heinkel 111's. The rear gunner of the second bomber put some holes in his Hurricane, damaging its oil pipe, port wing and tail. Flight Lieutenant R.P.R. Powell's oxygen failed at 19,000 feet and he fell to 5,000 feet before he regained consciousness, but the only permanent casualty was to Sergeant J. Robinson, who was wounded in the ankle, and force landed at Manston.

The Canadians of 242 Squadron, meanwhile, were in action in company with 229 Squadron, against more Heinkels and 109's. No less than thirty Messerschmitts came down on the squadron and a dog-fight began. Willie McKnight caught one 109 with a burst as it seemed to sail right in front of him. Flight Lieutenant Plinston put another into the sea as did Stan Turner, who first totally outmanoeuvred his opponent. Pilot Officer R.D. Grassick blasted another with two bursts, and saw smoke stream from it before he had to break away when attacked himself. Flying below, 229 Squadron confirmed seeing four Me109's fall into the sea. Pilot Officer Gordon Stewart who had only joined 242 on the 28th, coming from 607 Squadron with George Plinston, failed to return from this action and was later reported killed in action. The only other casualty was Plinston's Hurricane which caught an explosive bullet in the cowling, but he got home safely.

As all the engaged squadrons drifted back to their bases in southern

England, all knew they had been in a fight. In the final five flying hours of the day, the RAF had had ten of its aircraft shot down and had another written off in a crash landing. Only five pilots and one gunner being reported missing, however. In addition, several RAF aircraft had received damage.

It brought the day's losses to twenty-one aircraft but only eight pilots and one air gunner. This was far better mathematics than the 29th especially as claims against the Luftwaffe were between forty and fifty destroyed plus a number of probables.

The Fleet Air Arm had been represented by nine Albacores of 826 Squadron detached at Detling. They flew their unit's first operational sorties when they bombed Nieuport Harbour. Each machine carried six 250 pound bombs. On the return flight one Albacore with a hang-up, lost the bomb near Canterbury and demolished a Methodist Church and two houses.

Later in the day the squadron bombed a road junction at Westende, ending their day with an attempt to find E-boats off Zeebrugge that evening. One pilot came across a Heinkel but was unable to fire his gun as the air bottle wasn't connected!

*

At Dunkirk itself the evacuation had progressed well in the afternoon when the choppy seas had subsided, from the La Panne beaches especially after 4 p.m. while the RAF had been busy high above. Then at 7.20 p.m. that evening, all ships of the fleets were informed by the Vice Admiral, that the final evacuation of the BEF was expected on the night of 1/2nd June. Meanwhile, the evacuation of French troops from Dunkirk and St Malo beaches would continue from 1st June by both British and French ships. There was to be little respite for the gallant men of the Royal Navy and the volunteer sailors of the little ships. Equally, the next day would be full of incident and action for a very weary 11 Group.

CHAPTER NINE

Saturday, 1st June 1940

During the previous few days some squadrons had been pulled out of 11 Group's strength. Some had been mauled sufficiently to warrant their withdrawal, others had been relieved following a longer period of operational duty that had begun prior to Dunkirk.

Four new squadrons were made available to Park, 43 Squadron which had been ordered to fly down from Wick to Tangmere on the 31st and 66 Squadron whose pilots had flown from Coltishall to Kenley. On the morning of 1st June, 72 Squadron at Acklington received the call to move south, going to Gravesend, while 266 Squadron at Wittering were ordered to readiness, having recently moved down from Martlesham Heath.

There seems little rhyme or reason why some units were pulled out of the 'front line' and others were not. For instance, 54 and 74 Squadrons had both acquitted themselves well and although tired, had not suffered too badly. Indeed both units were just getting into their strides when rested. Both 17 and 19 Squadrons had been and would continue to be in action, since before the Dunkirk operation began. 17 Squadron had seen quite a bit of action before it began. 229 Squadron had lost eight pilots in four days but stayed at Biggin Hill. On 1st June 264 Squadron was rested but not pulled out of the group. However, they had flown their last patrol over Dunkirk.

June 1st started as all the other days had started with squadrons being called to readiness before dawn. Again it was the Hornchurch wing that took the first patrol slot, leaving the ground at around 4.20 a.m. The day was looking good weather-wise, fair with some cloud and good visibility. It would prove to be the heaviest day for the RAF during Dynamo.

The four Spitfire squadrons, 19, 41, 222 and 616, were above the French coast by 5 a.m. (616 having made rendezvous from the satellite airfield at Rochford) where they found some thicker clouds just inland. Of these units, only 41 would not be engaged.

Sandy Lane, leading 19 Squadron, spotted enemy aircraft at 5.40 – twelve twin-engined Me110's two miles to the north-east of Dunkirk at around 4,500 feet. 222, astern of 19, also saw 109's and the 110's in the layers of cloud.

Squadron Leader Marcus Robinson, leading 616 Squadron, became separated with his section but saw some Dorniers bombing shipping and above them a number of Me109's. As Robinson led his men down the Dorniers broke away and headed for the clouds while the 109's turned to engage.

Flight Lieutenant Lane led the attack, seeing the startled 110's begin to form their usual defensive circle. As they did so and before any of 19 Squadron had fired, one 110 staggered and then plummeted down with a strange pendulum motion as its tailplane broke off. He was later to learn that Tubby Mermagen had fired as he came into range and when his sights were on had 'stirred' his control column, thereby getting a hose-pipe effect from his guns. It worked and the 110 went down – not bad for a range estimated to be in the region of 1,200 yards!

As the Spitfires closed in, Lane picked out a 110, set its port motor on fire and saw it fall towards the ground. In his opinion these particular Messerschmitt pilots, compared to Spitfire pilots, were all novices and should never have been allowed out of their flying schools. It certainly seemed a valid comment for in the battle that followed, 19 Squadron claimed six 110's for sure, three probables, while 222 claimed three more and one probable. It became a different story when the Me109's came to their assistance, even if they were too late!

Douglas Bader (P9443) saw the 109's coming down through the clouds, going after 19 Squadron as they chased after the 110's. One Messerschmitt passed by his Spitfire, its twin guns atop of the engine cowling firing at a Spitfire ahead. Bader pulled in behind the 109 seeing his tracer hit it, then it burst in flames. Pilot Officer Hillary Eldridge (P9323) had a 109 overshoot him and he got in a long burst at it as it went by. The 109 slowed down, began smoking and burning from the engine cowling but Eldridge was then engaged by a 110 and he had to break away.

The 109's, however, picked off four of 222's pilots, Pilot Officer R.A.L. Morant, Sergeant L.J. White, Pilot Officer H.E.L. Falkust and Pilot Officer G. Massey-Sharpe. Meanwhile the other 222 Squadron pilots had also caught up with the 110's, three being shot down with another possible.

As the 109's had come out of the clouds behind 19 Squadron, Flight Lieutenant Wilf Clouston, coming up even further behind, found a 109 right in front of him. He and his Number 2, Flight Sergeant Harry Steere, shot it down, then Clouston pulled up after another which he sent down in a spin with its engine stopped. Pilot Officer L.A. Haines got 19's third 109 which left a glycol trail as it dived into the ground.

The 110's shot down by 19, went to Sergeant Jennings (two, one in flames with its pilot baling out), Flight Sergeant Unwin (one, which blew up right above him as he fired up into it). Another 110 was probably destroyed under his guns. Pilot Officer Gordon Sinclair got two, the first side slipping into the ground with one engine ablaze, the second being chased inland for about two miles before it ploughed into the ground. Pilot Officer H.C. Baker saw the 109's coming down, then saw four additional 110's just inland, then several others appeared. He knocked bits off one, then engaged another head-on. As it flashed over him, both engines began to trail glycol, then as he turned onto its tail firing again, it burst into flames and went down.

The squadron's only loss was Sergeant Jack Potter. He had followed the 110's round, firing all his ammunition into one but had to turn away when the rear-gunner of another 110 put a burst near his Spitfire. Without the means to continue the fight, he turned for home but as he reached the edge of the battle he heard a metallic bang and saw that a hole 8 inches by 2 inches had appeared in his port wing just above the oil cooler. He kept going but discovered oil and glycol smoke appearing as his engine began to sound rough. Finally the engine seized at 4,000 feet when about fifteen miles out from the English coast. Looking down he saw a small boat chugging along and staying with the Spitfire, glided down to a calm sea. He circled then went down to bellyland on the water.

The split-up 616 Squadron saw some of the action, Squadron Leader Robinson and his detached section chasing the Dorniers but this ended when 109's attacked. He damaged one while Pilot Officer Ken Holden attacked two 109's he saw circling a warship. Chasing one through cloud he set it on fire but lost it in the cloud. He later shot up another lone 109 which went down in a glide leaving flame and smoke behind it. Upon his return he ran out of fuel and had to crash-land at Rochester.

Flying Officer Johnny Bell engaged four 109's that were strafing a ship, claimed one but was then himself hit by a piece of shrapnel from AA fire. His engine lost power and he was about to bale out when it began to pick up again. Bell circled, looking for the rest of the squadron but failed to see them before two of the other Spitfire squadrons flew overhead. Joining up with these, he then spotted eight Me109's machine-gunning a ship. He tried to attract the other Spitfires (there was no inter-squadron radio at this period of the war), then dived.

One 109 was coming round for a second strafing run and clearly he had not seen Bell's approach, and above Bell saw the other Spitfires turning away, oblivious of the aircraft below. As he closed in on his chosen Messerschmitt, his first burst caused smoke to pour from it, the wings shuddered, then the machine went into the sea. He was then set upon by the other 109's, but found he could easily out-turn them but they caught him up whenever he tried to make a run for it. Finally there was a loud bang in the bottom of his engine which stopped. Yellow flames came from the exhaust and there was a distinct smell of burning. Being down to 500 feet a bale-out seemed undesirable so he glided towards a ship. Undoing his harness, oxygen lead and radio plug he pancaked onto the water, but the Spitfire's nose dug in and he was thrown forward. Struggling out under the water he bobbed to the surface and found the tail of the Spitfire still above the sea, so hid under it in case he was strafed. One 109 did make a quick pass but only fired a quick snap burst before going away. Bell then began to swim towards the ship which was about two miles away by the beach taking off men from the shore.

*

The battle and the patrol time ended, the remaining Spitfires returning to Hornchurch and Rochester. John Thompson's Treble-One Squadron had flown through the area for forty-five minutes and had not seen a single German aeroplane. The sky was vast and deep as aviators have found both in war and in peace. As Flight Lieutenant Lane of 19 Squadron climbed down to watch the others come in, the first pilot to taxi up was Sergeant Jennings, grinning from ear to ear.

'How many did you get, Sir?' he enquired.

'One,' replied Lane.

'Only one, Sir! I got two!'

'If people like you weren't so damned greedy,' said Lane, also grinning now, 'I might be able to get a few more.'

The squadron's only loss was Jack Potter. Like Bell, of 616 Squadron, Potter too experienced the nose of his Spitfire dig into the sea and had his forehead smash against the gun-sight as he was flung forward. It sank immediately but the dazed Potter struggled as his parachute pack caught on the sliding cockpit hood. When he finally kicked himself free he was several feet beneath the surface but as he swam upwards, saw the colour of the water gradually change from black to green, then he bobbed to the surface. For some seconds, he just floated on his back, the pack acting as a lifebuoy while his Mae West also supported the upper part of his body.

He had landed about fifty yards from the boat he had seen, which turned out to be a French fishing boat, the *Jolie Mascotte* with a crew of four, none of whom could speak English. They were on their way to Dunkirk but were lost, but Potter was able to tell them a course and showed them their position on their chart. He was given dry clothing, food and drink as the boat headed towards the French coast.

As they approached Dunkirk they saw a British destroyer (HMS

Basilisk). A motor boat came out from it and a RNVR lieutenant told Potter the engine was out of action due to bombing and so was the radio. The French crew agreed to try to tow the destroyer out to sea to escape further bomber attack. A line was rigged and a tow begun but then Potter saw about thirty Dorniers and Heinkels approaching with 109's above. He told the lieutenant his ship was about to be bombed and the destroyer cast off. Sitting about three quarters of a mile away, Potter and the Frenchmen watched the bombing. The British pilot watched with interest as the Germans attacked for there seemed little attempt at precision, rather they all let go their bombs at once hoping one would hit. They passed without scoring a hit and were harried by three Spitfires of his own squadron who had little idea that Potter was on the ship below them.

Taking up the tow again, the French boat pulled the destroyer only a short distance when about twenty Ju87's appeared. It was a sure sign that the RAF had left. Von Richthofen's dive-bombers were out. Again cast off, Sergeant Potter watched the Stukas dive down and release their bombs from about 400 feet. There were several hits and the *Basilisk* was mortally hit. The little French ship moved alongside and took off about 200 soldiers and crew, another destroyer (HMS *Whitehall*) arriving to rescue some others. The second destroyer then shelled the cripple until she sank.

It had been quite a morning for Jack Potter who eventually landed back at Dover having meanwhile been transferred to a coastal patrol boat.[1]

Roy Morant was also endeavouring to get back to England. One of the four pilots of 222 Squadron to be shot down, he wrote the following account in a letter to his parents shortly after the event.

> We left Hornchurch at 4.30 and joined up behind 19 Squadron. We were over Dunkirk at about 05.00. At 05.10 we sighted a large formation of aircraft NE of Dunkirk. The two squadrons turned and chased them. I was leading the end section at the bottom of the formation. The enemy aircraft turned out to be Me110 twin engine fighters. Being at the bottom of the formation I had to climb up to get at them. When they saw us they all made for the clouds. Formation was soon broken up and there were aircraft milling around all over the sky. I cannot remember exactly what happened but I did fire off at odd aircraft that passed across my sights.
>
> We then got on the tail of a Me110. He did a left-hand

---

[1] Sergeant J.A. Potter was shot down and taken prisoner on 15th September 1940.

climbing turn into the clouds. I followed him firing. I saw that I
was hitting him, but I did not see what result my fire had as just
then a number of Me109's dived from out of the clouds; one got
on to my tail and before I had time to break away a cannon shell
hit me with a bang in the engine. I went straight into a steep dive;
the cockpit was filled with glycol fumes. I tried to open the hood
but could not as I was going too fast. If I had got it opened I might
have jumped. Things happened so quickly that I really do not
know exactly what did happen. I remember looking at my
instruments to try and fly on those as I could not see out. My
gyro-horizon was upset as I had been dog-fighting. I eventually
managed to get my hood open but could still see very little owing
to the glycol fumes. I found that my engine was still running so I
decided not to jump as I knew that I was well over enemy
territory, and even if I was then high enough I would only be shot
on the way down or when I landed, as we knew they were not
taking prisoners. I got down to just above the ground which I
could just make out below me. I had luckily kept a rough idea of
where we were, as I steered a rough course to get me back to the
sands where I knew our troops were. I think that for part of the
way I was being chased. It was a fight against time before my
engine seized up owing to lack of cooling. I could make out
troops on the beach. I thought that they were firing at me, but I
was certain that they must be ours. It turned out later that they
were firing at me as they thought that seeing the glycol fumes
streaming from the aircraft, I was spraying them with gas.

I therefore landed just in the water hoping that the troops
would scatter when they saw me as I could not avoid them. Once
I had landed I jumped out very quickly and was confronted with
a crowd of troops levelling rifles and Bren guns at me. (I was told
later that one Bren gunner had fired at me but his friends
deflected his aim – luckily for me!) I can tell you I wasted no
time in reaching for the sky. I had a Bren gun held in my belly
until I had established my identity. Very luckily, I had an identity
card I was given at Digby.

Just after I had established my identity, two Me109's came
diving down on us. We were all glad of the protection of my
Spitfire which the troops round about sheltered behind and drove
the 109's off by rifle and machine gun fire. This finally
established my identity! (The RAF roundels on all our aircraft
had been modified just before Dunkirk by replacing the outer
white circle with yellow – this showed up less clearly from a
distance and was the standard marking for a period but eventually

the yellow circle was removed as that also broke camouflage. The Dunkirk troops had never seen the yellow markings before and said that it was not British).

When that was over I had a look at my Spitfire. The shell had blown two valves away and punctured one of the glycol pipes where it joined the cylinders. There were a number of machine gun bullets in different parts. The nearest one to me was about a foot behind me. It had hit my oxygen bottle which I had heard go with a bang.

I picked up the air intake which had broken off when I landed. I then showed the troops where the petrol tank was and got them to fire at it with their rifles. They punctured the tanks and then fired a tracer bullet at it which set it on fire. It burnt very well really considering it is all metal. It was a very sad sight to see my own aeroplane burning, but better that than let it fall into enemy hands.

I had come down about nine miles east of Dunkirk just in Belgium, I think. The troops whom I first joined up with were all stragglers. They had just reached the coast that morning. I started walking along the beach towards Dunkirk. We had been fighting that morning somewhere near Ghent as we had to chase them.

Just east of Bray Dunes I came across a crowd of troops trying to get a large boat down to the sea 100 yards away. They pinched a French car and tried to tow it, but with no avail as the sand was too dry. Seeing the boat I very quickly decided that that was what I wanted, so I very smartly joined up with them. They turned out to be the South Lancashires. I palled up with a second-lieutenant. He introduced me to his Colonel who was a VC, DSO, MC and bar, and real old soldier.

There were two destroyers lying off the coast; that is why we wanted the boat. I saw some men trying to reach the destroyers on small pieces of plank and in all sorts of small craft.

When we could not get the boat launched we went on to Bray Dunes where a large number of lorries had been run in a line into the sea and a structure put over them so as to form a sort of quay. There were a lot of troops here all waiting to be taken off. The quay was packed with troops when we got there, making an excellent target for the aircraft that were ground strafing us. I saw a brigadier produce his revolver and he soon cleared it. He put armed sentries on guard with orders to shoot the first man who tried to get on to it.

They carried out a number of bombing attacks when we were there, so I decided that it would be advisable to find a tin hat. There were a crowd of dead guardsmen there who had been machine gunned that morning. They wanted me to take one of theirs but at that time I was not callous enough. I luckily found a Belgian one that fitted me, so I used that – I still have it and a Belgian bayonet I picked up later.

The second-lieutenant (Bob Davidson), a platoon commander who was only twenty years old, and I sat in a Mercury car which was lying wrecked on the beach and watched two destroyers sunk, one damaged and a transport hit by bombs. It was like watching a film sitting in the comfort of a car and watching this about half a mile away. The dive bombers came first and disabled the destroyers and then the heavy bombers (Heinkels and Dorniers) came over and finished them off. The destroyer we had been trying to reach was hit amidships by the dive bombers. It must have been hit in the engines as it did not move. The Heinkels dropped salvoes of five heavy bombs. One salvo hit it and the destroyer just disappeared. You can imagine that we were rather glad that we had not got the boat launched.

What happened was that whenever the destroyers came near to the shore to take off the troops, the bombers would come over and drive them away. They were therefore very dubious of sending in any of their boats. They eventually signalled to us to move along to Dunkirk in small groups and they would try and get us off there. It was a long trek across the sand with flying boots on, which are certainly not designed for walking.

I have never seen such shambles as there were on these sands. Transport of all sorts deliberately wrecked; 'scuttled' as the troops called it. All sorts of equipment and, of course, a number of graves just marked by an upturned rifle. Also, of course, there were a number of unburied bodies. The mutilated ones were mostly covered, thank goodness. It surprised me how quickly the pigment turns yellow after death.

The troops were all very tired as they had been going since early that morning and they had been fighting the rearguard action. The Colonel therefore called for a number of halts to rest. It amazed me how he could lie down and go to sleep for ten minutes with bombing, AA fire and shelling going on practically continuously.

I saw a number of fights between our fighters and the enemy. I saw one fully loaded bomber come down in the sea with a huge splash and a Me109 explode in mid-air with a Spitfire on its tail – the pilot baled out. I saw one Spitfire go for seven Huns. He got a great cheer from the troops. It was very interesting watching things from the ground as I could see the difficulties the fighters are up against. At times we could see Hun bombers bombing from the cloud, while our fighters were about half a mile away obviously unable to see them. The troops could not understand that one could see an aircraft in thin cloud above one, but from the air one could not. One day while we were on patrol, I could see bombs bursting near a destroyer but I could not find the bomber as he was in thin cloud. Another thing that surprised me was the amount of AA fire that was thrown up without any apparent effect. The sky was black with puffs sometimes, mostly from the Navy.

Just east of Dunkirk, at Malo-les-Bains, French troops were settled in on the sands and what was left of the houses. They seemed very unconcerned of all that was going on in spite of the fact that they had to stay to the very last. One rather amusing thing I saw was a party of French soldiers who had dug two trenches in the sands and were using the ridge between the trenches, in which they sat, as a table; over it they had a clean white table cloth and were quite happily tucking in to a good meal on British rations while a bombing raid was going on about them. Apparently the French troops were reputed to be very good at bagging the British rations.

Malo-les-Bains and Dunkirk were both in a very bad state. Many of the houses were gutted and there were numerous fires. The amount of equipment was unbelievable. A lot of stuff had not even been removed from the quay and none of it was taken back. We saw a number of ambulances that had been machine gunned from the air. The things that I would have liked to pick up and bring back were uncountable!

When we got to Dunkirk we found that they were only bringing in one ship at a time. When we got there, there was a cross-Channel steamer alongside the quay. I was mighty glad to get on board but was rather sorry that it was not a smaller target. Its only defences were a few Lewis guns.

We had three-quarters of an hour to wait on board before the ship left and it seemed years. We had to wait for the stragglers coming in behind us. While we were waiting to leave a swarm of dive bombers came over. They had numerous tries to hit us but all missed, thank goodness. They shook the ship badly. The nearest miss was when a salvo of four bombs fell just on the other side of the quay to us. We all thought that our last day had come then. Some of the Tommies were amazing while this was going on. There was one who was standing and watching, giving a running commentary – such as, 'Gor' damn he's coming straight for us – Gor' four bombs, 'em's going to hit us.'

I must say that while these raids were going on I was beginning to wonder where the RAF was. It was the troops' chief complaint, but they did not realise that our fighter patrols were probably engaging the Huns out of their sight.

While we were waiting to leave we listened to the news on a wireless someone had salved. It was rather funny. The troops all said, 'Let's hear how the BEF is getting on'. The news said that the evacuation was being carried out in perfect order which amazed them no end. There was a loud protest when the announcer said that the evacuation was being covered magnificently by the RAF! I was glad to hear later that Churchill spoke well in our favour.

It was a great moment when the ship began to move out but at the same time it was rather a shaking sight, as just as we were moving out a party of wounded men came along and we had to leave them. (There was, in any case, no room for them; every inch of deck space on the ship was full of people.) They would, of course, be picked up by the next ship but one could not but help feeling for them.

On leaving Dunkirk we had to wend our way through the sunken shipping. There was one French destroyer, which was gutted and had its back broken, beached and its AA guns were still firing.

Once we left Dunkirk we were lucky enough not to be bombed, but at the same time there was the feeling that at any moment we might be. We had to go considerably off course to avoid mine fields. There was a continuous stream of shipping. I have never seen such a mixed collection of craft. The French Navy seemed to be in force. We passed one large ship lying on its side. There were a large number of small ships standing by to pick up survivors, so we went by. I heard afterwards from the news that it had been torpedoed.

It was a grand sight to see the cliffs of Dover. We called in at Dover but there was no room at the jetties and had to go round to Folkestone, where we disembarked; this was at about 6.30 p.m. The Church army and a number of civilians were there giving out food and hot drinks which were very welcome. We got into the trains not knowing where we were going and not caring save that we were in 'Blighty'. All the civilians along the line turned out and cheered as the trains went by. Cigarettes and chocolates were thrown in through the windows. This welcome was very moving for the troops, who, although dead tired, waved back.

We were travelling all through the night. At all the large stations along the line there were civilians serving out food and drink. They were also giving out post cards which they posted, sending telegrams and making 'phone calls to relatives of the troops.

It was a noble effort on those people's part. They had been at it night and day for the last five days.

The feelings against the Belgians ran very high and one lady told us at one station they had a train of Belgians and a train of Scottish in at the same time. The latter started to go for the Belgians and they had great difficulty in stopping them. Apparently there were large numbers of Belgian civilians who turned out to be Fifth Columnists and snipers. Bob Davidson only lost four men from his platoon and they were shot by Belgians.

We got out of the train at 5 a.m. next morning and were taken to a camp at Aldershot. We all had a wash and a good sleep.

I went to Farnborough which was an RAF Station nearby. I phoned up my CO from there and told him I was safe. He was very glad to hear it as apparently four of us were missing that morning. There was an account in the previous evening's paper which said only one of our aircraft was missing, so I thought all was well.

They flew me back from Farnborough to Hornchurch that afternoon. It was great to be back and I got a grand welcome from old 'Simon' (dog).

After I had rested I was none the worse for my adventure except that it took me a few days to get used to bangs etc. While in the train someone let one of the blinds up. It made a noise just like a shell and everyone instinctively ducked and were badly shaken.

Pilot Officer R.A.L. Morant, 222 Squadron

Johnnie Bell of 616, who was left swimming towards a ship two miles off the beaches, gradually closed the distance to safety. As he swam, he saw one Me109 crash on the sand dunes and saw several others strafing the beaches and small craft off-shore. Bell was finally picked up by a ship's boat crewed by a Naval rating and a British Tommy who had volunteered to come out to him. This was the last remaining small boat the ship possessed, which turned out to be the minesweeper HMS *Halcyon*.

As he was taken aboard, the minesweeper then sailed into Dunkirk harbour where it stayed for about forty-five minutes. All the time Ju87's were dive-bombing the harbour, the ships inside it and at the entrance.

Halcyon was replying with two 4-inch guns, Lewis and Bren guns, while others, including Bell, grabbed rifles etc. and kept up a steady barrage of small arms fire. He could see 109's strafing nearby beaches from time to time and was galled to see neat formations of RAF fighters flying some miles out to sea.

When *Halycon* sailed, RAF fighter patrols were seen frequently overhead and only one Ju88 made an attack but missed. The minesweeper, with Bell aboard, landed at Dover around 1.30 p.m.[1]

*

The relieving fighter wing comprised 145, 245 and 43 Squadrons, the latter unit making its first combat patrol over Dunkirk, led by Squadron Leader C.G. Lott (L1737). They were supposed to meet up with a French Bloch Squadron. 145 Squadron led but no enemy aircraft were seen.

> June 1st 1940, at the dawn of another of those bright and beautiful days which marked that summer in England. It was to be a momentous day to us though one to which the squadron was to become accustomed before it returned in the autumn, tattered and mauled but with undimmed ardour, to Usworth in County Durham.
>
> We had returned to our parent airfield at Tangmere the day before to take our place in the fighter force operating over France. Ever since the invasion of the Low Countries the boys had been getting at me to get the squadron moved to the Continent. It was small consolation when I told them that our time would surely come, and when it did they would all get their bellyful of fighting. Indeed it began to look as if they would get it anyway for their ranks were depleted steadily as replacements in the active squadrons were being made at our expense. One after another my best pilots were taken and my beloved squadron was diminishing before my eyes at an alarming rate.
>
> Both of the flight commanders went: Caesar Hull to earn undying fame in Norway, Peter Townsend to command another fighter squadron, No 85, with the greatest distinction. It was heartbreaking to have to let them go so that when the word came that we were heading south my spirits soared.
>
> The next morning was 1st June and we were assigned to patrol over Dunkirk with three other squadrons, two Hurricane and one Bloch (Frenchmen).

[1] Flying Officer J.S. Bell was killed in action 30th August 1940 aged 23.

Picking twelve out of fourteen did not present much difficulty and we accordingly leapt into the air at a quite indecent hour, full of high hopes, and, as far as I was concerned some trepidation. We were heading for a kind of trouble quite new to us, and although I was bursting with pride in my squadron I did not know just what to expect or just how we should cope. Furthermore, in an excess of zeal and defying all logic, I had chosen the oldest and slowest of our rather teased-out Hurricanes in which to lead, arguing that everyone else in the squadron should be able to keep up with me. It did not have even a 2-pitch prop but a fixed wooden one.

We set out with 145 Squadron from Tangmere and met up with 245 over Folkestone. Of the Blochs there was no sign, so off we set for Dunkirk. There was no difficulty about finding it. You could either fly along the smoke trail from Brighton to the blazing fuel tanks or follow the string of boats from the South foreland. Navigation was no problem at all.

My squadron was flying in the rear at what later came to be known as 'Top Cover'. There had been no time for cohesive wing tactics to be developed, let alone time to discuss them with our fellow squadrons. Add that we were flying in sections of three in Vic formation and there is nothing but the elements of hope and faith in our nebulous plans.

For forty-five minutes we stooged up and down the beaches at some 17,000 feet; too high to see much detail on the ground but high enough to see the wonderful and thrilling panorama of boats. Big boats, little boats, boats with brass funnels, boats with strings of smaller boats strung out behind them like a duck with her ducklings. In a never ending stream they crept over the water in both directions. The slowness of their movement was anguishing. Their vulnerability to air attack was so obvious as to make the spectacle truly heroic, and I could both have cheered and wept as I watched.

On land flames and smoke took my eye to the exclusion of all else. I did not see the gun flashes nor could I hear the noise as it was hard to realise just what a hell it must have been. At all events there was no interference from the air for forty-five minutes for we saw nothing during our patrol and in due course landed at Manson to refuel and await further orders. As one of our number had turned back with engine trouble we popped down with the remaining 11 and went to the Mess for breakfast. Manston, being the nearest airfield to Calais and Dunkirk, was a pretty busy spot just then but I give the station staff full marks; they did us proud.

> I remember that breakfast, not for what I ate but because I saw
> in *The Times* that I had been awarded a DFC. I could not believe
> it. I still wonder!
>
> *Squadron Leader C.G. Lott, 43 Squadron*

As these units returned, 19, 41, 222 and 616 Squadrons had been refuelled, re-armed, patched up and made ready. After some 'tea and wads' the pilots were back in the air by 8.25 a.m. There had, however, been a gap in the air cover and down below the Luftwaffe had used its Stukas in undisturbed attacks on the many ships off the beachhead. They and some Heinkels were still busy there when the Hornchurch units began to arrive.

Led by Sandy Lane (K9799), 19 Squadron flew just below a thin cloud layer. As he turned away from the harbour he glanced back over his shoulder to see what he hoped would be, for the Army below, an impressive sight of thirty-seven Spitfires. Up towards Nieuport, then back to Dunkirk flew the fighters. Suddenly there was a movement to Lane's left. It was an aircraft diving towards the shipping outside the harbour. It dropped a bomb which hit a destroyer which exploded and sank. Lane, furious not to have seen the German earlier, chased it into the clouds but lost it. He did, however, find three Dorniers. He and another Spitfire attacked, Lane severely damaging his target until it too went into cloud.

Flight Sergeant Grumpy Unwin, No 3 to Lane, had just begun to follow his leader when he felt a blow to his leg. He broke quickly, thinking he had been hit but then discovered that the radiator handle had shot forward, but by this time he had lost the other two Spitfires. Climbing above the clouds, he found numerous AA bursts and some Spitfires. Seeing two He111's, he chased one in company with some of 222 Squadron's Spitfires, some miles inland. The bomber's rear gun ceased firing and its starboard engine packed up before Unwin left it to three 222 Squadron pilots, Flight Lieutenant Robinson, Douglas Bader and Sergeant Johnson. It was claimed as probably destroyed.

It fell to Flight Sergeant Harry Steere to make the only certain kill by 19 Squadron, a Do215, when he found himself in the middle of about twenty of them. Despite crossfire which hit his Spitfire in several places, he knocked out the bomber's port engine and saw it spiral down trailing smoke, being harried by other Spitfires as it fell.

Flight Lieutenant Terry Webster (N3098) of 41 Squadron shot down two Dorniers, (one probable), while Pilot Officer Tony Lovell (P9429) and Pilot Officer Oliver Morrogh-Ryan (N3113) got a Heinkel. 41 also got two Ju88's. These victories cost them two pilots, Pilot Officer Bill Stapleton, later reported as a prisoner and Flying Officer Bill Legard. Squadron

Leader H.R.L. Hood, flying over the Channel, saw a Dornier bombing a ship and attacked, despite his guns being empty. He so upset the German pilot that he put his bomber into the sea without a shot being fired.

> On one of these antics Robin Hood had the unique experience when he dived on one enemy aircraft low down, although he was out of ammunition, and was amazed to see the chap dive straight into the sea!
>
> *Pilot Officer E.A. Shipman, 41 Squadron*

Denys Gillam led 616 Squadron and also got in amongst the bombers, mostly Ju88's. 616 were to the rear of the other squadrons, flying at 2,000 feet. Gillam saw a Dornier and chased it into cloud 1,000 feet above, and ran into a Ju88 as he came through. He closed in to 50 yards, fired a two-second burst and the 88 spiralled into the clouds, its fuselage seen to be splattered with bullet holes. Pilot Officer Roy Marples also chased the Dornier, met about thirty Heinkels and shared his ammunition out between five of them. Pilot Officer George Moberly saw a Ju88 come out of the clouds and head out to sea. He chased the bomber at full boost, his first burst scoring a hit but return fire damaged his own exhaust manifold. Chasing the 88 through thin cloud, a five-second burst simply smashed the tail right off and the 88 went into the sea about a quarter of a mile from a wrecked troopship.

Earlier that morning, at 8.34 a.m., an Anson V of 500 Squadron had taken off from Detling to patrol the Belgium coast. It was piloted by Pilot Officer P.M. Peters, his crew being Sergeant D.C. Spencer and Aircraftmen Pepper and L.G. Smith.

Two hours later, at 10.40 they saw nine Me109's at about 1,000-1,500 feet above Ostend. Three of the German fighters broke away to attack the Anson, one coming in behind it, two others from the starboard quarter. Phillip Peters took violent evasive action, throwing the Anson all over the sky, successfully turning and twisting about so as not to present the aircraft as a steady target. As he did so, the air-gunner A.C. Smith and navigator Sergeant Deryck Spencer kept up a steady return fire as other 109's came in to assist their comrades. The gunner's fire was so effective that two 109's were shot down into the sea and another damaged in a fight which lasted for fifteen to twenty miles at a height above the sea of around 50 feet.

When the remaining fighters flew off, Peters continued his patrol, landing back at base at 12.37. There the crew found two bullet holes in the wing, one through the flaps and a fourth through the cowling of the port engine.

Peters, Spencer and Smith were subsequently decorated with the DFC
and two DFMs respectively.

By late morning three more squadrons had been brought to Readiness,
43, 145 and 245. Each provided three sections – nine Hurricanes – a
total of twenty-seven fighters.

At 11.25 a.m., 145 Squadron detached itself from the patrol when it
saw some German bombers; 43 and 245 continued on, then 245 went
down towards the dog-fight which had begun. 43 were then alone and
found the top cover German fighters.

> I led the chaps away the second time that morning. We went off
> in the same order as before and were soon on patrol again. On the
> second leg I saw another squadron. They looked in the distance a
> little smaller than Hurricanes and then it dawned on me that they
> were the Frenchmen in their Blochs. So along we went, and back
> once more with the fourth squadron above and behind on the port
> quarter. On the second turn I looked back just in time to see their
> leading echelon wing over and dive. In plan they were easy to
> recognise as Messerschmitt 109's!
>
> I shouted loudly over the radio, '109's coming down behind',
> and swung round into the attack. As far as cohesion was concerned
> that was the end and I found myself alone amidst what seemed like
> hordes of Huns in a matter of seconds. They came from all
> directions and I had a mad struggle for survival. First one and then
> another would get on my tail; twice I was down to 3,000 feet and
> twice back to 17,000; twice I flocked into a spin. Not once did I get
> a chance to shoot back. I am not sure that I even thought of it. In
> the distance I saw a ball of vivid yellow flame plummeting to earth,
> but whether friend or foe I know not, and never will.
>
> There was a brief lull, then from above and ahead, two 110's
> approached; I pulled up and over in a most crude and unpolished
> twist and managed to finish up behind the second, though at some
> distance. They both were diving gently and with a quick look
> round behind I followed. Steady and straight he flew, and I
> gained a little. I put the bead of my reflector sight slap on him; I
> was thinking most extraordinarily clearly for some reason, and
> calmly and methodically lifted the sight just a little to allow for
> the longish range. It was about 400 yards. Firmly I pressed the
> firing button, and almost immediately first one engine and then
> the other poured black smoke. I kept the button pressed for a long
> burst with the sight remaining rock steady. I must have hit him,
> yet I wish only one engine had smoked for then I should not be

wondering still if it was because he slammed his throttles open that his engines belched black smoke. He plunged into a cloud layer at about 3,000 feet and I pulled away. He had been flying straight and steady too long and, so had I! The sky was empty.

I was steaming and my hands were shaking a little, and I decided I had learned enough for one day and set off for home. I felt some relief and just a little pride to find that I was the last to return.

The first had been Tony Woods-Scawen. He was a small, slight fair-haired boy; not really a clever fighter-pilot but a good one for he had the heart of a lion and was all guts. He had had a similar experience to mine. All the Huns in the Luftwaffe had taken a pot at him but some had shot more accurately than others and pretty well plastered him. 'I took a crack at dozens of 'em', he said, 'but I don't think I hit one.' His hydraulic system had been shot to pieces covering the cockpit and all that was in it with oil. It was over his clothes and hands and face; the plane was riddled with holes; one longeron was practically shot through.

When he arrived over the field he put his undercarriage down. I say 'put' it down but as he said the plane was so teased that the wheels just fell down out of exhaustion. And they stayed down. The flaps would not work but he landed successfully and taxied in. The mechanics rushed out to meet him and fazed, awestricken, at the spectacle his plane made. Full of holes and smothered in oil it really did look a wreck. And Tony! covered in oil from head to foot; face as black as a tinker. 'Ooh! How did you get on, Sir? What was it like?'. Tony grinned all over his face and answered in one word, 'De-e e e licious,'he said.

When I counted noses we were two short. Sergeant Gough was dead and Pilot Officer 'Crackers' Carswell, shot down in flames, was burnt quite badly but had been picked up by a destroyer. It had been his first operational mission since ditching in the North Sea some four months previously. Poor Crackers; he recovered, came back for some more in September and first time out was again shot down in flames and burnt again. Once more he recovered but this time the medics pinned him to the ground.

On the other hand our score had been nine confirmed and six probables.[1,2]

Squadron Leader C.G. Lott, 43 Squadron

[1] Original manuscript of an article by Squadron Leader Lott for *Blackwoods Magazine* in 1940. AVM George Lott provided his manuscript for inclusion in this book.
[2] Tony Woods-Scawen, Hurricane, L1592, coded FT-C went for repair to a maintenance unit. It flew again with 615 Squadron in August 1940 and was damaged and repaired again. After three more years in use at various flying training units it was earmarked for preservation and is now on display in the Science Museum in London.

Top scorer in this action was Sergeant Jim 'Darkie' Hallowes (N2585) who shot down four German fighters. The first was a 109 which was attacking a Hurricane. When Hallowes went for it, the German pilot looped but came directly into Hallowes' line of flight. Firing from 150 yards the 109 burst into flames and dived into the sea. A second 109 he attacked caught fire and lost a wing, then he shot the tail from a 110. The fourth, another 109, he chased fifteen miles inland, leaving it shedding pieces and heading for the ground. Sergeant P. Ottewill (L1726) shot down two 109's, the first exploding in a ball of flame, the second spinning into the sea with smoke pouring from its engine. He then damaged a 110 before his ammunition gave out. Flight Lieutenant John Simpson (N2665) also bagged two, one in the sea, one diving into the ground. Then his windscreen was covered in oil and he was chased towards England for some considerable distance by a 109. Flying Officer J.D. Edwards (L1736) was shot up by a 110, then shaking this off, shot down a 109 which broke up in the air. He then sent a 110 down on fire, counted as a probable.

The pilots of 145, meantime, had engaged the bombers' lower escort – estimated at around seventy Me109's and Me110's. The 110's formed a defensive circle as the Hurricane attacked. Pilot Officer Nigel Weir cut across the circle, his burst of gunfire slicing off the nose of one Messerschmitt and knocking off part of its port engine. The 110 stood up on its tail, then fell away to crash into the sea. Weir then sent a 109 down but he was attacked himself so was unable to see if it too crashed.

The squadron claimed five 110's and three 109's, Flight Lieutenant Roy Dutton getting a 110 and two 109's, Flight Lieutenant A.H. Boyd one of each. Two pilots, Dutton and Weir, were attacked by Hurricanes in the fight but were not hit. They did, however, lose one pilot, Pilot Officer H.P. Dixon, and Pilot Officer L.D.M. Scott's machine was hit in the radiator but he got it back to Manston (N2497).

Squadron Leader E.W. Whitley (N2707), a New Zealander, led his 245 Squadron into the battle from below. They had seen Dorniers but became embroiled with the fighters and did not get to the bombers. They shot down six 109's, four confirmed and two probables. Pilot Officer John Redman's victim disintegrated, with its wings falling off, the rest of the machine failing in pieces. Pilot Officer Southwell sent one into the sea, while the pilot of a second baled out. Pilot Officer G.E. Hill found his starboard four guns jammed when the transporter took the wrong groove but his port guns smashed a 109's tail and it went into the sea with flames flickering beneath the pilot's cockpit. The squadron lost two pilots, Pilot Officers R.A. West and A.L. Treanor.

*

The Luftwaffe had mounted a series of heavy air attacks during this morning period, not only above and off Dunkirk and La Panne but out over the sea on the shipping routes to England. They had started at 5 a.m., then again at 8.30. More had come at 10.00 and 10.40 a.m. and again at noon. After that there was a lull until nearly four o'clock when the Germans launched heavy dive bombing attacks on Dunkirk harbour and all shipping located nearby for over half an hour.

The lull from mid-day till four was only broken by three small actions in mid-afternoon, 111, 151, 17 and 609 Squadrons were on patrol and each had brief encounters.

John Thompson's Hurricanes saw nothing, but Flight Lieutenant Peter Powell had taken off late because of engine trouble and engaged a lone Do17 5,000 feet over Dunkirk. He attacked but observed no damage before it escaped.

Leading 111 and 151 was Teddy Donaldson. He saw a single Ju88 about to bomb some ships towards the end of their patrol time and emptied his guns into it. Shortage of fuel forced him to give up the chase but it had been driven off.

The other two squadrons, 17 and 609, were also in action. 17 had flown to Manston, landing at mid-day, Sergeant Sewell being delayed by engine trouble. Another developed engine trouble so they took off for their afternoon patrol with nine aircraft, joining up with 609's Spitfires. 609 too were down to nine aircraft.

Flying at 9,000 feet, 17 Squadron saw a Ju88 three thousand feet below, five miles off shore, and five Hurricanes dived to the attack but to no effect. The 88 returned fire from the rear gunner, scoring hits on Flight Lieutenant Toyne's and Pilot Officer Ken Manger's machines. Another 88 was attacked by Pilot Officer Whittaker but this too escaped inland.

The Spitfire pilots had become split up and Flight Lieutenant 'Hack' Russell's section was reduced to just himself and Flying Officer A.R. 'Paul' Edge when their No 3 was lost in a turn. As they were looking for him, a lone Me110 surprised them from behind to fire into Russell's aircraft. Edge saw it surrounded by bursting shells and tracer before it began a long slow spiral into the sea. Edge took on the 110 and in a head-on attack in which it seemed to the British pilot that the German was intent on ramming him, Edge scored hits on the 110 which went vertically down to the sea. In 609 Squadron's History it crashed but the RAF only credited a probable victory, probably because it was not seen by another pilot to go into the sea.

What was a fact was that Hack Russell was dead. An experienced veteran whose DFC had just come through, this gallant American had destroyed a dozen German aircraft and possibly six more.

Several squadrons were ordered off to patrol during the mid-afternoon, 64 and 66 Squadrons from Kenley, the latter flying their first patrols and 229, 242 and 610 from Biggin Hill. They met mixed fortunes.

The Luftwaffe mounted a large dive-bombing raid by a large force of Ju87's escorted by Me109's and Me110's. The Hurricane pilots of 242 Squadron saw the Stukas dive-bombing the ships anchored to the northwest of Dunkirk harbour just after 4.30 p.m. The British boys were at 2,500 feet and they estimated the enemy force at around fifty strong. There were only seven Hurricanes and while one section immediately went down on the Stukas, Flight Lieutenant Don Miller saw about forty Me109's come out of cloud above, then dive upon them. Miller pulled up and attacked the leading Messerschmitt to give it a three-second burst from ahead and below. The 109 rolled partly onto its back and went over his Hurricane seemingly out of control. Stan Turner also engaged a bunch of 109's, giving one a long seven-second burst which sent it diving into the sea. He then turned on two more, hammering out long bursts till he stalled and fell away. As he regained flying speed and looked up he could only see one of the Messerschmitts.

The first section meanwhile were in amongst the Stukas. Pilot Officer Stansfeld caught one as it released three bombs. He held his thumb on the gun button for a full 10-seconds, the 87 rolling onto its back as he shot past it. He also saw one ship hit on its stern by a diving Stuka. Willie McKnight followed a diving Stuka, firing as he went and the Stuka just did not make it and fell straight into the sea. He then climbed up behind another and his fire caused smoke to come from it then this too dived steeply into the sea. He repeated these manoeuvres twice more, each time severely damaging two more of these deadly gull-winged dive-bombers.

In total the Canadians were credited with three Stukas and one 109 destroyed, two Stukas and two 109's as probably destroyed – all without loss.

Harold Maguire's 229 Squadron chalked up three Stukas, one definite and two probables. Flying Officer Robert Smith got the confirmed kill, attacking it just after it had bombed and was pulling out of its dive. He opened fire at 200 yards and its engine belched fire as it fell away into some cloud. As Smith dived through the cloud he saw the Stuka crash into the water. He later shot up another Stuka, stopping return fire from the gunner. Pilot Officer R.E. Bary chased another Stuka across the coast at twenty feet. He left it severely damaged and rocking from side to side.

No 64 Squadron were credited with one Stuka destroyed plus three possibles but they lost one pilot, Pilot Officer Hey, who failed to make it back. 66 Squadron were not engaged and 610 Squadron, flying at 8,000 feet, therefore above the main fight, found themselves in cloud.

They saw three 109's for a brief moment but lost them almost at once, then the Spitfires became separated. It was their final patrol.

> On the afternoon of 1st June 1940 we were up over Dunkirk yet again flying at 20,000 feet above 8/10th cloud. We saw no enemy aircraft. This was our last patrol and in the afternoon the squadron was ordered to move north to Acklington.
>
> *Flight Lieutenant J. Ellis, 610 Squadron*

Three Hudsons of 220 Squadron had taken off at 3 p.m. and at 4.45 became embroiled in the battle with the Stukas. Again we see the action through the eyes of Hilton Haarhoff, air gunner, from his diary:

> This was to be my great day, earning me a DFC together with the same decoration for Selley, my pilot and Jouault, the pilot of the third Hudson in the battle flight. Only sheer bad luck prevented Sheahan, our leader, from further distinguishing himself – he had already been awarded the DFC.
>
> Our flight was ordered off to carry out the third relief of the Dover Dunkirk patrol taking off at 1400 hours. We relieved the earlier battle flight at the Dover end at 14.35 and set course for the other side. The weather was delightful, sunny, with a thin layer of cloud at 4,000 feet. The surface of the Channel was as smooth as a mill pond. The shipping was still in the form of a continuous stream coming from Dunkirk with only a few tugs, Channel steamers and destroyers going in our direction. As we approached Dunkirk a black pall of smoke was to be seen – this came from the oil tanks which had been fired by our RE's.
>
> In the Channel approaching the harbour, a destroyer was to be seen lying on its side and smoking furiously. This destroyer, a French ship, had been heavily bombed by dive bombers on the previous day. The beaches of Dunkirk, whence most of the embarking had been effected throughout the two previous days and nights were now nearly deserted, but the sands showed a mass of shell holes and shelter trenches which were hastily dug by our troops. Nearer the water's edge the sand was littered with discarded equipment, clothing and rifles.
>
> Several buildings in the town were burning, while many more were smouldering, and frequent gun flashes were to be seen. One or two balloons were to be seen over the docks, so we were not able to fly directly overhead, but it was evident that the place had received heavy damage from bombing and shelling. We completed our circuit of the embarking point and turned for

Dover. We were still flying in our old formation – Selley on the left and Jouault on the right of Sheahan, who was leading. Our old arrangement, if we were attacked by fighters still stood; then Selley was to take the lead so that I could act as fire controller. We had sighted a formation of Spitfires overhead flying at about seven thousand feet and well above the layer cloud but there was no sign of any Jerries, though a destroyer seemed to be 'letting loose' at something up above but we left our fighter boys to look after them, as we had strict orders to stick to our beat to ward off any Jerries who attempted to interfere, from a low level, with our boys who were getting away on the ships. We turned for Dover, then back to Dunkirk, where we were now able to see quite distinctly a line of lorries which had been driven out into the sea to form a jetty for the boats. We had not seen this previously as it was at the extremity of the beach. At a rough estimate I placed the number of lorries at about a hundred. The foremost one was all but covered by the sea, and must have been driven out at low tide.

We did not stay at Dunkirk very long as we could still see the Spitfires up above, so turned for Dover once more covering the patrol without event. We were approaching the other side for the third time when while we were still about ten miles away, Sheahan called up on the RT and said there appeared to be some trouble ahead. Just below cloud level we could see a whirling mass of aircraft, and as we drew closer we could pick out Ju87's, about twenty of them with three Spitfires in their midst. Sheahan kept our flight edging away and we were all expecting to see the 87's fall out of the sky, but they were turning inside the Spitfires, which were not able to do a thing. All the time different Ju's were peeling off and carrying out attacks on our ships.

I saw one 87 go down in a vertical dive, release his bombs and then start climbing again. I looked for his target, an inoffensive tug towing a barge loaded with troops. The bomb, and it must have been a big one, fell just in front of the tug, and an enormous shower of water was shot up into the air completely blotting out the small tug. I did not expect to see the tug again but in less time than it takes to tell, the tug was still steaming forward and the shower of water decreasing as it fell; the gallant little tug was quite unharmed and I gave it a cheer.

All this time we were flying round the scene of action and suddenly Sheahan gave me the signal to attack, so in we went – I saw Jouault immediately get on the tail of an 87, firing as he went. I tested my guns and suddenly heard Selley say, 'There's a bunch on our left, shall we have a go at them, Boet?' I agreed as about three miles away I could see about twenty 87's all in a large circle. We made right for the centre of them, firing as we approached and Selley tried to get on the tail of the nearest but they were very quick in turning off. As we approached we could see the tactics they were employing to carry out their bombings on the shipping. Wheeling around in a large circle of roughly two miles diameter at about 2,000 feet, one aircraft would 'peel off' and go up into a steep climb, which brought him to the centre of the ring and above the target. Reaching this point about 1,500 feet above, the ring of other EA, the '87' would be near stalling point and would then 'whip' over in a stall turn and go down almost vertically, drop his bomb and then reform the circle, to be followed by another 87.

Our first attack was made on an EA as it went down in its dive but Selley's shots were well short while I did not do much better and had to content myself with putting up a curtain through which the Jerry flew, but I was not able to see whether he 'caught it' or not, as Selley and I were now discussing things and we decided to get the centre of the bunch and to attack the 87's as they went up in their climb prior to doing a dive attack. As we followed the first one up I opened fire from long range and my burst, which was a nice long one registered and I saw the 87 lurch, but it continued on up.

Then Selley swung the Hudson to get his guns on, and my turret 'cut out', but a nice short burst from the port guns did the trick, and the Ju whipped over and went down in a spiral, hitting the water with a tremendous splash. Selley levelled out and made for another, and I got a nice bead on an EA on our port side. He was apparently just starting his climb and flew from our port side over our tail and at about seventy yards range. I was firing at him for about three seconds and he never finished the climb, as he spun and I saw him going down in a cloud of smoke. Fletcher, our navigator, confirmed his crashing – almost on top of a tug.

Our next target was another 87 going up in its climb and again I fired as we approached with Selley finishing him off at short range. With this one Selley must have continued firing up to about thirty yards and then climbed over him because I saw him going down, and the next second just as I was giving him a short good-bye burst I saw one of the crew leave by 'chute. I never saw what happened to that chappie, though I presume he landed safely, as when I last saw him the canopy had spewed and the Jerry was swaying to and fro. It now occurred to me that I was employing the wrong tactics, as my bursts were perforce from long range as I was firing at a target for which Selley was aiming, and as soon as he brought his guns onto the target my turret cut out leaving me immobilised at the critical moment.

Accordingly, I commenced picking out my own targets over the side and tail. In all while Selley carried out three more climbing attacks I picked out 87's and fired at them as I could, generally from fairly long range. I was not able to press the attacks to the end but I'm sure at least two of them were certainties, while two others went home, if they got home, with bits of British lead aboard. The EA were now dispersing and Selley chased on towards Dunkirk where the Jerry finally crashed going down in a slight spin. We returned once more to the scene of the combat, and Selley made for the only remaining EA which was starting a climb, we were still a long way off when we started our climb and as Selley afterwards admitted, he was so intent on watching the EA and his own gun sights that he forgot to look at the instrument panel, and suddenly our Hudson gave a sickening shudder and then fell over the starboard and started a spin. When I recovered from the strange sensation I started to decide what had happened and the realisation that Selley was out of action flashed across my mind. As we were only at 3,000 feet when we went into the spin I thought it was all 'UP', but Selley and Fletcher heaved on the stick and we eventually straightened and flattened out scarcely one hundred feet above the water. I don't know how Selley and the others felt just then, I was bathed in perspiration, but when I spoke to Selley shortly afterwards, he was still shaky.

The Jerry aircraft had now disappeared, and by my watch, everything had happened in just thirteen minutes. We looked around for our two other machines and spotted Sheahan first and joined him. Over the RT he told us that as he went in to attack his bunch the Spitfires that were already there, came straight for him, and he spent all his time in getting recognition signals off, and eventually when the fighters left him alone, the fun was over. Sheahan was cursing soundly in his inevitable way and he did not break off to rate Selley for wandering away from the rest of the battle flight, but we knew he was peeved, and felt damned sorry for him for having had such bad luck. We continued circling and at first thought Jouault had caught it as he was nowhere to be seen but eventually he was seen coming from the direction of Dunkirk. His explanation was that after tackling one 87 which he was positive had gone down into the sea, but which none of his crew were able to verify, he got on to the tail of another and followed it, firing all the while, all the way to Dunkirk, eventually shooting it down on the far side of the tower. We swapped experiences and on making examination found that none of our Hudsons had been damaged at all by enemy return fire, though I could see that our starboard mainplane had been badly 'wrinkled', probably due to our spin and subsequent pull out but I did not draw Selley's attention to this till we had finished our patrol. Jouault and Selley, in addition to our navigator, Fletcher, all were convinced that the Ju's returned our fire but I'm afraid my attention was too taken up with getting any right on target to have noticed any tracer from the 87's, which the others had seen.

We continued our patrol and as if miraculously everything was quiet once more, the shipping continuing on as if nothing had occurred. We could see the men on several of the ships cheering and waving as we flew past, so it was probable that they had seen and were pleased at the result. After leaving Dover for the second time after this previous incident, we were approaching Dunkirk in a tight formation as we could see a destroyer firing its pompoms. We approached cautiously to take stock of things, when suddenly there was a series of flashes immediately below us on the water. Sheahan pointed upwards and through the wispy cloud we saw three He111's, making off like h –. They had dropped a stick of bombs across us!! Fortunately we were higher than they supposed, but for all that the burst of the bombs gave me a severe jolting. We went up after the He's but they were not having any and soon out-distanced our Hudsons. We did one more return trip and on leaving Dunkirk once more, we sighted to the south an object on the water, and on going to investigate found it was a large ship's lifeboat, with about ninety men aboard. The engine had evidently broken down, and having no oars they were just drifting. As the boat was about eight miles away from any other shipping, Sheahan signalled Selley to remain behind while he and Jouault went for help. Selley took advantage to carry out some of his spectacular flying for the benefit of the troops in the lifeboat. As we flew over them at a height scarcely above the sides of the boat, I could see the troops waving their caps furiously at us.

It was while we were thus engaged that three Ju88's were seen approaching at about 3,000 feet. It seemed that they were making for the lifeboat, so Selley told me to get ready as he was going to head them off. As we turned towards them, however, they swung away and though we chased them we were not able to close the range, which was too large for firing. As Selley broke off the chase, I caught sight of two Me109's flying about 5,000 feet above the 88's and I drew Selley's attention to them and we were none too happy, expecting them to come at us at any moment but they went their way. Sheahan and Jouault had, in the meantime, managed to divert a tug to take the lifeboat in tow and we could see the tug in the distance. After an hour the lifeboat was in tow behind the tug, which was already towing two barges and we escorted the 'train' back to the line of ships. As our time of patrol had long since expired we set course for our base and landed safely. An examination of our aircraft showed the wings to be badly buckled and wrinkled, and it was handed over for repairs. Our combat with the 87's had already been radioed to base and our CO and the Station Commander were there to hear the story. A bottle of whisky was brought out and while we made our report a toast to 'many more jerries' was drunk! In passing I must give due credit to the pilots of that squadron of 87's with which Selley and I were involved. The combat lasted for nearly a quarter hour, and during that time we were putting one machine after another out of action, and yet the pilots of the remaining 87's carried out their bombing attacks for a considerable period before breaking off.

That evening over a glass of beer, we were told that Selley, Jouault and I had been recommended for an immediate award of the DFC! I could hardly believe my ears and gulped my mouthful of beer to cover my surprise, though delighted.

Flying Officer H.A. Haarhof, 220 Squadron

The final actions of this first day of June came well after 6 p.m. 111 and 151 Squadrons flew a patrol beginning at six but poor visibility hindered them and they saw nothing. At 6.15, 17 and 609 Squadrons headed over to find three Ju88's in a Vic at 7,000 feet about to dive bomb shipping some two miles out to sea. Yellow Section of 17 Squadron climbed up from 6,000 feet but were unable to close and their long-distance firing caused no visible harm. Nevertheless the Germans' return crossfire hit Pilot Officer Ken Manger's Hurricane and he went down leaving a trail of white glycol smoke before going into cloud.

Squadron Leader Emms followed through the cloud and later saw what he believed was Manger's machine on the beach. However, Manger had baled out, splashed down into the sea and was rescued by a French vessel before being transferred to a British troop ship. He was back with the squadron the next day.

The squadron having completed some twelve patrol missions over Dunkirk, and achieved some successes and a few casualties, it was a great surprise and somewhat annoying to hear from the returning BEF Army, 'Where the hell was the RAF?' and 'Why weren't they there to protect them from the bombs on the beachhead?' The RAF could understand the bad feelings, particularly when the pilots had witnessed the appalling congestion on the beaches at Dunkirk. Continuous aerial combats were taking place all around and many miles from the beaches, thus greatly reducing the number of attacks on the endless queues of troops waiting to get on board ships. It was hard for the Army to understand and bad blood between the Services remained for a long time thereafter. The experience that Pilot Officer Manger had after he was shot down from the crossfire of three Junkers 88's over Dunkirk brought the matter to our attention on 2nd June. He parachuted onto the beach area and gradually made his way to the front of the soldiers queue to get on board a destroyer. An Army officer in charge of boarding very rudely informed Manger that all boats were for the Army and not for the RAF and refused to allow him to pass. Manger being an amateur boxer took a good swipe, scored and sent the Army officer into the sea, whereupon Manger calmly stepped on board. Next day at dawn Manger was once again flying in protection of the Army over Dunkirk!

Pilot Officer H.A.C. Bird-Wilson, 17 Squadron

The Spitfires of 609 Squadron also flying in difficult weather – it was 9/10th cloud at 8,000 feet – found three Heinkels which were attacked and damaged by Flying Officers Frankie Howell (N3024) and John Dundas (L1096). Number Three in this section, Flying Officer J. Dawson, also waded in but failed to see some covering Me110's coming down behind them. Some Very lights were fired as a warning, possibly by the Navy way below and Howell and Dundas broke away. Dawson did not and was shot down.

At 7.40 p.m. 72 Squadron flew their first offensive patrol to Dunkirk, in company with a four-man top cover from 64 Squadron. The sixteen aircraft set course from Deal where they had made rendezvous at 8.05, arriving over Dunkirk to find 10/10ths cloud. Squadron Leader R.B. Lees (P9458) saw fires on the ground through breaks in the cloud and judged he was over the harbour. They patrolled for fifteen minutes above the cloud then descended through it, losing Yellow Section in the process. Coming out at 3,000 feet five miles to the east of Dunkirk, the Spitfires were greeted with AA fire. A few minutes later one of Ronnie Lees' pilots dived over the top of his aircraft and he also heard something indistinguishable over the RT. Thinking they were either under attack or the other pilot had seen a hostile aeroplane, the squadron followed him up into the clouds and became split up, and so later they returned to base.

The final air action of the day fell to a Hudson crew of 206 Squadron operating from Detling. Three Hudsons were out on similar duties to 220 Squadron and at 8.15 p.m. they saw some Fleet Air Arm Skua aircraft being engaged by nine Me109's. The Hudsons flew to the rescue, split up the Messerschmitts and several hits were claimed on them. At least two were seen to go down into the sea and the others turned and fled. Flight Lieutenant William H. Biddell led the Hudson trio (in N7251) and was awarded the DFC for his action, his air gunner, LAC Walter Caulfield, receiving the DFM.

*

This ended the first June day over Dunkirk. Seventeen fighter pilots had been shot down but five got back, one being wounded. More than fifty German aircraft had been claimed destroyed with nearly forty more possibles.[1] From Dunkirk over 64,000 troops had been picked up, bringing the total since 27th May to just under 260,000.

The serious side, however, was that the RAF had been unable to contain the Luftwaffe attacks with the means at its disposal. Serious losses in ships had occurred and the troop embarkation had been continually interrupted. The cross-Channel sea route had also been heavily attacked, not only by German aircraft but by heavy and accurate artillery fire from the shore.

It was clear that the evacuation that had now lasted officially for six days and nights must soon be stopped. The cost of saving men in France was rapidly reaching too high a price in ships, sailors and airmen not to mention aircraft, aircraft that would soon be needed to defend Britain. The orders for the end of Dynamo were decided upon, then issued.

---

[1] Officially the enemy aircraft destroyed figure was seventy-six; the Luftwaffe records the loss of twenty-nine, (ten fighters plus nineteen bombers) with a further thirteen aircraft seriously damaged.

CHAPTER TEN

Sunday, 2nd June 1940

Evacuation of troops continued throughout the night of 1st-2nd June. Considerable doubt existed concerning the exact total of British soldiers still to be off-lifted from Dunkirk; a figure of 2,000 plus some 4,000 men of the rear-guard was estimated. In contrast the numbers of French soldiers seemed to be increasing from 25,000 on the evening of 1st June to anything between 50,000 and 60,000 by the 2nd.

The dawn patrols were off at first light – a regular feature now for the British fighter pilots. Home-based units went to their dispersal areas, others flew from bases further away to refuel in readiness for operations. The Tangmere squadrons flew up to their forward base.

> We were operating over the Pas de Calais each day and it was necessary to fly from Tangmere up to either Hawkinge or Manston at first light to refuel so as to get the maximum time over the patrol area.
>
> Each day started the same with the batman bringing in a cup of tea while it was still dark and I would have five minutes to think about the day to come and used to pray just that I could have a cup of tea again the next morning – I thought no further than that. I remember one particular morning when the three squadrons, 43, 145 and 601, took off together in formation and I happened to be Green Three which put me right on the very outside of the thirty-six Hurricanes. All the aeroplanes started to move together and it's a picture that I will never forget, the Hurricanes lifting off together in the dawn's early light and flying along the English coast.
>
> *Pilot Officer J.E. Storrar, 145 Squadron*

These first patrols found no hostile aeroplanes and it was not until way past eight o'clock that the first clashes came. It was a warm cloudless morning with good visibility. There were several squadrons airborne between 7.15 and 9 a.m. and quite suddenly the air was full of aircraft in what was to prove virtually the final air actions of the campaign.

No 92 Squadron, who had been out of the battle since 29th May, returned to Martlesham from Northolt and became part of a wing show to the Calais-Dunkirk area. Other units in the wing were 32, 611 and 266, the latter flying its first war sorties. 32 was top cover (23,000 feet), 66 below, 611 below them plus 92 the lowest at 14,000 feet.

> We were over Dunkirk on the second last day of the evacuation with more than our squadron. We went over in layers between 15,000 and 25,000 feet. Our squadron led the armada. We disobeyed our orders and came down to 9,000 feet where we ran into thirty He111's which we drove back, destroying about eighteen of them. However, below us the dive bombers were operating the whole time.
>
> *Pilot Officer A.C. Bartley, 92 Squadron*

It was just on eight o'clock. Bob Tuck was leading the squadron and saw three Heinkels below to his left, then six more came into view to the right. Tuck led Blue Section down, his attack producing a stream of oil from the right-hand machine. His Number Two, Pilot Officer Bob Holland, also damaged a Heinkel but Blue Three, Pilot Officer Alan Wright, looking back, saw Me109's coming down and warned the others.

The first 109 put some bullets through Tuck's tail and fuselage as he began the break. He pulled round even harder and the 109 pilot shot past his Hurricane, allowing Tuck to get behind him. Waiting until the German pulled out of his dive, Tuck got right in behind it and fired. Fifty rounds slammed into the Messerschmitt from point blank range and it exploded.

Bob Holland had thought initially that the 109's were Spitfires and it was not until he formated on them that he realised his mistake. He fired a five-second burst into the last one and it went down in flames. Three others then turned on him so he dived into some cloud. Alan Wright zig-zagged downwards, after another 109, setting its engine on fire when just 1,000 feet above the ground. As he was about to watch it hit there was a crash behind him as another 109 got on his tail and put sixteen holes in his Spitfire. Out of ammunition, Wright dog-fought the 109 pretending to be dangerous until he shook it off.

Squadron Leader P.J. Sanders, soon to take full command of the squadron, saw Tuck's section engage the Heinkels, then led his Green Section down, knocking large bits and pieces off two of them despite attempts by Me109's to intervene. Yellow Section's leader, Pilot Officer H.D. Edwards, also engaged a group of six Heinkels, followed by six more. He called his section into line astern, but they failed to hear him and so he went into attack three bombers on his own. He singled out one, and his first burst caused flames to shoot out from the Heinkel's port motor. It went down staining the sky with a long black smoke trail and went into a thin layer of cloud. Edwards then found himself above three Heinkels, their gunners firing up at him. He was about to half roll onto them when 109's came down on him from the bright morning sun and he had to fight his way out of trouble.

Bob Tuck, meanwhile, having flown through the cloud, found a Heinkel right below him. He gave it three three-second bursts and one engine exploded in flames. The bomber spiralled down, its crew taking to their parachutes before it crashed inland from Dunkirk. Again 109's pounced on him but he out-fought them, damaging two of their number.

Leading Red Section was Flight Lieutenant Brian Kingcome who also dived onto the Heinkels, but seeing two other sections tackling them, winged over to the right as three more bombers flew below him. His wing-over was so quick that he temporarily lost his wingmen but hammered his eight guns at the right-hand Heinkel and it fell away with flames coming from its port engine, smoke issuing from the other and its wheels dropped. The air was laced with return fire from all three bombers and then oil covered his Spitfire from the crippled one as it went into cloud.

As his two Section men closed up with him, Kingcome led an attack upon another Vic of bombers. All three were liberally sprayed with .303 rounds by the Spitfires and all three went into the clouds with burning engines and shattered hydraulics.

Yellow Two, Tony Bartley, was also well in amongst the Heinkels, although the Section had been strung out when Edwards began his first attack. Closing in on a Heinkel, Bartley saw that its port motor seemed already on fire, and his attack set the other burning. He then slid in behind another bomber and fired two or three bursts, and both motors caught fire and its undercarriage too fell down. Having throttled right back, Bartley, with his speed down to that of the Heinkels, was able to shift his aim to the third Heinkel in the Vic and again his fire produced smoke, flames and dropped wheels. The latter two Heinkels began to go down but by this time Bartley had lost the rest of the squadron.

A few minutes later he spotted five Heinkels flying to the east away from the sea. Again throttling back to their speed, he shot up two of them who also began to go down on fire. Another pass on two more bombers produced no visible results but one of their gunners put two bullets into his Spitfire. He made one last pass on yet another Heinkel but again he saw no result.

In his prolonged action, Tony Bartley had shot up at least five Heinkels, all having gone down with burning engines and some with wheels hanging down. How many of these failed to get home is unknown but they knew they had been in a fight.

The squadron diary noted fourteen bombers and four 109's shot down for no loss. The RAF credited them with eleven He111's and two 109's confirmed plus six Heinkels and a 109 probably destroyed.

The other two squadrons were not so fortunate, both sustaining losses. They were heavily engaged with the Heinkels' fighter escort, Me109's and Me110's.

Squadron Leader J.W.A. Hunnard (P9333) had led his 266 Squadron down from Wittering to Martlesham at dawn, and when the wing flew out they took a slot at 22,000 feet. While 92 Squadron were tackling the Heinkels at a lower altitude, 266 flew serenely on for another twenty-five minutes, unaware of the battle below the clouds. Yellow Section became separated from the patrol and then Red Three was lost in a turn which reduced the squadron down to eight aircraft.

As the end of the patrol time approached and Hunnard was about to turn for home (it was 8.31 a.m. and 32 Squadron at 24,000 feet above had already turned towards England) 266 were bounced from above by two Me109's. Squadron Leader John 'Daddy' Hunnard (he was thirty-three years old) saw tracer shells zip over his hood and as his Number Two turned to engage, Hunnard himself went into a quick climb, then stall-turned behind the other Messerschmitt. He fired two three-second bursts and the 109 dived vertically.

Pilot Officer Nigel Bowen, the Number Two, had been hit in the 109's first attack, cannon fire damaging his wings, starboard exhaust stubs and the magneto leads. However, he went after the 109 as it flew by and two long bursts caused smoke to pour from its engine. As it went into a spiral dive, Bowen had to pull up as the other 109, being attacked by his commanding officer, flew across in front of him. Pilot Officer A.W. Cole saw three Me109's above and as they attacked he weaved and broke away having first fired a quick burst in their direction. He then met one of the Messerschmitts head-on, both pilots firing, both missing. They both broke to the right and Cole dived, only to find the 109 on his tail. Twisting and turning Cole eventually hauled round onto the 109's tail, fired a five-second burst and the 109 rolled onto its back and dived towards the sea.

The other section, led by Flight Lieutenant James Coward, saw one of Hunnard's section shot down by the 109 that Cole shot down. He then saw another 109 behind another Spitfire and Coward attacked. A six-second burst and the 109 dived into cloud on its back at an estimated speed of over 400 miles per hour.

Meanwhile, the separated Yellow Section found some Me110's in a circle and engaged. Two pilots, Flying Officer N.W. Burnett and Pilot

Officer R.M. Trousdate, a New Zealander, both scored hits on separate 110's, Norman Burnett claiming a damaged, Dick Trousdale a probable. 266's losses were Pilot Officer J.W.B. Stevenson and Sergeant R.T. Kidman[1] missing, while Spitfire N3169 was damaged on landing, its pilot Pilot Officer N.G. Bowen being uninjured. On the credit side, 266 were credited with one 110 destroyed (sic) and six 109's possibly destroyed.

Baron Worrall's 32 Squadron, as already mentioned, had turned for home shortly before 266. Somehow they had lost two pilots, Sergeant Flynn and Pilot Officer R.F. Smythe. Smythe, however, had merely become separated and to add to his problem his radio had packed up. As he descended through the cloud he found a Ju88 and attacked. Two bursts forced it down on its back and it was credited as destroyed. Regaining height he then ran into six Me109's, fired at one and saw no result although RAF records credit a possible. He landed back at Biggin Hill late, victorious but safe.

> You may find it difficult to believe but 32's interceptions and fights with the Luftwaffe were few over Dunkirk. This was because we flew as top cover to other squadrons doing their best at lower levels and low over and around the beaches. For example: squadron patrols over St Omer-Dunkirk-Boulogne on 24th and 25th May, one was at 23,000 and 3 at 18,000 feet; on 2nd June squadron patrol at 23,000 feet over Dunkirk; on 3rd June squadron patrol at 18,000 feet Abbeville-Amiens-Péronne. Each time we left the English coast whether on fighter patrols or on bomber escort duty each of us expected combat and would have welcomed it. We always wondered if we would see England again, but I do not remember ever feeling scared. However, 32 had been well trained and was a team which had the good fortune to suffer comparatively few casualties.
>
> *Squadron Leader J. Worrall, 32 Squadron*

Squadron Leader J.E. McComb led 611 Squadron from Digby to Martlesham soon after dawn having been ordered into the battle zone at 1 a.m. Apart from a brief patrol on 28th May, 611 had remained at Digby and not been further involved in the Dunkirk operation.

When the bombers had appeared and 92 Squadron engaged, 611 were almost immediately in action with the fighter escort, thereby allowing 92 an initial Messerschmitt-free attack. The squadron had been flying above the coastline, above the edge of the cloud layer which stretched inland but not over the sea. The 109's were seen flying on a similar course just below the cloud level.

[1] Sergeant Kidman, 26, from Cambridge was buried in Dunkirk Town cemetery.

Leading Red Section, James McComb saw two Me109's approaching from his right, firing their cannons. He turned the squadron into the attack but the 109's turned away. McComb pulled after them and fired at the rear machine with a five-second burst. Petrol streamed from the left side of the fuselage, right behind the pilot as it disappeared in a left-hand spiral dive.

Becoming separated from the others, McComb then saw five He111's and seeing no sign of any sort of escort, attacked the leader. He fired into the bomber but then found a Me110 on his tail. McComb half-rolled, tried a tight turn to get behind the Messerschmitt but finished up in a spin. Falling away he found his tailplane completely stalled and thought his controls had been hit but he eventually regained control at 2,000 feet. Looking up, he could now only see four Heinkels.

> I remember the first enemy aircraft I saw was an Me109 which flew across my bows and I was so surprised I forgot to press the firing button. I remember after spending some time getting an Me109 off my tail and losing a lot of height in doing so, I looked around for anything that had not got a black cross on it and way up above was a Spitfire up to which I climbed and found Flight Lieutenant Jack Leather, my second-in-command. Jack always flew with his hood open; said he could get out quicker that way! As I closed with him and saw his red grinning face, he called me up with 'Kee-rist this is dangerous' and roared with laughter.
>
> *Squadron Leader J.E. McComb, 611 Squadron*

Jack Leather (N3054) had just been in action with a 109 which he had seen attacking a Spitfire thought to be the one flown by Flying Officer Don Little. The Spitfire began to go down in a gentle spin with white smoke – probably glycol – streaming from its engine. Leather got in a five-second burst from 50 yards and the 109 slowly turned over and whipped into a spin. He was then attacked by another 109 which put six holes in his machine and did not see his 109 again.

Another Spitfire, flown by Pilot Officer C. Jones (N3050), was also hit as he went after a 109 attacking a Spitfire. The 109 broke away and down into cloud, Jones following still firing. The German pilot appeared to be trying to abandon his aeroplane but then bullet holes began to appear in his left wing and he had to evade rapidly. Flying Officer D.H. Watkins found two 109's behind him, pulled the 'plug' and climbed away into the sun. Upon turning, he saw the 109's crossing his path 300 feet below, flying in line astern and 200 yards apart. Watkins went down on the rear machine, and fired from 200 yards. Bits of the 109's left wing broke off, the machine shuddered violently, climbed, then dived vertically out of sight.

Pilot Officer M.P. Brown (N3056) was also battling with 109s, being followed down by one while his engine was coughing and spluttering. At low level over the beach and in the smoke, his engine picked up but the 109 was still with him so he too opened the boost cut-out and pulled away. Climbing back to 10,000 feet he saw two groups of Stukas but with a rough engine and a damaged Spitfire, decided to retire. His Spitfire had been hit in the wing, rudder, fin and fuselage and port tyre, but he got it down safely at Southend.

Flying Officer Barrie Heath also found the Stukas, coming down on the tail of one of the leaders, giving it a ten second burst which knocked out the rear gunner. The Stuka shuddered, turned over and fell towards the sea. He then attacked another which was diving on a ship. Hits blasted the Stuka's fuselage before Heath ran out of ammunition and broke away, having had his radio mast hit by return fire.

> Dunkirk was seen from miles away by a huge column of black smoke going up to over 30,000 feet. We did two tours at 24,000 feet along the beach and then we saw a large formation of Ju87s below us. At that moment we turned and Sergeant Sadler missed the turn, so I went out to bring him back and one of my colleagues told me later that as I broke away an Me110 took my place which was lucky for me. We shot down a number of Ju87s, but of course the whole squadron had split up. I got mine and my hand was shaking so much that I went on firing into the sea as I was pulling out of my dive.
>
> *Flying Officer B. Heath, 611 Squadron*

Flight Sergeant Sadler saw the battle with the Stukas and Spitfires but was then attacked by a 109. Evading this he saw six Me110s in a circle above some Spitfires. He attacked and saw one 110 go down out of control.

> I recall that one way of getting a Hun off your tail was to dive into the thick black column of smoke over Dunkirk, do one and a half turns inside it and squirt out the other side. I recall Pilot Officer 'Sneezey' Brown adding to the end of his combat report, which described how he had been chased half round France by an Me109, and getting rid of it by diving under a gantry on the dockside, that 'he did not feel that he had done much to raise the morale of the BEF'. Another occasion was when I saw above me a Spitfire (it turned out to be Flight Sergeant Sadler) dive into five circling Me110's and then get trapped in the circle. They could out-dive him but he could just turn inside them so that their

shells and bullets just went under his tail. Each time they fired and missed, Sadler leaned out of his cockpit and made a vulgar gesture with two fingers.

Squadron Leader J.E. McComb, 611 Squadron

The squadron was inflicting damage but also getting hit in return. Pilot Officer D.A. Adams (N3066), Number Two to Flying Officer R.K. Crompton, followed his leader down on two 109's but a 109 slid in behind Crompton and fired. Crompton pulled to the right but then Adams lost sight of him in the tussle. Adams then saw four Ju87's in a box formation just above. He shot at one and it fell in a smoking dive, then left a trail of flame. Cross-fire from the other Stukas hit his machine twice and then two 109's attacked. He fought these, and even got in a shot at one but saw no result. The other flight commander, Flight Lieutenant K.M. Stoddart (N3058) was attacked by 109's, shot up and dived clear but managed to get back. Hit by cannon shells just behind him, a hole was torn in one side of the fuselage which blew off the cockpit canopy and left the other side like a sieve. The armour plating, only recently fitted to the Spitfire, was splintered at the back with bullet and shrapnel marks. His control wires had been damaged, some holding together by just two strands.

> Being shot up was a case of inexperience and bad recognition. I was separated from the squadron and went to join up with a friendly looking aircraft which appeared from nowhere and was in fact a 109! Not a very glorious first sighting of a German aircraft!
>
> *Flight Lieutenant K.M. Stoddart, 611 Squadron*

We landed back at base where we were given a champagne breakfast after which we had the unpleasant task of sorting out who was missing, which turned out to be Donald Little and Ken Crompton, both Auxiliaries and important members of the squadron.

We went again a few times after that but without major engagement as we were instructed to keep top cover and leave the Hurricanes to mix in with the German Air Force.

Flying Officer B. Heath, 611 Squadron

On the day those close friends were killed we had laid on a drinks party for wives, in the Mess before lunch. We were ordered to Dunkirk and one of my chaps said, 'Shall we cancel the party?' I told him that if he could keep a Spit in the air for those hours he was a smart pilot and anyway we could not have Hitler interfering with our drinking habits.

As we were about to take off, Donald Little leapt onto my wing and said, 'Feed my dog tonight'. I bawled at him to get back into his cockpit and only after we were airborne did it occur to me that he could feed his dog himself but there was 'radio silence' so said nothing. Little and Crompton with their 19-year-old brides shared one half of a cottage in Wellingore near Digby whilst my wife together with Barrie Heath (now Sir Barrie) and his wife shared the other half. That morning we ran into a cloud of Messerschmitts and got into all sorts of trouble and lost these two young pilots. We arrived back in ones and twos over a period of time, some having to land and refuel. Meantime the party had started, broken with a cheer as someone else turned up. Came the time when Lel Crompton realised with June Little that no more were coming back. Without a tear or a word they quietly slipped out of the ante-room and went back to the cottage.

Squadron Leader J.E. McComb, 611 Squadron

The squadron had been in a real scrap and was credited with two Ju87's destroyed, one Stuka, one Me109 and one Me110 as probables. The other confirmed Stuka was shot down by Pilot Officer C.H. MacFie. He was Green Three to Ralph Crompton and lost both him and Adams when they went down on the 109's. Seeing AA fire out to sea, he then saw six Ju87's with a single Me109 above. He attacked the highest Stuka which broke and dived. MacFie chased it through the smoke over Dunkirk, found it on the other side going down on shipping off the harbour. As the German pilot pulled out of his dive MacFie got in a long burst and its nose dropped, then it hit the sea and broke up. It was then he saw a Spitfire spinning down without a tail, thought to be Crompton's aeroplane. It crashed on the beach.

The Spitfire pilots of 66 Squadron fared no better than 611. Early in the day they flew from Duxford to Martlesham Heath, taking off at 7.00 a.m. to fly over Dunkirk.

They arrived on station at 7.45 patrolling at 27,000 feet but found no sign of enemy aircraft at this height. At 8.30 Squadron Leader Rupert Leigh observed a formation of Ju88's and dived with his section in line astern. As Leigh was about to open fire he saw three Spitfires attack individually. The next moment the air seemed full of Me109's and Me 110's. Leigh loosed off a long range shot at a 109 then felt a bang followed by a smell of petrol. He pulled his Spitfire into a very sharp turn, lost control and spun. Regaining control at 3,000 feet he saw several 109's above him so flew into cloud and set a course for home, landing at Debden at 9.15.

Others managed to get in amongst the Ju88's and undoubtedly the Spitfires Leigh had seen were other sections of his squadron. Flight Lieutenant Ken Gillies saw the 88's – five in number – way below at 11,000 feet. He dived with his Red Section, while Flight Lieutenant H.F. Burton, Green Leader also dived. The 88's held their formation well and on breaking away from his pass, Gillies saw he was near other bombers and their 109 escort. He shared his ammunition out amongst them but when his guns were empty was forced to dog-fight his way out of trouble.

Billy Burton found his windscreen icing up as he dived and when he broke away over Dunkirk found too that the air was full of aircraft. He attacked two 109's, then one of a Vic of He111's. The Heinkel began to lose height and start smoking. He was about to attack again when he spotted smoke coming from his engine and the temperature rising so broke off and flew home. Flying Officer E.W. Campbell-Colquhoun lost his leader in the fight but got in a deflection burst at a 109 from 100 yards, which shot away the Messerschmitt's windscreen.

Yellow Section, led by Flying Officer Reg Rimmer, also attacked the five Ju88's. As he closed in, he heard Sergeant F.N. Robertson, his Number Two, call out that he'd been hit. Looking back he could not see him. Later he too attacked some Heinkels, severely damaging one before lack of fuel forced him to return to England.

Sergeant Frederick Robertson's Spitfire was struck by cannon fire and he caught a machine-gun bullet in the leg. He had fired at one Ju88 and as he dived away saw the Junkers diving with smoke coming from both its engines. As Robertson levelled out his machine was hit again, this time by AA fire. The shell blew away the aileron of his right wing and then smashed into the cockpit, destroying the machine's controls. Robertson was left with no choice, and baled out, landing on the beach five miles west of Dunkirk but he succeeded in getting a boat – one of the last, to return to his squadron.

Two other pilots were shot down in this, 66's first real combat. Sergeant D.A.C. Hunt, like Robertson, took to his parachute, but Flight Sergeant M.W. Hayman was not so fortunate and was posted as missing.

*

With daylight evacuations now ended, there was a total lack of air activity following these early morning fighter actions. Only those ships still on their way back and near the English coast were still at sea.

Other than some Hudson and Anson patrols over the mid-Channel areas or off the Belgian coast, there was nothing flying until shortly after

6 p.m. Operation Dynamo was near its end and as the evening heralded the dark hours when the final flurry of the evacuation occurred, the RAF were out yet again. Seven squadrons flew patrols in the final three hours before darkness – three seeing action.

At 6.40 72 and 609 Squadrons took off, twelve from 72 but just five of 609. Following an inauspicious first war patrol the previous evening, 72 were looking for more constructive participation in the Dunkirk show.

The squadron's orders were to patrol Dunkirk and to provide air cover for a hospital ship off the harbour. One Spitfire of 609 aborted the mission, the rest flew on. Red Section of 72 Squadron flew at 10-12,000 feet, Yellow Section at the same levels but to seaward, while Blue worked in pairs forming a rear-guard one thousand feet above. The four machines of 609 flew top cover 4,000-5,000 feet above and behind 72. As can be seen, 72 were flying sections of four rather than the more usual threes.

At five minutes to seven o'clock, six Ju87's came into view and were attacked. 72 had now come down to 8,000 feet when the bombers were seen, a call from Red Two, Flying Officer O. St. J. Pigg, warning the others of their approach.

Squadron Leader Lees led Red Section down and to port. The Stukas were about four miles away, heading north – out to sea. He rocked his wings as an order to close up and ordering Yellow Section to guard the rear, Lees put the others into line astern.

Almost immediately, the Stukas attracted an AA barrage and the leading three Stukas began to peel off into their attacking dives. Lees attacked these first three Stukas ordering Yellow Section to engage the second three who were still flying straight and level. Two bursts from Lees and his victim went into a right-hand spiral. A third burst of six seconds from 75 yards set the 87 on fire and his Two and Three saw it crash. Flying Officer Pigg attacked the second 87 and it too crashed in flames. The third Stuka turned and came head-on towards Pigg, its pilot putting a burst into his Spitfire damaging its starboard wing, port aileron and air pressure system. He was also hit in the leg giving him a slight wound but it did not prevent him from making a successful wheels-up landing at Gravesend.

Red Three, Pilot Officer D.C. Winter, attacked this Stuka but overshot it. Suddenly there was another Stuka in his sights and he silenced the rear gunner as smoke came from the engine. It turned over but Winter lost sight of it at 200 feet. Number Four in the section, Sergeant B. Douthwaite, chased another Stuka twenty miles, before leaving it smoking heavily.

Yellow Section got one Ju87, Flying Officer T.A.F. Elsdon (K9940) hit his target which went down in a spiral until lost to view. Blue Two, Flying Officer E.J. Wilcox set another Stuka ablaze, and saw one of the crew bale out. He fired at another Junkers but overshot it although not before causing smoke to stream from it. By the time he had turned, the Stuka had disappeared in the smoke above Dunkirk.

The four covering Spitfires of 609 apparently kept any high-flying 109's away from the fight. Had the Luftwaffe pilots known who were in the Spitfires they might have acted differently. Flying Officer Peter Drummond-Hay led three novice pilots on this, their first patrol. They had originally been assigned as stooge patrol over the Thames estuary but this was changed at the last minute and only they were ready for action. Luckily they did not need to prove themselves on this occasion!

The other two squadrons to become engaged were 111 and 151 Squadrons. 151 flew high – 20,000 feet. They had flown over at 6.30 and by 8 p.m. had not seen a single sign of German aircraft. Above them flew 111 as top cover. At just after 8 p.m., Squadron Leader Thompson in front of his 111 pilots made out a Vic formation of German machines 2,000 feet below. Two sections of 151 went down at them while Thompson patrolled above keeping watch on a bunch of Me109's 4,000 feet above. Climbing up-sun towards them Thompson lost sight of the 109's but found a circle of Me110's below. Leading his men down, he gave out a burst but then his engine cut out and as his oxygen bottle gave out he had to reduce height.

Flight Lieutenant Peter Powell, climbing with his section after the 109's, reached 25,000 feet to find just one Me109. He attacked it and it fell away pouring out smoke from its fuselage. The others then went down on the 110's, Pilot Officer P.J. Simpson probably destroying one, Flight Lieutenant Connors hitting one on the tail of a Hurricane, then damaged a second one as well as silencing its rear gunner. Flying Officer D.C. Bruce damaged a 109 (P2886) while Pilot Officer R.R. Wilson destroyed another. Wilson had initially broken formation when his gravity tank ran dry. Switching tanks he saw a 109 coming up behind him and when evading found another ahead. Firing at it the 109 dived, leaving a trail of smoke, then he attacked a 110. Smoke came from its port engine but its rear gunner put a burst into his Hurricane. Two shells hit his port wing, two more hitting the cockpit. Smoke started to come from the engine but with six Me 110's closing in from behind he had rapidly to evade. Putting his fighter through a barrel-roll, then a steep turn, he shook them off, then headed for home. He almost made the English coast but finally the fumes became too much so he baled out. His Hurricane went into the sea but he floated down about a mile from Manston aerodrome.

The pilots of 151 Squadron, finding an empty sky suddenly full of aircraft, took part in some fierce fighting but the only certain kill went to Squadron Leader Donaldson who destroyed one Me110. Others were shot-up, the squadron being credited with one Me110 damaged plus a damaged Ju87.

*

These last battles on the evening on 2nd June were the last, officially, of Operation Dynamo. In the morning and evening dog-fights, more than twenty German aircraft had been claimed as destroyed, thirty as possibles or damaged. Eight RAF pilots had been shot down but two were safe. Another had baled out while another had crash-landed with a slight leg wound.

The evacuation of the British Expeditionary Force was completed on the evening of the 2nd. At 11.30 that night the Senior Naval Officer Dunkirk reported BEF evacuated. Hopes of picking up further French soldiers that night and in the early hours of 3rd June were dashed when ships arriving at the harbour and nearby beaches found no troops at all. Further attempts over the following two nights were more successful and brought back 28,000 men before the evacuation was finally terminated.

For the BEF, the Royal Navy and the Royal Air Force – the Dunkirk Evacuation was over.

> Our team was getting very weak and the only person who was enjoying himself was Tuck, who took over the command of the squadron. And then it was over, as suddenly as it had begun. The evacuation of Dunkirk had been completed. A decimated, bloody but unbowed squadron was pulled out of the front line to lick its wounds and reform its ranks. The first stage of my war had ended, and we were moved to Duxford.
>
> *Pilot Officer A.C. Bartley, 92 Squadron*

CHAPTER ELEVEN

The End

The BEF had escaped. Defeated it may have been and it had lost virtually all its equipment but it was safe. 338,226 Allied troops had been brought back, not bad when put against the 45,000 estimated when Dynamo was put in motion. The operation had also lasted nine days rather than an expected two. Although the whole episode might be termed a victory, wars are not won, as Winston Churchill pointed out, by evacuations.

Despite the army's belief that the RAF were mostly absent, it was very much in evidence, as the previous chapters show. However, when one is tired, hungry, wet, scared, being bombed and shot at it, it is natural to look for reasons why this might have been avoided. The man on the beach simply believed that if the RAF wanted to it could shoot down all the Stukas, Heinkels, Dorniers and Ju88's that were trying to kill him and see off all the Messerschmitts buzzing above his head. Life isn't that simple.

Britain's still limited Air Force had been badly mauled in and over France since 10th May (over France and for the period of the evacuation, an accepted figure of 432 Hurricanes and Spitfires had been 'expended' between 10th May and 4th June – or put another way, the equivalent of approximately twenty fighter squadrons). So as Dunkirk approached Dowding had been quite right to persuade Churchill to end the mammoth drain of his limited fighter force. He would not have been thanked if Britain's defensive element had been lost to no end in France when the Luftwaffe was finally unleashed against England in August 1940. Already under strength it would not have taken much to destroy Fighter Command's means to fight, defending or attacking. As we now appreciate to the full, his course of action was totally correct.

At Dunkirk one has to remember the Hun could concentrate in Time and Space; whereas we were on thin standing patrols at extreme range and scanty and confused radar. The C-in-C was concerned to husband his resources for the coming Battle of

Britain and he was absolutely right. We had no organised air defence systems over the Beach Head and any of ours shot down were lost and reserves were thin.

The great thing about Dunkirk was that it was successful. It would not have been if Hitler had got his priorities right, but he was obsessed with the capture of France and thus the whole of Europe. He failed to appreciate the effect of Britain being left in one piece could have on his final strategy.

Wing Commander H. Broadhurst,
Station Commander, Wittering

One could of course argue that defence of Britain might have started with Fighter Command being ordered to attack constantly the Luftwaffe in France. This, however, like so many arguments, is fine when actions are looked at in retrospect. At the time, it is easy to see how Dowding and Air Ministry were reluctant to pursue a more aggressive policy at Dunkirk. It is true to say that Fighter Command could have been more aggressive on paper, but the war in the air was still in its early WW2 days in May 1940.

Nevertheless, Dowding needed to give full support to the evacuation of the BEF and he gave all he felt he could. Although he was charged to provide a continuous air umbrella over the evacuation, this was impossible to achieve. With only a daily average of sixteen squadrons – many untried and many under operational strengths, this fighter force had no chance of filling the sky with fighter aircraft. As each hour of the evacuation passed the serviceability rate declined.

Keith Park tried to speed up the replacement rate/time of Hurricanes and Spitfires. The time taken to obtain a replacement varied from 24 to 48 hours due to the somewhat cumbersome procedure that had to be adopted. Park suggested to 'higher authority' that during the crisis, squadrons should merely inform No 41 Maintenance Group direct of their requirements, forwarding copies of their demands by signal. This recommendation was not adopted for administrative reasons – resulting in the continuance of the delays. When aircraft replacements were received on the squadrons, their guns had not been harmonised and they had items of equipment tied in parcels hanging up inside the airframe. This, of course, delayed still further the time it took to get the replacement machines operational.

The Royal Air Force had to operate at long range from their English bases, something not envisaged in Britain's defensive policy. Often they had to fly and fight over unknown territory and under heavy anti-aircraft fire – both hostile and 'friendly'! Many damaged aircraft were forced to ditch in the Channel when trying to return to England.

All our sorties were in some way tests in economical engine
handling and on the longer ones there was not much fuel left on
landing. At least two didn't make it, one force landed at Manston
and another, wheels up, somewhere between the coast and
Hornchurch.

Pilot Officer E.A. Shipman, 41 Squadron

Casualties in Hurricane Squadrons were the heaviest because they were
the longest in the battles, and prior to the beginning of Dynamo were the
only fighter squadrons to operate inland over the French and Belgian
coast. The Spitfire units, despite flying on occasions up to four patrols
a day during critical periods, were ordered not to fly over the hostile
coast although several pilots, in the heat of combat, did chase German
aircraft inland over France.

On many occasions the number of trained pilots in Hurricane
squadrons fell below nine men and remnants of two squadrons had to be
employed together to make up a squadron formation.

There were times when you were down in numbers and didn't
have your full twelve aircraft, partly because of losses, partly
because some were on maintenance or unserviceable. There were
occasions when we'd be down to eight or nine aircraft, so we
then made the number up with another squadron who were in a
similar position.

Pilot Officer P.L. Parrott, 145 Squadron

Frequently aircraft needed repair after being shot up which might
take days. Allocation of replacement aircraft took a day or two
and they needed careful inspection to ensure everything ticked
before flying in combat – guns tested, sights harmonised, R/T
correctly crystalised and so on.

Also, there were aircraft available but pilots had been
wounded. Newly arrived pilots lacked experience and were given
further training on the squadron before being flown operationally.

In both of these instances it was necessary to make up to ten
or twelve aircraft by pooling resources – ergo composite
squadrons.

Squadron Leader J. Worrall, 32 Squadron

At the beginning of the Blitz in France when all squadrons were below
their paper establishment of pilots, Air Ministry withdrew batches of
pilots from 11 Group squadrons to replace wastage in Hurricane
Squadrons in France. Replacements could not be obtained from
operational training units, so Air Ministry posted pilots into 11 Group
from flying training schools. These, however, remained non-operational

as they had not yet even flown front line operational aeroplanes. The squadrons themselves had not the time to spare to train these replacements as all these pilots were fully occupied over Dunkirk. The state of affairs forced the operational nucleus of the squadrons to tire more quickly as the pilots were unable to take a day off to rest. This resulted in the total squadron becoming fatigued very quickly. When these squadrons had finally to be pulled out of the front line, they were replaced by the more recently raised squadrons who suffered heavy casualties owing to the relative inexperience of their leaders. It should be remembered, however, that up until 10th May, practically all squadron and flight commanders were operationally inexperienced. As Keith Park reported, if his squadrons had been kept up to establishment in the first place, it would not have been necessary to keep withdrawing units from the line just as they were becoming proficient in air fighting.

Park had a total of thirty-one squadrons through his Group for Dunkirk, the average being sixteen for any one day. At first Air Ministry ordered 'weak' fighter patrols to be flown throughout the eighteen hours of daylight. As Park forecast, this resulted in heavy casualties due to the superiority in numbers of the Luftwaffe. 11 Group, after strong representation to Air Ministry, was permitted to fly patrols of two, three or more squadron strength. Even so it appears at times that 11 Group put up a number of squadrons at a specific time but they were not always totally aware that they were part of one major patrol or wing. Even then it was too new a tactic to be used successfully. There had been no pre-war training in any kind of 'wing' formation flying, especially in conditions of cloud. As mentioned in earlier chapters, it was unpopular due to a lack of continuity of aircraft, leaders and because there was no inter Squadron radio links. The squadrons over Dunkirk were out of radar and radio control from England.

> The first thing I remember about the move south to Hornchurch was that we had some hurried alterations, retrograde we thought, made to our radios in order to fit communications with other squadrons at Hornchurch. We were unhappy about it and we found the communications with Hornchurch when over the Channel quite nil as I remember. Certainly it was impossible to co-ordinate with other squadrons. We were usually high cover with the Hurricanes well below on low cover.
>
> At first, we operated as a squadron but towards the end were to fly as wing, meeting another squadron over the Channel – I don't remember seeing them or even hearing from them. We were usually above cloud although on several occasions we could see what was going on below – the thick black smoke from the oil

tank fires drifting in a long plume south-westerly across the Channel, and also the confusion of shipping, of course.

Robin Hood, our CO who could be most forthright in his comments was heard to say on the RT when we couldn't contact control or other squadrons' 'What a bloody f – up. Nothing but shit and corruption!' and how very true!

Pilot Officer E.A. Shipman, 41 Squadron

Peter Parrott recalls the feeling that as fighter pilots they wanted to be independent and that wings were too unwieldy and they would get in each other's way in a fight. Fighting wings would come later in the war but at Dunkirk it was all too new to contemplate or to have even the time to contemplate it.

Although we flew over in a wing, formation flying of any sort was out once we arrived over Dunkirk. Except on one or two occasions the sky seemed full of German aircraft and we were quickly split up. In a short space of time it was everyone for himself. Within minutes we'd done our business and then it was a case of getting back for more fuel and more ammunition and get ready to go back again. Most of our fighting was either inland or out to sea so little wonder that the Army said they never saw us. Also the amount of AA fire the Navy was shooting up at us, kept us at a high altitude!

Flight Sergeant G.C. Unwin, 19 Squadron

Again, when any sort of wing reached the battle area, the leader, to cover the maximum area, would split up his force, some being engaged with the Luftwaffe, others seeing no sign of the enemy.

This is the true story as I saw it over Dunkirk and Calais. Fighter Command were at first disinclined to send the Spitfires out of England at all. We are primarily home defence. Anyhow we went, and at first, just as single squadrons (12 Spitfires). You have had my accounts of how we used to run into fifty and sixty German machines every time we went over there, and fought them until our ammunition ran out. While this battle was going on up at 10,000 feet, the dive bombers which did the chief damage, were playing havoc down below us. The fact was that they had layers of bombers and fighters, with which twelve Spitfires had to cope.[1]

Pilot Officer A.C. Bartley, 92 Squadron

[1] From a letter by Bartley to his father, June 1940.

As a direct result of employing from two to four squadrons at a time with the limited squadron resources available, there had to be gaps in the RAF's air umbrella. The higher numbers eased combat losses and achieved a higher success ratio but added to the army's feeling that the RAF were absent – which for periods it was. It was apparent from RAF pilots who were themselves in Dunkirk trying to get back to England, that bombers seemed to appear when the RAF left. It would seem logical to suppose that the Germans would have had air observers behind Dunkirk who would at such moments be able to call-up their aircraft to come into the battle zone. As the Luftwaffe rapidly took over recently evacuated French and Belgian airfields, it was able to put more sorties over Dunkirk and its aircraft could be turned around more quickly. Another factor was the cloud layers which hid either high or low flying German aircraft, not to mention the constant layers of smoke. Again pilots in Dunkirk reported seeing RAF fighters on patrol above cloud while the Luftwaffe were bombing from below cloud. It was also a fact that the army and the navy fired at practically all aircraft on a 'shoot first' basis. This would help perpetuate the myth that all the aircraft were German so where were the RAF!

One lesson which appears to have been remembered by the RAF from World War I was that the men who have the height control the battle. Yet at Dunkirk, patrols flown a little lower would have engaged a more low-flying enemy whose targets were troops and ships. Nevertheless, the fighter pilot's natural tendency is to fly higher than his enemy.

> What Dunkirk did for air fighting was that it moved the fighting, which we had always thought we would do from around 7,000 to 10,000 feet, straight to over 20,000 feet in about four days. For every time we went over we said, right we must be higher than they are so we'd go up another 4,000 feet and when we got there they would be about 2,000 feet above us. In no time at all air fighting changed from the traditional pattern where one could see the ground to right on top where you couldn't see it at all. This is one of the reasons I'm sure the Army has often said, 'Where are these fighter pilots?' They were there all right but they couldn't see them.
>
> *Pilot Officer H.M. Stephen, 74 Squadron*

Tactics were another factor at Dunkirk. For years the RAF had been trained in certain 'by the book' flight formations and fighter attacks. It was hard to change overnight and like all war preparations, everyone thinks they've got it right until it's proved otherwise. For the RAF at Dunkirk and even later during the Battle of Britain, old tactics proved costly – and deadly!

The set flying formation was four Vic sections of three aeroplanes to make up a basic squadron patrol of twelve aeroplanes. It was quickly established that it was too inflexible and the two wingmen had to spend much of their time keeping station with the section leader. Some squadrons quickly adapted to three sections of four which could subdivide into pairs when action was joined. Oddly enough either the word did not penetrate down to all squadrons or else these other squadrons did not agree the new formation was better.

> It was a measure of the discipline which existed among the pilots in a way. Flying in Vics of three never changed while I was in 145 and certainly when I later joined 605 who were at Croydon at the end of September they were still flying in Vics and we were still flying in these Vics when I was shot down again on 1st December 1940, but by that time we had got to the stage of having two weavers, one above and one below the squadron. I was hit when the Squadron made a turn and baled out. The funny thing was and this was the measure of those wretched Vics, the squadron landed back and somebody said, 'Well, where's Peter?' Nobody knew where I was and no one had seen me shot down and had flown the rest of the patrol without a top weaver.
>
> *Pilot Officer P.L. Parrott, 145 Squadron*

> We were still using the outdated Vic 3 formation which as you know proved ineffective in later operations and was replaced by the more flexible finger four formation with the basic element of two aircraft. Perhaps the powers that be, in their wisdom, kept a tight control on the fighter squadrons used in the Dunkirk operations as they knew that they would be required in a much more crucial role in the near future. But looking back, I feel the squadron would have achieved much greater success if it had been allowed to patrol in small flexible units searching for and intercepting aircraft on the approaches to Dunkirk. However, Dunkirk was no doubt a most valuable exercise in introducing the squadron to the realities of war and easing us gently into the big battles which were soon to follow.
>
> *Pilot Officer J.N. MacKenzie, 41 Squadron*

As one pilot told this author, he has always felt that four Vics were retained for so long because they 'looked nice'!

> We found all we had been taught before the war was totally useless. Flying in Vics of three was just not on. Any rapid turn in

any direction would usually lose the outside wingman who would find himself alone. Our CO was taught by the book, kept to the book and in consequence was shot down by the book! In our first real action his whole section went down when the Messerschmitts hit us.

Flight Sergeant G.C. Unwin, 19 Squadron

Fighter Command was also trained in copy-book attack methods. Number One Attack was made in line-astern whereby the leader fired, followed by each succeeding fighter in either his section or whole squadron. Number Two Attack called for two fighters flying side-by-side to attack two enemy aircraft or possibly two lines of fighters flying a co-ordinated version of the Number One Attack. Number Three Attack, which was more complicated, involved three fighters simultaneously attacking from the rear, beam and rear quarter. Devised in the peacetime 1930's Air Force, they were untried in actual combat and for the most part seemed to be only really effective if the enemy aircraft flew straight and level without taking too violent evasive action.

The more thinking fighter pilots over France and Dunkirk quickly realised that these tactics in the main were useless and adopted a far more fluid attack with freedom of movement. They also learned to get in close before firing and in consequence had their guns' harmonisation brought down from 400 yards to 120 yards. In many ways Dunkirk was an end – and a beginning.

I am not sure we knew what we were doing then, never mind trying to recall today the tactics we used. The fact was we had no tactics other than what we were told to do by AFDU of Air Ministry. They claimed as the Air Fighting Development Unit, to know that we should fly around in sections of three and have our guns ranged to give a pattern at 400 yards that would result in 60% of the bullets hitting the target. This assumed that no pilot was a better than 60% good shot. We also were expected to have one pilot 'weaving' about at the back so that he could note any aircraft creeping up behind. All this was nonsense, of course. The 'weaver' was the first chap to be picked off and if that did not happen he was likely to run out of petrol. At 400 yards our bullets had not, at that range, penetrating power; so after the first day I ordered all our guns to be fixed to a single point at 250 yards. We discovered some time later that the enemy, that flew around in pairs, were more versatile than our Vic formation of three. Incidentally, I eventually concluded that except in level flight the outside guns of the Spitfire did not, through flexing of the wings,

send bullets where the other six were going. The Hurricane with
its guns closer in to the fuselage, was a better gun platform.

Squadron Leader J.E. McComb, 611 Squadron

Churchill, in his speech to the House of Commons of 4th June, stated
that 'there was a victory inside' the deliverance of the BEF evacuation.
The victory by the RAF over the German Air Force. True the Luftwaffe
had suffered its first reversal and had been stopped in achieving its aim
although it could be said this aim was an impossible one. Had
Kesselring and his air commanders concentrated more on the ships
rather than men on sand dunes or sheltering amidst the rubble in
Dunkirk itself, then matters and casualties might have been very
different. Drowning 500 men at sea in one ship with one bomb was far
better than killing one or two men on the ground with one bomb. It was
very much a case of these air commanders not fully appreciating the
potential of the force they had. Raids on the harbours of Dover,
Ramsgate, Sheerness or Folkestone would have wreaked havoc amongst
returning troops and ships. Sneak raids on RAF bases such as Manston
or Hawkinge would have caused tremendous problems for the British
fighters.

Yet what was the victory achieved by the RAF? At the time it was
thought that for every RAF fighter lost at Dunkirk, four German aircraft
had been destroyed. A figure of 106 RAF aircraft was quoted as being
lost in the battle. This figure is almost impossible to reconcile from
squadron records for damaged aircraft were often written off days after
the date of the action while others might eventually be repaired. The
claims against the Luftwaffe totalled around 390 by Air Ministry,
although in Park's subsequent report he lists 258 destroyed and 119
probably destroyed or damaged. After the war captured German
documents indicate Luftwaffe losses for the Dunkirk period to be 156
'on all parts of the front'. Of these nineteen can be listed as lost away
from Dunkirk, reducing the figure to 132 aircraft. This would include
those lost to AA fire – the Royal Navy itself claimed 35 shot down.

The RAF flew no fewer than 3,561 sorties, of which 2,739 were
fighter sorties. According to the records I have gone through, Fighter
Command lost, between 26th May and 2nd June, 55 pilots killed, six
Defiant air-gunners killed, eight pilots taken prisoner (of which one
later died), eleven pilots and one air gunner wounded, and one pilot
killed in a flying accident.

In terms of leaders, Fighter Command lost three squadron
commanders killed, one taken prisoner, six flight commanders killed
plus another taken prisoner. About a dozen section leaders were also
lost, including two senior NCO pilots.

Over the same period thirty-nine fighter pilots who had either baled out over the sea or force-landed on or near the beaches had managed to get back. Other pilots brought down in France before Dunkirk had also made their way home, including Pilot Officer Bryan Wicks. It will be recalled that he had been shot down on 23rd May and following various adventures, and with the help of Belgian civilians, he reached Dunkirk late on 2nd June.

Dressed as a Belgian peasant, he had a job trying to convince the Army that he was an RAF pilot. Finally he was allowed to get in a queue for a ship and managed to get away in one of the last to go on the morning of 3rd June. On his return to his squadron he found all his belongings had been inventoried and his car sold. He went on to win the DFC in the Battle of Britain and rose to the rank of squadron leader. Sadly he was later killed in action.

The RAF, nevertheless, deserve to call Dunkirk a victory. It carried out its assigned task to the best of its ability with the limited numbers at its disposal. It had also been blooded and as far as experience was concerned was in a far better position for the Battles over Britain to come than it had been.

*

The end of Dynamo did not herald an immediate end to the fighting, either on land or in the air. The evacuation might have ended officially but the odd ship still got away from the vicinity of Dunkirk on 3rd June, while others were still at sea from the previous night.

At first light half a dozen RAF squadrons were either sent off or was mostly clear of hostile aircraft. 92 Squadron were recalled almost as soon as they were airborne because of low mist and fog. 616 flew one patrol despite heavy ground mist in the first morning light and 17, 43 and 145 Squadrons flew a patrol at 7.30 a.m.

These three units made rendezvous at Manston, then took off towards Dunkirk. Pilot Officer Dave Hanson saw twelve Ju87's and one Me109. Flying Officer Meredith was seen by Hanson and Pilot Officer R.C. Whittaker to go after the 109 but he was not seen again. Meredith had flown all through the Dunkirk operation, only to die when it was over. Hanson himself damaged one Stuka but had to break off when the others attacked him. His Hurricane received two cannon shells in the port wing, one bullet through the fuselage which knocked out his radio. One piece of shrapnel caught him in the left leg. Whittaker meantime also chased after the 109 but was unable to close in and his long range firing appeared to miss.[1]

---

[1] Pilot Officer R.C. Whittaker was killed in action four days later.

The rest of the day stayed clear for the most part and subsequent patrols both this day and on the 4th, the sky was empty of German aeroplanes. Flight Sergeant Unwin of 19 Squadron remembers the scene of desolation on his squadron's last patrol over the now empty beaches. Litter and debris covered the beaches and dunes. Fires still burned in the town and wreckage bobbed about at the water's edge. The smoke still stained the sky from the oil refinery, but otherwise the whole area seemed deserted.

Number 616 Squadron also flew a last patrol on the 4th. The weather turned bad and they were unable to land at Rochford. Pilot Officer E.W.S. Scott tried to get in, crashed and was killed. The others landed at Tangmere.

It was over.

*

Flight Lieutenant D.E. Gillam, 616 Squadron
Most of 616 Squadron sorties were in close support to Army – up and down the beach at 1,000-2,000 feet; consequently we couldn't intercept but got involved only as the Germans dived away.

Compared to later campaigns it was not a great occasion for us but at the time we felt that we had been really blooded.

Pilot Officer J.N. MacKenzie, 41 Squadron
Looking back on events at that time I feel Dunkirk, as far as 41 Squadron was concerned, was a fairly negative operation mainly because the squadron was too tightly controlled. My recollection of the Dunkirk operation is of flying in formation on patrols over Dunkirk and surrounding area and seeing only one enemy aircraft (which appeared out of and disappeared quickly back into low cloud) during a period of ten days and a total of ten offensive patrols.

Squadron Leader J.M. Thompson, 111 Squadron
We spent most of our time east and south-east of Dunkirk to try and intercept the Germans before they could reach Dunkirk. This may have accounted for the fact that the Army said they rarely saw any fighters.

One always remembers the sight of the black smoke from the blazing oil tanks nearby, the hundreds of boats off shore and plying to and from England and the masses of men on the beaches. It was a godsend that the weather was good or I doubt if we would have been able to evacuate as many as we did.

I remember one evening going to Victoria station to pick up a pilot who had come back after being shot down and rescued. There was a large number of British soldiers on the platform at the same time who had also just come back from Dunkirk. We got a really good verbal pasting from them about how the RAF was never seen, where were we and what the hell were we doing, etc. Little did they know or appreciate what was happening or what we were trying to do on their behalf.

For some obscure reason we were never allowed to attack targets on the ground, although the opportunities were there in abundance; petrol tankers, lines of German transport and troops going towards Dunkirk. Perhaps the powers that were at the time were concerned about the civilian casualties which would almost certainly have resulted amongst the large number of refugees who were on the roads at the same time.

Pilot Officer H.M. Stephen, 74 Squadron

We were all learning how the thing should be handled and those who were senior were also learning the art of leading. I could see the very beginning of the two by two formation coming out at this time.

It was all just sheer endeavour, professionalism and hard work disciplined into us youngsters – we were all in our twenties. It just shows what an extremely high standard the professional RAF was.

Squadron Leader J.E. McComb, 611 Squadron

Frankly of tactics we knew nothing but unlearned a lot we had been told. I would sooner fight two more Battles of Britain than another Dunkirk. The odds there were a fraction too sporting for me.

Pilot Officer A.C. Bartley, 92 Squadron

No wonder the soldiers did not see us up at 10,000 feet, but little do they realise that we saved them from the 'real bombs', 500 pounders carried by the Heinkels. What reasons Fighter Command gave for forbidding us to go below 15,000 feet I don't know.

Pilot Officer A.C. Deere, 54 Squadron

There is no doubt that our peacetime training was invaluable in terms of the discipline we had and the ability of those, known at the time, as operationally qualified, in other words had sufficient hours and time on the squadron. 54 Squadron's losses were disproportionately high, looking back, but that was because it was our first combat against the Germans who had already had experience in Spain, Poland and the Low Countries. Our people were leading from the front and it was most of the leaders that got shot down.

When they took us out, and when I arrived back from Dunkirk I found the squadron had been moved north, we were tired. It had been something new for us, like playing your first game of Rugby – eighty minutes seemed a long time. I had flown ten days non-stop and it was pretty tiring. Especially as we were losing a disproportionate number of chaps it seems. We lost a lot of experienced pilots – Max Pearson, Tom Linley (Deputy Flight Commander), Sergeant Phillips, Johnny Allen and George Gribble were shot down but got back, I was shot down and got back. The period of Dunkirk was as intensive as any period of the Battle of Britain for me, except one when I flew seventeen days non-stop. Added to that fact was that we were flying over foreign territory. We were over that strip of water, well outside range of communication – we had bad radios anyhow – the old HF radios – and so we had the mental thing that, 'I've still got to get back! – which is the way home!' It was that extra worry about getting back or getting lost, getting in combat and not having enough fuel left.

Pilot Officer H.A.C. Bird-Wilson, 17 Squadron
The period during the evacuation of the British Expeditionary Forces from Dunkirk was a most strenuous one, but the true seriousness of the situation was not fully appreciated by most of the young pilots, even when witnessing the heavily laden Royal Naval destroyers and the mixture of all sorts of pleasure boats which were ploughing their way back and forth from the beaches of Dunkirk to England. Pilots were too busy with their own survival to apprehend the ghastly catastrophe that was happening to the BEF. The Hurricane and Spitfire Squadrons of 11 Group shared out the continuous mounted patrols over Dunkirk and Number 17 Squadron were flying on approximately two patrols a day. If the squadron was ordered to patrol over the beach head at 04.30 hours in the morning, it meant real pre-dawn awakening and to allow ample time to fly out and be in the Dunkirk area on time, then the next patrol would be around midday. Cloud conditions played a great part in helping the Luftwaffe carry out their attacks against undefended ships. Such conditions did not make the task of interceptions by RAF fighters easy, although

many combats took place between Ju88's, Me109's and Me110's. It was during this time that the Me110 tactics of their defensive circle was first observed and only at a later date were tactics introduced by attacking head-on in a counter direction. A very exciting and somewhat dangerous manoeuvre!

One of the greatest inspirations came to the squadron when they were resting in the officers' mess at Manston between patrols, when in walked Air Vice-Marshal Keith Park, the Air Officer Commanding Number 11 Group, still in his white flying overalls. (Mess regulations had been slightly relaxed during this period!) There was a general discussion about our dawn patrol over Dunkirk, then to our surprise he mentioned that he likewise had been flying his Hurricane over Dunkirk. This to us was a great morale booster and a lesson in true leadership. Such action by AVM Park is not generally known, even by his own 11 Group pilots.

Squadron Leader H. Edwardes Jones, 213 Squadron
Everyone felt that they had given a good account of themselves, especially operating thirty to forty miles away from the English coast and in a bit of a shambles of a show. Better still, they felt confident they could see off the Luftwaffe if it tried something over England.

Air Chief Marshal, Sir H.C.T. Dowding,
Commander in Chief, Fighter Command
My dear fighter boys. I don't send out many letters and signals but I feel I must take this occasion with the intensive fighting in northern France, for the time being over, to tell you how proud I am of you and the way you have fought since the Blitzkrieg started. I wish I could have spent my time visiting you and hear your accounts of the fighting, but I have occupied myself in working for you in other ways. I want you to know my thoughts are always with you and it is you and your fighting spirit that will crack the brow of the German Air Force and preserve our country through the trials which yet lie ahead. Good luck to you.

*

The whole period of the Dunkirk evacuation as far as the RAF was concerned can be seen through the recollections of just one of its fighter pilots. Pilot Officer Allan Wright, aged twenty, was a pilot with 92 Squadron and fought, like so many of his contemporaries, his first air battle above Dunkirk. This is his story:

Even at the time the whole episode seemed a dream, although it became real enough. On our very first patrol over Dunkirk – 23rd May – Pilot Officer Pat Learmond, my closest friend from RAF Cranwell days, and, at the time, rival in love, did not return – he was shot down and killed. We were just twenty years old and I was overwhelmed with shock and disbelief. When I first saw a few Me109s on that sortie, not far away and glinting in the sun, they were just other aeroplanes to me; it just didn't occur to me to attack or realise the danger – how green can one be! But this is so true of initiation into battle, Dunkirk or the Falklands, or any other.

During the week or so of Dunkirk, briefings were almost nil, either about the enemy on the ground or in the air. At the time, the system of thorough aircrew briefings had not been thought of. We were, however, given the limits of our patrol area, warned not to patrol below 10,000 feet and told to attack any German aircraft seen. We were also warned to conserve fuel and to leave the battle area with sufficient fuel to get back. Not easy to assess in the heat of battle. No information at all was given on what was going on down there until it was all over and all our troops had already landed back in England. A surprise no doubt for Pilot Officer Casenove when his aircraft was damaged and he managed to land on the beach and found that the army reckoned he had less right than they to get into the boats.

Up to the time of Dunkirk we had practised air combat individually or in sections of three against bomber targets. It must be remembered that until the Germans advanced into France, it had always been assumed that their bases would be kept behind the Maginot Line. There had been no thought that the German fighters and our own would be within range of each other and also that their relative speeds would be too high for dog fighting as known in the Great War.

With my experience confined to flying in a section of three, you can imagine my surprise when we flew into Martlesham Heath on 28th May to find other squadrons already there and when we flew in the second time on 2nd June, we took off as part of a wave of four squadrons. I thought of the Hendon Air Display, but I cannot remember any particular wing formation or discussion of tactics. I don't think there were any. We were just aware that we were involved in something very big.

The patrols over Dunkirk were hair-raising experiences. I took part in six, was engaged every time, fired my guns every time and it seemed every time, turned into a dog-fight. On one occasion I saw a mêlée of aeroplanes a few miles away and charged in. After a while I became aware that I could not catch any enemy aircraft in my sights and that all the aircraft around me were passing at great speed, often head-on. It then dawned on me that they were all circling in one direction while I was circling the opposite way round! A stall turn put matters to rights but then I found that I was as much a target as an attacker. It was after this episode that on return to base a spent bullet was found in the bottom of my fuselage, quite undamaged. We decided that it must have been fired partly upwards from a great distance away, probably at someone else and having arced through the sky, fell into my Spitfire with only enough force to penetrate one skin of aluminium. A chance in a million.

There seemed to be more dog-fighting over Dunkirk than later, in the Battle of Britain or when escorting bombers over France. By then one side or the other was only too well aware of the distance and fuel necessary to get back to base. Then it became a matter of 'bounce', from up-sun if possible, attack and climb up again out of the way. The Germans, when attacked over the UK, and occasionally over Dunkirk, would usually open the taps and dive for home. There was good reason for this. Other things being equal, the Spitfire had the edge in the climb over the 109, while the 109 had the edge in the dive flat out. The Me109 pilots also found out over Dunkirk that the Spitfire had the tighter turned circle, which meant that after a turn or two of a two-plane dog-fight, the Spitfire would have the 109 in its sights. At Dunkirk we were discovering these things.

On one sortie, about mid-day, I held on to a 109 in my sights and was firing at it and closing to 100 yards or so when it pulled up apparently vertically into the sun. I hung on as best I could but it was impossible in the glare of the sun to hold in my sights or see him properly. I also had no idea what he was doing with his throttle, whether he was coming or going so to speak. We could not go on like this without falling like leaves out of the sky, out of control and in inevitable collision. So, as the stick became almost useless I pulled away and lost him. One up to him.

On another occasion, I had fired at one Me109 somewhere about 10,000 feet up and after a few strikes down he went at full bore. There seemed a good chance of getting him, so down we both went, each coaxing as much speed as we could out of our aeroplanes. The speed built up rapidly, the controls stiffened, elevators were trimmed. It is remarkably difficult to move the nose around at high speed to get the sights steady on target and needs all one's strength and concentration. I fired several times and the range closed. The ground was clearly rushing towards us, in fact I can remember seeing houses, gardens and streets of suburbia. But I got the sights on again and pressed the gun button. His engine caught fire and his dive steepened. As he was about to hit the ground there was an almighty bang in my cockpit. I thought the speed had been too much and my aircraft was breaking up. An unfamiliar smell and smoke filled the cockpit. (I was to recognise the smell of cordite at other times.) We were going much too fast to manoeuvre, but heaving back on the stick I let the ground rush past and dragged the aircraft up and around. There was another Me109 attacking me, but I had no ammunition left. All I could do was to go on pulling round as if to attack, and then head off home, weaving and neck-twisting on the long journey back across the North Sea, and able at last to count the fourteen bullet holes after landing back at Martlesham Heath.

We used to say, even when engaged in attack, one must be aware of the danger behind. It was for this reason that the German fighter pilots, having learned their tactics from fighting in the Spanish Civil War, used to fly in loose pairs, each one of the pair guarding the other's tail. I don't think that the Dunkirk affair lasted long enough for us to learn the value of this tactic, in fact we were flying in close vics of three in line astern with two weavers above, well into the Battle of Britain.

As aircraft became damaged it was possible to release pilots individually from duty for periods of up to 24 hours at a time, leaving sufficient to fly the remaining aircraft. I was released at mid-day on 24th May in just these circumstances. Bourne End was where my girl friend (later my wife) lived. We and a friend of hers spent the afternoon sailing on the Thames. I remember well thinking as we lay rocking gently on the water in the sunshine, what an extraordinary and seemingly impossible situation to be in – from fighting for one's life over France in the morning – to this – with the prospect of killing or being killed the next morning.

Pilot Officer A.R. Wright, 92 Squadron

Claims and casualties

The following list gives the combat claims by 11 Group fighter squadrons during the period 26th May to 3rd June 1940. It has been compiled from 11 Group's record of combats and casualties, and from squadron diaries. Both have certain inaccuracies in them and these have been amended here. Other information to make the list as accurate as possible has come from interviews with the men who were there and from the Ministry of Defence. It is not claimed as being 100% accurate even now and it must be remembered that the claims and credits are those which were made at the time in good faith by the pilots and squadrons who flew at Dunkirk.

Date/time 26 May	Sqn	Pilot	Dest	Prob/dam	Losses	
0440-0615	17	PO H A C Bird-Wilson	Ju88		F/S W T Jones +	N2528
		FL C F G Adye			FL C F G Adye +	P3483
		PO R C Whittaker				
		PO K Manger				
		PO D W H Hanson				
		?				
0505-0645	65	FO G V Proudman	Me110		FO J Welford +	P9437
		FO S B Grant	Me110	Do17		
		FS W H Franklyn	Me110	Me109		
		SL D Cooke		Me109		
		PO J B H Nicholas				
0505-0645	54	FL J A Leathart	Me110		PO J L Allan – b/out	N3188
		FL J A Leathart	Me110	Me110		
		FL J A Leathart	Ju88	Me110		
		FL M C Pearson				
		PO A C Deere	Me110	Me110		
		PO A C Deere	Me110			
		PO D McMullen	Me110			
		PO B H Way		Me110		
		FS P H Tew		Me110		
0735-0915	19	SL G D Stephenson	Ju87		SL G D Stephenson – PoW	N3200
		PO M D Lyne	Ju87	Ju87	PO P V Watson – b/out	N3237
		FL B J E Lane		Me109	FO G E Ball – W	'L'
		FL B J E Lane				
		FO F Brinsdon	Ju87			
		Sgt J A Potter	Me109			
		FL W G Clouston	Ju87			
		FL W G Clouston	Ju87			
		FS H Steere	Ju87			
		FO G E Ball	Me109			
		FO G L Sinclair	Me109			
0818-1009	65	FO G V Proudman	Hs126	Me109	PO K G Hart OK – FL on beach	K9912
		PO T Smart	Me110			
		FO Walker	Me110	Me109		
		FO J B N Nicholas	Me109			

Time	Sqn	Personnel	E/A	E/A	Remarks	Serial
1013–1159	17	FS W H Franklyn	Me109	Me109		
1308–1430	32	SL D Cooke	Me109	Me109		
		FL G A W Saunders	Me109	Me109		
		FL C G C Olive		Me109		
		PO K G Hart				
		PO R C Whittaker				
1318–1445	605	FL M N Crossley	Ju88		PO I J Muirhead – b/out	N2346
		PO T P M Cooper-Slipper	Ju88		Sgt C A Irwin +	P9305
1440–1700	19	FL B J E Lane	Me109	Me109	PO M D Lyne – W	L1031
		FO G W Petre		Me109		
		FO G L Sinclair				
1840–2030	145	PO P L Parrott	He111	He111	PO P L Parrott – force landed – OK	
27 May						
0435–0640	54	–	Do17		FL M C Pearson +	N3030
		SL D Cooke	Do17		FO G Proudman – W	N3128
0640–0845	65	FS R R Macpherson }	Ju88			
		FS W H Franklyn				
		FS W H Franklyn				
		FO G V Proudman				
0752–0945	74	FL A G Malan	Me109	Do17	PO P C F Stevenson –	L1084
		FO J C Freeborn		Me109	OK – force landed	
		PO H M Stephen		Me109		
		WO E Mayne		Me109		
		FL W P F Treacy		Me109		
		PO P C F Stevenson				
0830–1020	264	SL P A Hunter }	Me109	Me109		
		Sgt F H King				
		PO M H Young				
		LAC S B Johnson }				
		PO R W Stokes				
		LAC Fairbrother				
0837–1023	605	–	Me109	Me109	FO N Forbes – PoW	L2119
		FL N G Cooke				
		Cpl A Lippett }				
1120–1300	264	PO T D Welsh	He111			
		LAC L H Hayden				

Time	Sqn	Crew	Claims		Casualties	Serials
1300-1510	65	SL P A Hunter Sgt F H King PO H M Young } LAC S B Johnson FL E A Whitehouse } PO H Scott ? ?		He111 He111 He111		
?	145	PO T Smart PO T Smart PO S B Grant Sgt N T Phillips FL G A W Saunders SL D Cooke ?	Do17 Do17	Do17 Do17 Me110 Do17		
		PO J E Storrar ?		Me110 Me110 Me110	PO A Elson + PO P H O'C Rainer+ Sgt A Bailey +	P2723 N2713 N2711
1321-1450	601	PO J K McGrath PO P B Robinson FO C Riddle		Me110 Me110		
			Me110	Me110 Me110		
1407-1600	54	SL J A Leathart PO A C Deere } PO J A Allen } PO A C Deere		Ju88 Ju88 Do17		
1440-1555	17	FO R V Meredith Sgt G A Steward	Do17	Do17	SL G V Perry + FO P J Danielson +	P3423 P3581
1440-1555	605	-				
1516-1700	74	FO W G Measures } PO P C B St.John } FL W P C Treacy PO H M Stephen } Sgt W H Skinner } FL A G Malan PO D H T Dowding PO D G Cobden	Do17 Do17 Do17	Do17 Do17 Do17	FL W P C Treacy –Evaded	K9875

Time	Sqn	Crew	E/A	E/A	Result	Serial
1545–1650	56	SL E V Knowles		He111	PO M C Maxwell – OK – force landed	P3478
		SL E V Knowles	He111		FL R H A Lee – OK	P3311
		Sgt R D Baker }		He111		
		FL J H Coglan }				
		PO L Ereminsky }				
		FO Fisher				
1610–1810	213	FL R D G Wight	Me109			
		FL R D G Wight	Me109			
		PO H D Atkinson				
		FO E G Winning				
1830–2015	610	FO E B B Smith	He111	Me109	FO A R J Medcalf +	L1016
		PO P Litchfield	Me110	Me109	Sgt W T Medway +	L1006
		SL A L Franks	Me110			
		FO G M T Kerr				
1830–1940	56	FL A T Smith	Me110	Me110	FO Fisher – W	P3355
		SL E V Knowles	Me110	Me110		
		Sgt G Smythe	Me110	Me110		
		FS C J Cooney				
1900–2025	79		Me110	Me110		
			Me110	Me110		
1900–2025	145	FL A H Boyd	Me110	Me110	PO D N Forde – OK	N2710
		FL A H Boyd	Me110		PO E C J Wakeham – OK	P3314
					PO J H Ashton – OK	N2713
1900–2025	601	FO W P Clyde	Me110		FO C Lee-Steere +	P3486
		FO T E Hubbard	Me110		FL Sir A Hope – OK	P2568?
		?	Me110			
		?	Me110			
1904–2105	19	FL W G Clouston	Do215	Do215		
		FO G W Petre		Do215		
		FS H Steere }				
		Sgt B Jennings }				
		FS G C Unwin	Hs126			
28 May						
0430–0645	54	PO A C Deere	Do215	He111	PO A C Deere - ftl Dunkirk, ret'd	N3180
0545–0855	213	FL R D G Wight	Me109		FO E G Winning +	P3354
		FO W M Sizer	Me109		FO T Boyd – OK	P2721

Time	Sqn	Crew / Pilot (claim)	E/A claimed	E/A (loss)	Casualty & fate	Serial
app 0640 / 0900-1050	242	FL D R Miller	Me109			
		FS G C Unwin	Me109			
		FS H Steere	Do17			
0900-1050	19	SL D Cooke	Do17			
		FS W H Franklyn } Sgt J R Kilner	Me109			
				Me109	FO G W Petre – W	L1029
0900-1050	65			Do17	PO T Smart – ftl Dunkirk, ret'd	P9435
0900-1050	616	PO K Holden	Me109			
		FO G E Moberly	Me109			
		PO E W S Scott	Me109	Me109	Sgt M Ridley – W	K9947
1020-1150	229	Sgt J C Harrison	Me110	Me109	SL M Robinson – OK	K9804
		SL H J Maguire	Ju88	Do17	FO R O Hellyer – OK	N2551
					Sgt S A Hillman +	
1020-1150	213	PO H D Atkinson	Me109			
		Sgt S L Butterfield	Me109	Me109	Sgt S L Butterfield – b/o, rescued	P2817
		Sgt S L Butterfield	Me109		PO G G Stone +	P2792
		Sgt S L Butterfield	Me109		Sgt J A Lichman – W	P2834
		FO W A Gray	Me109			
		FL R D G Wight	Me109			
		FL R D G Wight	Me109			
1135-1315	242	PO P S Turner	Me109	Me109	PO A H Deacon – PoW	N2651
		PO W L McKnight	Me109	Me109	PO D F Jones +	L1746
		FL D R Miller	Me109			
1135-1315	264	SL P A Hunter } Sgt F H King	Do215		FL E A Whitehouse +	L6959
					PO H Scott +	
		Sgt R Thorn } LAC F J Barker	Do215		PO A McLeod +	L7007
		"			PO J E Hatfield +	
					Sgt L C W Daisley +	L6953
					LAC H Revill +	
29 May						
0415-0640	222	PO K Manger		Do215	PO J W Broadhurst – OK	
1238-1410	17	SL G D Emms } PO K Manger } FL W J Harper } PO H A C Bird-Wilson				
		PO J T Whittaker		Me110	PO D W H Hanson – W	
		PO D W H Hanson				

Time	Sqn	Crew	E/A	E/A	Notes	Serial
1238-1410	245	?				
1437-1610	151	PO D H Blomley	Do17	Do17	PO K C Dryden – ftl Dunkirk, ret'd	N2659
1437-1610	56	Sgt G Smythe	Me110		Sgt J W Elliott +	L1972
			Ju87		LAC E J Jones +	L6957
					(PO D M S Kay – OK)	
1445-1630	264	PO E G Barwell }	Me109			
		LAC F J Barker }	Me110			
		FL N G Cooke }	Me109			
		Cpl A Lippett }	Me109			
			Me109			
		PO G H Hackwood }	Me109			
		LAC P Lillie }				
		PO G H Hackwood }	Me110			
		LAC P Lillie }				
		PO M H Young }	Me109			
		LAC S B Johnson }	Me110			
		SL P A Hunter }				
		Sgt F H King }				
		Sgt E R Thorn }	Ju87			
		LAC F J Barker }	Me110			
		PO R W Stokes }	Me110			
		LAC Fairbrother }	Me109			
		PO T D Welsh }	Me110			
		LAC L H Hayden }	Me109			
		PO M H Young }	Me110			
		LAC S B Johnson }				
1445-1630	213	PO H D Atkinson		He111		
		FS C Grayson		He111		
		Sgt R T Llewelyn	Ju87	Me109		
		Sgt M E Croskell	Me109	Ju87		
		FO W A Gray		Ju87		
		FO W M Sizer	He111	He111		
1512-	500	PO G H Wherry }			Ditched in sea;	OY-X
		FO Alington			48 Sqn crew att'd	
		LAC Harding			to 500 Sqn.	
		LAC L S Dilnutt }	Me109		Rescued by drifter.	

Time	Sqn	Crew	Claim	E/A causing loss	Remarks	Serial
1627-1955		PO A Leeson / Sgt J H Hoskins / Cpl R G Rogers / LAC R G Honnor			All crew injured; Shot down by Me109, ditched and rescued by destroyer	N5065
		PO Chaffey – OK / PO Jones – OK / LAC F S Cunningham – W / LAC Elvidge – OK / PO J B Latta – c/l OK		Me109		R3312
1627-1955	242	PO W L McKnight	Me109			
		PO W L McKnight	Do17			
		FL J H Plinston	Me109			
		PO D G MacQueen	Me109			
		PO J B Latta	Me109			
		PO P S Turner	Me109			
		PO R D Grassick	Me109			
1630-1800	229	PO R R Smith	Me109	Me109	FL F N Clouston +	P3489
		PO V M Bright	Me109		FL P E S F M Brown +	P2636
		PO R Clifford Brown	Me109		Sgt J C Harrison +	P2876
					FO W G New – b/o	N2473
					PO A S Linney – b/o	N2521
					FO G M T Kerr +	L1006
					FO J Kerr-Wilson +	N3289
1630-1800	610	SL A L Franks	Me109			
		FL J Ellis	Me109			
		FO G L Chambers	Me109			
		PO S C Norris	Me109			
1630-1800	64	FL D B Hobson	Me109	Me109	SL E G Rogers +	L1052
		FS C Flynn	Me109		PO R T George +	K9832
		?	Me109		PO H B Hackney + / FS C Flynn – OK	K9906
		?				
1900-2022	264	PO E G Barwell / PO J E M Williams	Ju87			
		FL N G Cooke / Cpl A Lippett	Ju87			
		"	Ju87			
		"	Ju87			
		SL P A Hunter / Sgt F H King	Ju87			

(+2 Ju87s shared)

Time	Sqn	Crew		Notes	Serial
		PO D M S Kay }	Ju87		
		LAC W E Cox }			
		Sgt A J Lauder }	Ju87		
		LAC Wise }			
		PO R W Stokes } Ju87			
		LAC Fairbrother }			
		Sgt E R Thorn } Ju87			
		LAC F J Barker } Ju87			
		PO T D Welsh } Ju87			
		LAC L H Hayden }			
		PO D Whitley }			
		LAC R C Turner } Ju87			
		PO M H Young } Ju87			
		LAC S B Johnson } Ju87	Ju88		
		PO G H Hackwood } Ju88			
		LAC P Lillie } Ju87			
		PO G L Hickman } Ju87			
		LAC Fiddler } Ju87			
		Sgt A J Lauder } Ju87			
		LAC Wise }			
1930-2100	56	FO L Ereminsky Me109			
		FS F W Higginson Me109			
1930-2100	151	FL J H Coghlan }	Ju88	FO K E Newton – b/o	P3303
		FL J H Coghlan }	Ju88	PO R N H Courtney – b/o, wounded	P3321
		Sgt R D Baker Ju88	He111	SL A L Franks +	N3177
1930-2100	610	SL E M Donaldson }		Sgt P D Jenkins +	L1062
		PO J R Haymer }			
		–			
1930-2100	213	Sgt R T Llewelyn He111	He111	PO J F Howitt – inj	L1756
1930-2100	242	–			
30 May 0928-	500			PO I S Wheelwright +	N5227
				Sgt H N Johnson +	
				LAC R G T Soper +	
				LAC F H Giles +	

Time	Sqn	Crew	Claim	E/A	Remarks	Serial
app 1315	245	FL J A Thomson		Do17	FL J A Thomson – OK	N2496
		PO J S Southwell			Sgt P Banks – ftl	P2597
		PO D Pennington			PO G Marshall – ftl	N2709
					PO R A West – ftl	
1425-1610	213	FL R D G Wight		Do17	FO G D Ayre +	L1086
1420-	609	-			FO J C Dundas – ftl	L1063
					FO F J Howell – ftl	N3203
					FO J Dawson – ftl	
31 May						
0434-0655	222	-	Me109		PO G G A Davies – ftl Dunkirk, OK.	N3295
-0640	41	FL J T Webster	He111			
		FL J T Webster				
		PO A D J Lovell				
		PO T A Vigors				
-0640	222	-	Me109	He111	PO K B McGlasham – ftl Dunkirk, ret'd.	N2702
1220-1400	245	PO K Manger	Me109	Me109		
1220-1400	17	Blenheims	Me109			
		FL R G Dutton				
1220-1400	145	FL R G Dutton	Me109			
		FO M A Newling				
1345-1535	609	FO I B N Russell	He111	He111	FL D Persse-Joynt +	N3202
		FO J Dawson	He111			
1400-1535	264	PO E G Barwell	Me109	Me109	PO G L Hickman +	L6968
		PO J E M Williams			LAC A Fidler +	L6961
		SL P A Hunter	Me109		PO D Whitley – ftl	L6980
		Sgt F H King			LAC R C Turner – ftl	
		PO M H Young	Me109	Me109	PO M H Young – b/o	
		LAC S B Johnson			LAC S B Johnson – b/o	
		PO G L Hickman			(latter two collided	
		LAC A Fidler			over Dunkirk)	
1400-1535	213	FL R D G Wight	Me109		SL H D McGregor – b/out	P3482
		FL R D G Wight	Me109		FO K N G Robinson – b/out	P2763
		FO Robinson	Me109		PO W M Sizer – ftl	P3424
		PO W M Sizer	Me109		FO W N Gray +	P3361
		Sgt S L Butterfield	Me109		FO T Boyd +	P3419

Time	Sqn	Crew	E/A	E/A	RAF casualty / result	Serial
1555-1745	229	Sgt P P Norris	Me109			
		PO V M Bright	Me110	Me110	PO V B S Verity – b/o	L1982
		PO V B S Verity	Me110		Sgt D F Edgehill – W	P3553
		Sgt D F Edgehill	Me110			
		Sgt D F Edgehill	Me110			
1555-1745	242	FL G H Plinston	Ju88			
		PO D G MacQueen	Do17			
		PO N K Stansfeld	Me110		Sgt G H Hatch – PoW/+	K9813
		PO W L McKnight	Me110		FS C Flynn – OK	P3969
		PO W L McKnight	Me110		Sgt A E Binham – OK	L1057
1555-1745	64	FO D M Taylor	Me110		FO G L Chambers +	N3274
		PO H P F Patten	Me110		FO G Keighley – b/o	L1013?
		FO H J Woodward	Do17			
		PO J O'Meara	Me109			
1555-1745	610	FL L F Henstock		Me110		
		FL J Ellis	Me110	Me110		
		PO P Lichfield		Me110		
		?				
1840-2000	264	Sgt E R Thorn }	He111	He111	FL N G Cooke +	L6975
		LAC F J Barker }			Cpl A Lippett +	
		PO E G Barwell }		He111	PO E G Barwell – OK	L6972
		PO J E M Williams }			PO J E M Williams – OK	
		PO G Hackwood }			PO R W Stokes – ftl	L7019
		LAC P Lillie }		He111	LAC Fairbrother – b/out	
		SL P A Hunter }				
		Sgt F H King }		He111		
1855-2130	242	FO P S Turner	Me109			
		FL G H Plinston	Me109		FL G H Plinston – OK	P2884
		PO J B Latta	Me109			
		PO R D Grassick	Me109			
1855-2130	609	FL I B N Russell }	He111		FO J C Gilbert +	L1081
		PO C N Overton }			Sgt G C Bennett – W	L1087
		FL I B N Russell	He111		ditched off Dover.	
		FL I B N Russell	Me109			
		PO C N Overton	Me109			
		PO P Drummond-Hay	Do17			

Time	Sqn	Pilot			Remarks	Serial
1840-	111	PO J R Buchanan	He111			
		FO J C Dundas	He111			
		FO J C Dundas	Do17(½)			
		SL J M Thompson		Me109	Sgt J Robinson – W	L1973
		FO H M Ferris		Me109	Sgt W L Dymond – OK	P2884
		PO J A Walker	Me109	Me109		
		Sgt J T Craig		Me109		
		Sgt R W Brown		Me109		
		Sgt W L Dymond		He111		
		Sgt W L Dymond		He111		
		Sgt J Robinson	Ju88			
		FL S D P Connors		EA		
1 June 0418-0630	19	PO H C Baker	Me110	Me110	Sgt J A Potter –ditched – OK	K9836
		FL W G Clouston	Me109	Me110		
		FL W G Clouston }	Me109			
		FS H Steere				
		PO L A Haines	Me109			
		Sgt B J Jennings	Me110			
		Sgt B J Jennings	Me110			
		PO G L Sinclair	Me110			
		PO G L Sinclair	Me110			
		FS G C Unwin	Me110			
		FL B J E Lane	Me110			
0418-0630	222	SL H W Mermagen	Me110	Me110	PO R A L Morant – ftl Dunkirk, OK	P9377
		FL D R S Bader	Me109	Me110		
		FL A I Robinson	Me110		PO H E L Falkust – PoW	P9317
		PO T A Vigors	Me110			
		Sgt S Baxter	Me110			
		PO H P M Edridge		Me109	PO G Massey-Sharpe +	
0418-0630	616	PO K Holden	Me109		Sgt L J White +	P9337
		FO J S Bell	Me109		FO J S Bell – OK ditched, rescued	N3232
					PO K Holden – c/l	K9948
0822-1015	19	PO L A Haines		He111		
		Sgt B J Jennings		Do215		
		PO G L Sinclair		He111		

Time	Sqn	Crew		E/A		E/A	Result	PO G L
Sinclair		Do215						
0825-1055	222	FS H Steere		He111		He111		
		FS G C Unwin		He111	1973	He111		
		FL A I Robinson ⎫			2884			
		FL D R S Bader ⎬						
		Sgt R B Johnson ⎭						
0825-1055	41	PO A D J Lovell		He111		Do215	PO W Stapleton – PoW	N3107
		PO O B Morough-Ryan		Do215		Do215	FO W E Legard +	P9344
0825-1055	616	FL J T Webster		Ju88		He111		
		?				Ju88		
		FO G E Moberly				He111		
		Sgt P Copeland				He111		
		FL D E Gillam			9836	Ju88		
		PO R Marples				Ju88		
		PO H K Laycock				Ju88		
		PD D S Smith						
		FO R Miller						
		FO R Miller						
app 1040	500	PO P W Peters ⎫		Me109		Me109	a/c MK-V	
		Sgt D C Spencer ⎬		Me109				
		LAC Pepper						
		LAC L G Smith ⎭						
1053-1245	145	FL R G Dutton		Me110			PO H P Dixon +	P2952
		FL R G Dutton	9377	Me109			PO L D M Scott – OK	N2497
		FL R G Dutton	9317	Me109				
		FL A D Boyd		Me110				
		FL A D Boyd		Me110				
		PO R D Yule		Me110				
		PO M A Newling		Me110				
		PO A N C Weir		Me110				
1053-1245	43	SL G C Lott	9337	Me110		Me109	Sgt T A H Gough +	L1758
		FO J D Edmonds	3232	Me109		Me110	PO M K Carswell –WIA/rescued	N2584
		Sgt P Ottewill	9948	Me109		Me109		
		Sgt P Ottewill		Me110				
		Sgt H J L Hallowes		Me110		Me109		
		Sgt H J L Hallowes		Me109				

Time	Sqn	Pilot				
1100-1215	245	Sgt H J L Hallowes	Me109	Me109		
		FL J W C Simpson	Me109	Me109		
		FL J W C Simpson	Me109	Me109		
		FO W C Wilkinson		Me109		
		FO W C Wilkinson		Me109		
		FO C A Woods-Scawen		Me109		
		PO G E Hill	Me109	Me109	PO R A West +	N2709
		PO J Redman	Me109	Me109	PO A L Treanor +	N2658
		PO N J Mowat		Me109		
		PO J S Southwell	Me109			
		PO J S Southwell	Me109			
		FL J Thomson		Me109		
1415-1615	151	SL E M Donaldson	Me109	Me110	FO I B N Russell +	L1058
1415-1615	609	FO A R Edge		Ju88		
1545-1730	229	PO R R Smith	Ju87	Ju87		
		PO R E Bary		Ju87		
1545-1730	242	PO N K Stansfeld	Me109	Ju87	PO G M Stewart +	P2732
		PO P S Turner	Ju87	Ju87		
		PO W L McKnight	Ju87	Ju87		
		PO W L McKnight		Me109		
		FL D R Miller		Me109		
		FL D R Miller				
1545-1730	64	FO A J O Jeffrey	Ju87	Ju87		
app 1645	220	PO R A Selley		Ju87	} on the ground	
		FO H A Haarhoff	Ju87	Ju87		
		PO R J Jouault	Ju87	Ju87		
1810-2030	17	– FO F J Howell		He111	PO K Manger – b/o	P3476
1810-2030	609	FO J C Dundas		He111	FO J Dawson +	N3222
app 2016	206	FL W H Biddell } LAC W D Caulfield	Me109	Me109		

Time	Sqn	Pilot	Claim	Claim	Casualty	Serial
2 June						
0715-0900	266	SL J W A Hunnard		Me109	PO J W B Stevenson +	N3169
		FL J T B Coward		Me109	Sgt R T Kidman +	N3092
		PO N B Bowen		Me109		
		PO A W Cole	Me110	Me109		
		PO R M Trousdale		Me110		
		FO N W Burnett		Me109		
		?				
0715-0900	32	PO R F Smythe	Ju88	Me109	Sgt D Flynn – PoW	P2727
0715-0900	92	PO H D Edwards	He111			
		Sgt R A Fokes	He111			
		PO R H Holland	Me109	Me109		
		SL P Saunders	He111			
		FL R R S Tuck	Me109			
		FL R R S Tuck	He111			
		PO T G Williams	He111			
		PO A R Wright	Me109			
		PO A C Bartley		4/He111s		
		PO J S Bryson		He111		
		Sgt P R Eyles		He111		
		FO C B F Kingcome		He111		
		FO C B F Kingcome		He111		
0715-0900	611	SL E J McComb	Me110	Me109	FO R K Crompton +	N3064
		SL E J McComb		He111	FO T D Little +	N3055
		PO C Jones		Me109	FO B Heath – OK	N3054
		FO D H Watkins		Me109	FL W J Leather – OK	N3050
		FS H S Sadler	Me110		PO C Jones – OK	N3056
		FO B Heath	Ju87	Ju87	PO M P Brown – OK	N3058
		PO D A Adams	Ju87		FL K M Stoddart – OK	
		PO C H MacFie			(all 4 a/c damaged)	
0745-0845	66	FO W A Smith		Me109	FS M W Hayman +	N3047
		FO E W Campbell-Colquhoun	Me109		Sgt D A C Hunt b/o	N3028
		FL H F Burton		He111	Sgt F N Robertson – b/out	N3033
		?		Me109		
1840-2035	72	SL R B Lees	Ju87		FO R F Rimmer OK	K9924
					FO O StJ Pigg W	

Time	Sqn	Pilot			Notes	Serial
1850–2140	111	PO D C Winter		Ju87		
		FO T A F Elsdon		Ju87		
		FO E J Wilson	Ju87	Ju87		
		Sgt B Douthwaite		Ju87		
		FO O StJ Pigg	Ju87			
		FL R P R Powell	Me109	Me110	PO R R Wilson – b/o	L1564
		PO P J Simpson		Me109		
		PO R R Wilson		Me109		
		PO R R Wilson		Me110		
		FO D C Bruce		Me110		
		FL S D P Connors		Me109		
		FL S D P Connors		Me110		
1850–2140	151	SL E M Donaldson	Me110	Me110		
		?		Me110		
		?		Ju87		
3 June app 0730	17	PO D W H Hanson		Ju87	FO R V Meredith + PO D W H Hanson – OK	P3477

11 Group strength as at 30th May 1940

Sqdn	Station	Officers	NCOs	A/C Ready	A/C Ready 12 hours	A/C at MUs
609	Northolt	20	1	15	3	–
92	Northolt	17	5	13	–	3
151	Nrth Weald	10	4	16	3	1
601	Tangmere	14	2	13	2	2
145	Tangmere	13	1	16	2	–
19	Hornchurch	8	4	13	–	–
41	Hornchurch	13	6	15	2	–
65	Hornchurch	1	1	1	–	2
222	Hornchurch	11	5	11	4	–
626	Hornchurch	13	3	9	3	–
56	Nth Weald	7	5	15	1	–
17	Kenley	9	3	11	2	4
64	Kenley	12	6	11	2	2
32	Biggin Hill	1	–	3	1	1
79	Biggin Hill	–	1	5	1	1
213	Biggin Hill	6	7	9	1	1
229	Biggin Hill	6	3	8	–	–
242	Biggin Hill	11	–	11	–	2
610	Biggin Hill	11	1	9	3	2
111	Nth Weald	13	9	17	1	–
245	Hawkinge	not known				
	Totals:	**196**	**67**	**221**	**31**	**21**

These figures have been taken from a report compiled by AVM Keith Park but I have only included those squadrons who were in action at Dunkirk in day operations or who were operational at this date. 264 Squadron for instance had returned to Duxford on the 30th to rest. Likewise, 32 and 79 Squadrons had been pulled out of the front line but had a small number of fighters still in the Group.

11 Group statistics from Keith Park's report dated 8th July 1940

Air operations over France and Dunkirk by his squadrons for period 10th May to 4th June 1940.

Period	Patrols	Hours flown	EA Destroyed/	Damaged	RAF Casualties
10/12 May	10	167.30	6	3	6
13/19 May	28	722.00	45	30	18
20/25 May	74	1463.00	93	49	30
26 May to 4 June	101	4822.00	258	119	87
Totals			**402**	**201**	**141***

*A number of these pilots eventually returned.

APPENDIX D

German Fighter Claims 26th May – 3rd June 1940

26 May

I./JG1	4 Spitfires
I./JG2	10 Spitfires, 1 Blenheim
I./JG3	1 Hurricane
II./JG3	1 Hurricane
I./JG53	1 Hurricane, 1 Battle
III./JG53	1 Hurricane
I./JG77	1 Spitfire
I.(J)/LG2	1 Spitfire
II./ZG76	1 unknown type

27 May

II./JG26	1 Spitfire
III./JG26	2 Spitfires
II./JG53	3 Blenheims
V.((Z)/LG1	2 unknown types

28 May

III./JG2	5 Hurricanes, 1 Spitfire
I./JG26	8 Spitires
II./JG26	2 Spitfires, 2 Hurricanes
III./JG26	4 Hurricanes
II./JG51	3 Spitfires, 1 Hurricane

29 May

I./JG2	2 Wapitis
I./JG3	2 Wellingtons
II./JG3	3 Hurricanes
III./JG3	6 Spitfires
I./JG20	1 Spitfire
II./JG20	2 Spitfires
II./JG26	4 Spitfires, 2 Ansons
III./JG26	5 Spitfires, 1 unknown
Stab./JG27	2 Blenheims
I./JG27	2 Blenheims
II./JG51	2 unknown types
I/(J)/LG2	8 Hurricanes
II/ZG26	3 Spitfires

30 May

nil

31 May

II./JG2	1 Spitfire
III./JG3	2 Hurricanes
I./JG20	3 Lysanders, 6 Spitfires
	2 Skuas*, 1 Hurricane

1 June

I./JG2	1 Lysander
II./JG2	1 Lysander
I./JG20	1 Blenheim
I./JG26	2 Spitfires

187

31 May (cont)

Unit	Claims
I./JG26	1 Spitfire
III./JG26	11 Hurricanes, 4 Spitfires,
	2 Lysanders
II./JG27	1 Lysander
I./JG53	2 Wellingtons
III./JG53	2 Spitfires, 1 Biplane, 1 u/k
II./Tr.Gr.186	1 Spitfire
II./ZG26	5 Spitfires

1 June (cont)

Unit	Claims
II./JG26	6 Hurricanes, 1 Spitfire
I./JG27	2 Wellingtons
III./JG53	4 Hurricanes
I.(J)/LG2	1 Spitfire
I./ZG1	3 Hurricanes
II./ZG76	2 Spitfires, 5 unknown

2 June

Unit	Claims
II./JG2	1 Spitfire
II./JG26	4 Hurricanes, 2 Spitfires
III./JG26	1 Hurricane, 3 Spitfires
Stab./JG27	3 Spitfires
I./JG27	4 Spitfires
II./JG51	1 Hurricane

3 June

Unit	Claims
II./JG3	2 Hurricanes
I./JG53	1 Spitfire
III./JG53	11 Spitfires, 5 Hurricanes

* The Skuas were from 801 Squadron FAA, operating from Detling, L2917 and L3005 (with another which crash-landed afterwards with one man wounded). One Skua crew claimed a Me109 destroyed and another probable.

On 28th May 806 Squadron FAA, from Manston, were attacked by what was thought to be a French fighter and one Skua was shot down (crew rescued) and another shot-up, wounding its gunner.

On 29th May 806 Squadron FAA, from Manston, claimed a Ju88 late afternoon NE of Ostend, and damaged another.

Bibliography

The Sands of Dunkirk, Richard Collier, Collins 1961
The Nine Days of Dunkirk, Davide Divine, Faber & Faber 1959
Dunkirk – The Great Escape, A.J. Barker, Dent & Sons 1977
Fighter Command, Chaz Bowyer, Dent & Sons 1980
Fighter Squadrons of the RAF, John Rawlings, Macdonald & Janes 1969
Aces High, C.F. Shores & C. Williams, Grub Street 1994
242 Squadron – The Canadian Years, Hugh Halliday
A Clasp for the Few, K.G. Wynn, 1981
Under the White Rose (609 Sqdn), F.H. Ziegler, Macdonald 1971
Spitfire, B.J.E. Lane, John Murray 1942
Fly for your Life, Larry Forrester, Muller 1956
Nine Lives, Alan C. Deere, Hodder & Stoughton 1959

Index